PHILOSOPHY
AND DESIRE

CONTINENTAL PHILOSOPHY VII

PHILOSOPHY AND DESIRE

Edited with an Introduction by
Hugh J. Silverman

ROUTLEDGE
New York • London

Published in 2000 by
Routledge
29 West 35th Street
New York, NY 10001

Published in Great Britain by
Routledge
11 New Fetter Lane
London EC4P 4EE

Library of Congress Cataloging-in-Publication Data
Philosophy and desire / edited, with an introduction
  by Hugh J. Silverman.
       p.   cm. — (Continental philosophy ; 7)
    Includes bibliographical references.
    ISBN 0-415-91956-8. — ISBN 0-415-91957-6 (pbk.)
    1. Desire (Philosophy)   I. Silverman, Hugh J.   II. Series.
B105.D44P48   1999
128' .4—dc21   98-50356
                                                                    CIP

Previously published volumes in the series *Continental Philosophy*
Hugh J. Silverman, editor

CONTENTS

Introduction

Hugh J. Silverman

I. Erotic Practices / Erotic Transgressions

II. Desire for the Other: Levinas

III. Desiring Subjectivity: Sartre and de Beauvoir

IV. Reading Feminine Desire: Irigaray

V. Writing Desire: Barthes and Derrida

VI. Productive Desire: Deleuze and Guattari

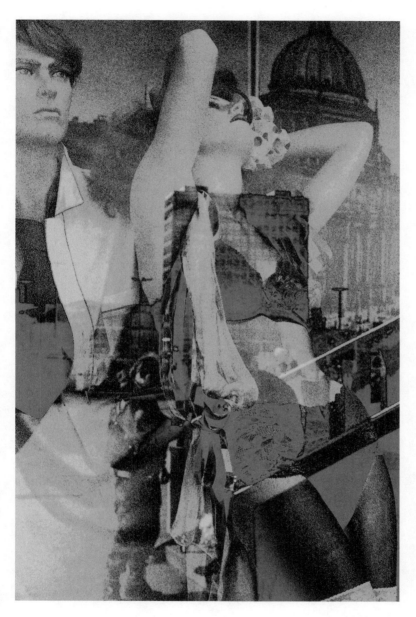

INTRODUCTION

TWENTIETH-CENTURY DESIRE AND THE HISTORIES OF PHILOSOPHY

Hugh J. Silverman

Freud (sex) and Hegel (power): With respect to the question of desire, twentieth-century continental philosophy has been pre-occupied with two alternative formulations—desire as sex and desire as power. These two views oppose and complement each other. They form a frame within which the question of desire takes shape.

Sex or the libido characterizes a certain energy, drive, passion, or enthusiasm for the object of one's desire. *Jouissance* is charged with directionality, excess, and release of energy. The libidinal is affective, desiring, and often out of control. Sex is ecstatic—it takes one outside oneself. Power, by contrast, arises out of concrete relations with others. The reading of the master-slave relation in Hegel's *Phenomenology of Spirit* is based upon a notion of desire. The slave desires the position of the master. This desiring relation gives the master power over the slave since the master really only gets his/her position from the slave's interest in supplanting the master. The master could not be master, could not exert power, if the slave did not desire the master's position. Unlike the sexual relation, the power relation uses desire to constitute domination and control, but also to achieve self-consciousness at the same time. For Hegel, we can be aware of ourselves only when others are conscious of us—the master is a master only when the slave desires to be master.

In the sexual relation, the desire to surrender to the other includes a concomitant desire not to supplant the other. When desiring to exert control over the other in the sexual relation, then libidinal desire becomes excessive, converting itself into something like the Hegelian model of power. When desire is simply excessive, the id gets out of control—a control the ego is supposed to exert over the libidinal desires. But this means that there is another desire—a desire to keep the animal drives in check, under control. And the ego often invokes the ego ideal or super-ego to help provide reasons why the ego should maintain control over its libidinal desires.

These two models dominate twentieth-century continental philosophy. They are reiterated in different ways in a variety of contexts, many of which are taken up in this volume. The binary pair—desire as sex/desire as power—as the basis for an understanding of desire in the twentieth century is itself situated in the context of the whole history and text of Western metaphysics.

Plato, for instance, thought that desire could serve different ends. In the *Symposium,* desire can be for another human being (*eros*), for friendship with another human being (*philia*), for a kind of intellectual companionship (*nomos*), and for harmony and unity with the world of ideas (*theoria*). Socrates's account of what the wise woman Diotima taught him demonstrates how these four levels can be experienced even by the same person. The first type is consistent with the account Aristophanes is given to report, namely, a physical desire of one person for another—his narrative of strange beings with four legs, four arms, two heads, and so on, who were split apart and are forever seeking to get back together, is an explanation for sexual desire. But in the Diotima speech, desire to have friendship with another, rising above sexual, erotic desire, is clearly more significant. This kind of desire can be either heterosexual or homosexual. And given the value placed on homosexual love in Greek daily life—as illustrated by Alcibiades, who arrives at the end of the *Symposium* seeking an expression of Socrates's interest—the line between *eros* and *philia* is not always so clearly demarcated, particularly as Socrates entices young men with his rhetorical skills.

Desire at the level of friendship can also lead to a coincidence of minds—desire for union with other minds, a kind of community of intellect. But even if successful, there is no assurance that this community of intellect will also provide knowledge of the ideas or forms. Although a community of intellect—as in an academy, a research institute, or the like—might help provide a context in which direct knowledge of the ideas might be possible, it does not necessarily follow that it will. Knowledge or intuition of the true, the good, or the beautiful comes from training in many things, including dialectic, but these do not guarantee knowledge of the ideas. The account of the philosopher-king in the *Republic* is a story of persons who seek to achieve this knowledge, but only after long training of body and soul, and even then there is no guarantee that they will achieve it.

In the *Republic*, Plato offers a description of the three parts of the soul. He says that the soul has (1) an appetitive part, (2) a spirited part, and (3) a rational part. The appetitive part is what acts out not only desire for food and drink but also erotic desires, bodily desires. The rational part directs itself to the ends of reason and follows those ends scrupulously. The third part, which guides the soul in one direction or the other, what Plato called *thumos,* is a motivational element in the soul. It can lead the soul to follow the appetites or to follow reason. This spirited element is also a form of desiring but not a desire for a particular object. Rather, this spirited part of the soul is the soul desiring what it takes to be good for itself. *Thumos* thereby directs the soul to make reason agree with the appetites or, when properly directed, to make the appetites conform to reason. Thus desire can be appetitive or rational, and the spirited element of the soul both animates this desire and helps the soul carry out its ends—whether for purposes of sex, friendship, community, or knowledge.

Many have noted similarities between this tripartite Platonic view and Freud's tripartite structure of the psychic realm: the id, the ego, and the superego. And while the ego should be in a position to determine whether it follows the "advice" of the id (libidinal desires) or of the superego (the moral ideals of the culture), it is not always successful at this invocation. Similarly in Plato, the spirited portion of the soul can sometimes allow reason to conform to the appetites rather than the appetites conforming to reason—a perversion Plato clearly does not appreciate.

For Plato, as long as reason is properly guided such that the appetites follow its dictates, then it will seek what is good for the soul. This is no guarantee that the soul will achieve such a high end, but at least it will be properly guided. Along with the proper use of reason, the conditions are in place for the soul to know the good (or the beautiful or the true). Knowing the good, for Plato, ensures that one will do the good. That is, if the soul truly achieves knowledge of the good, it will act accordingly. Love of ideas, the universal truths, and so forth will help the soul to know the good, but only knowing the good will bring about such action.

Aristotle provides an alternative to Plato by giving even more weight to desire. For Aristotle, knowing the good is not sufficient to do the good. For Aristotle, desiring to do the good is also part of the relation between knowing the good and doing the good. He claims, in his *Nicomachean Ethics,* that the virtuous person is someone who knows the good, desires to do the good, and does the good. A continent person knows the good, desires something else, and nevertheless does the good. An incontinent person knows what is good but desires the bad and does it. A brutish person ignores the good, desires the bad, and does the bad. Hence, for Aristotle, desire plays an important role in ethical behavior. And knowledge as well as action also needs to take desire into account. Aristotle's model allows for cases of human action characterized by continence or incontinence—both of which have no place in Plato's account. The only way to bring these features into Plato's version is to consider the role of *thumos* in the soul, orienting the soul to conform to reason, but this does not constitute the kind of desire that Aristotle proposes. In Aristotle, desire gives depth to any action. What we do is either in compliance with or against our desires.

Aristotelian desire is not the same as *eros, philia, nomos,* or *theoria;* nor is it a form of love. Aristotelian desire functions between knowledge and action. It confirms or disconfirms our actions. A good action that is nevertheless colored by contrary desires is still a good action, but one that demonstrates a certain conflict in the process of choosing. This type of desire has to do with a kind of power over oneself and one's emotions as opposed to a feeling or passion for another person or object. And this is the major difference between the Platonic view and the Aristotelian one. Clearly the Aristotelian version has more to do with the kind of psychological account one finds in Freud, where self-control is always a factor. Only to the extent that Hegel offers a notion of self-consciousness does it resemble Aristotle's account—but even in Hegel, self-consciousness is reflective, directed toward oneself and not a constraint upon oneself and one's actions.

Aristotle's view of desire is incorporated into early Christian thought—intention matters. Evil thoughts in the mind, even if never acted upon, mean that there are bad intentions, for evil thoughts *are* bad intentions. And bad intentions are sinful. Sinfulness is not just by virtue of sinful acts; even sinful desires are considered to be sin. Desires are now turned into something to be worried about. The desire to be good, to achieve salvation, to follow in God's path is a desire to live the Christian life. To deviate from such a desire is to pervert desire. Augustine's problem with desire is that it could lead to a surrender to bodily interests. Desire that is anything other than desire for a *visio Dei* is misguided. And so desire is distinguished from will. Will keeps one on track, directing one's goals and interests to that which is good, to doing good works. Weakness of will allows one's desires to have priority over one's calling to follow God, to seek oneness with the divine, to achieve a vision and harmony with the divine, and ultimately to experience God's love *(agapé)*. The appeal to bodily interests becomes sinful when one follows those interests. Self-awareness must be awareness of how the body can deceive, how the body can demonize, how the body can pervert the proper goals of the soul.

The Platonic search for unity and the corresponding denigration of the bodily interests is reiterated in St. Augustine. The desire to follow the path of goodness needs to be a free choice. One must recognize one's own sinfulness and deny one's bodily desires. Self-knowledge means self-control. Love means loving another person, loving friendship, loving Church and community, loving God. And ultimately, loving God is the desire that is to be encouraged.

With Thomas Aquinas, the Aristotelian structure of virtue, continence, incontinence, viciousness, and brutishness is repeated, only now in the eyes of God. God knows when we have sinned. God knows when we have allowed the desires of the body to take over. God knows when love is not his love. The difference between Augustine and Aquinas is that the former simply wants to overcome the corrupting call of bodily desires in favor of faith. Aquinas, however, believes that we have a more rational ability to make choices in which we contain our desires, hold them in check, and nevertheless act morally—as far as anyone else can tell.

But in the Renaissance, the crucial difference is that desire is again a yearning to know—to know all things, to know the universe, to know our bodies, to know how machines can be made, to know the depths of nature, and so forth. The grand figures of Leonardo da Vinci, Galileo, and Machiavelli, to name a few, are all committed to turning desire into knowledge—knowledge of the human body, its anatomy, and its contexts, knowledge of the heavens, and knowledge of human society and personality. Desire is focused on achievement in the arts, sciences, and politics. Personal desires must ultimately conform to these higher desires for knowledge. And sometimes—as Machiavelli makes perfectly clear—desire can take the form of a will to control, to maintain power, to use every means available to achieve such ends. This latter form of political desire, is of course, consistent with the notion of power as mastery over others. And the parallel between mastery over other people (as in Machiavelli's recommendations to his prince) and knowledge as mastery over nature (Bacon, da Vinci, Galileo) exhibits a common structure. The Book of Nature is rich, and only through knowledge can it be delved into properly.

So strong is the desire for knowledge, the use of reason, and the fullest use of the intellect in the various fields of human endeavor that in the neoclassical age (the seventeenth century) a conflict arises between reason and passion. If desire is the proper exercise of reason, then significant achievements in self-knowledge are possible. But if desire becomes passion—even excessive passion—there is a problem, for often this conflict produces a conflict of choice as well. Many seventeenth-century French plays—such as those of Corneille and Racine—are filled with this dilemma. Phèdre is torn between her passionate desire for her stepson and her need to follow what is right, and what reason tells her is right. Desire in the seventeenth century is converted into passion, and passion alone. Reason has nothing to do with desire. Reason cannot allow desire to take over—and yet, so often, this is precisely what happens. And when it happens, the individual is torn apart. *The Princess of Clèves* shows how important this kind of choice can turn out to be. And even in other works—such as Descartes' *The Passions of the Soul* and La Rochefoucauld's *Maxims*—passion becomes a taxonomy of desires, a list of alternative passions. The fascination with the multiplicity of passions is set off against the obsession with reason.

On one side of the English Channel is an appeal to experience and knowledge derived from the senses; on the other side is the strict reliance on reason. For empiricists such as Hume, the multiplicity of the passions is like the multiplicity of sense impressions. Each one has its own characteristics, each one can be described in detail, and each one can amount to the expression of desire without having explicitly to deny knowledge about them.

Knowledge of one's passions will help to achieve self-knowledge. Both Descartes and Hume offer a catalogue of the passions but to different ends. Yet both are concerned ultimately with self-knowledge—one through reason, the other through sense experience. Neither has a separate place for feeling, sentiment, emotion.

Out of the conflict between reason and experience, the feelings must be given a separate place—and this place is offered in Romantic theory, Romantic poetry, and Romantic painting. Rousseau's sympathy for the appeal to feelings provides a third term to be added to reason and experience. And Rousseau's need to understand feeling is a need to understand oneself as well. Self-consciousness also involves understanding reason, experience, and feeling. And feeling is where desire most fully expresses itself. Feeling is the expression of one's innermost nature and the best way to achieve harmony with Nature itself. Knowledge of one's feelings is knowledge of oneself. The Renaissance ideals of knowledge are now fully addressed to one's own feelings, sentiments, emotions. And these emotions are not to be denigrated, as in Augustine, or to be conflicted, as in the seventeenth century. Rather, feelings are to be explored and developed to the highest sensitivity.

Rousseau sets the stage for the binary form of desire as exhibited in the twentieth century—the dichotomy between the Freudian and Hegelian models. With the celebration of feeling and the need for self-knowledge, Rousseau leans in the direction of Freud. Hence the appearance of Kant as setting the conditions for the limits of knowledge, choice, and experience demonstrates in effect the limits of desire. Desire cannot take one everywhere. Desire, as illustrated in Goethe's *Faust,* has to have its limits, and if those limits are not respected, something like damnation is the certain fate. One cannot strive to know, experience, and feel everything without giving up one's very humanity. Just as Faust demonstrates what happens when one seeks to go beyond the limits of human knowledge, experience, and feeling, Kant delineates intellectually where those limits are located. The conditions of the possibility of metaphysics are also the conditions of the possibility of what can be said about what is beyond those conditions. Desire has its limits: Kant's lesson taught, Faust's lesson learned.

After Kant and Goethe, desire is no longer concerned with the limits of knowledge and self-knowledge. Desire is desire to encompass everything—through the fullest expression of the passions (de Sade), through the call to totalize (gain power over) all that can be known (Hegel), through revolution in the very fiber of bourgeois society (Marx), through the celebration of the individual subject (Kierkegaard), and through the critique of all ideals of any culture in favor of self-overcoming (Nietzsche). Nineteenth-century desire is no longer content to accept the limits that Kant articulated and that Goethe's Faust enacted. Nineteenth-century desire wants it all through affirmation, and this is ultimately the achievement of power: to overcome the other through desire, to overcome oneself through will to power, rejecting established values, ideals, and expectations. On the one hand, desire wants power by taking the place of the other, and, on the other hand, desire wants to express itself fully and without limitations as the individual expression of freedom.

This dichotomy between desire for power and libidinal desire frames the twentieth-century continental tradition. Desire in continental philosophy is either erotic, poetic, loving, transgressive, and insidious, or an encounter with the other—productive, creative, and discursive—and expressive of power. When desire is of the Freudian variety, it can also become the basis for a social theory. When desire is of the Hegelian variety, its negations constitute the other, give meaning to desire, and reaffirm oneself.

Erotic Practices/Erotic Transgressions (Part I) outlines some types of eroticism as derived from the Freudian model and then shows two alternative ways of understanding the erotic. Martin Dillon distinguishes between what he calls "biological reductionism" and "semiological constructivism," and attempts to open a theoretical space capable of accommodating the "truths" to be found in both. One version reduces the erotic to a physiological condition, while the other turns the erotic into a discursive practice. For Dillon, both of these accounts—one the medical side of Freud, the other the narratological side of Lacan—do not adequately account for the lived body, which constitutes a historically situated natural condition and which founds a circumscribed plurality of competitive social forms in the domain of erotic norms and praxes. This (Merleau-Pontean) account of the lived body avoids the reductions of the medical model but also seeks to shy away from accounting for the body in the language of the body. It seeks to see the erotic as charged with energy but contextualized by social norms in relation to bodily erotic practices.

By contrast, LaFountain's reading of Bataille examines alternatives to erotic norms and seeks to understand erotic transgression. Here the Freudian model is animated by the Hegelian dialectic. If there might be some possibility of "being whole again"—an idea that the Hegelian totality could be understood not only as the achievement of mind or spirit in its self-actualization but also as some former unity that the erotic calls out for—this condition marks the confrontation with death and excess (the experience of *le petit mort*). Death and excess present limits to totality. The erotic, orgasmic body confronts death and excess by trying to simulate them. A disruption in the dialectic between the socially accepted and the transgression of those norms produces an indecidability. This indecidability is the place in which the dialectic

8

breaks up—where it becomes "insidious." Death and excess would be expressions of what Dillon means by the "lived body." When textualized, the very question of the role of a textual death, one in which the erotic-textual body of the writer/reader is the practice of eroticism, introduces this moment of indecidability—a moment of eroticism, a moment of textual *jouissance* (as Barthes would call it).

Desire for the Other: Levinas (Part II) takes a radical departure from the Freudian libido turned erotic. Brian Schroeder focuses directly on Hegel's "logic of Desire" in the *Science of Logic* as opposed to his *Phenomenology of Spirit*. He takes up war as the most extreme form of interpersonal violence and reformulates the problem in the light of Levinas's notion of otherness. In short, he is looking for a way in which otherness for Levinas is something other than Hegelian negation. Schroeder asks whether the negativity, that is, otherness, that desire negates in its movement as Spirit renders the relation with the Other obsolete; or does it bring one into a genuine relation with the Other? And what is the role that desire plays in the promotion and/or overcoming of the violence that is war? Reading Levinas with and against Hegel sees the relation with the Other as a logic of relation that is faced with the possibility of violence. But does violence reaffirm the face-to-face, or does it reaffirm a dialectic of negativity?

Bettina Bergo comes at the question by asking whether it is not Heidegger rather than Hegel who frames the Levinasian concept of desire. She shows how Levinas's reconfiguration of Heideggerian notions of space and time results in a radically new conception of desire. Levinas's notion of desire can be formulated in terms of need and enjoyment as existential notions as opposed to transcendental ones. Is desire something that we feel, experience, live in relation to the other human being, or is it a condition for our understanding of the possibilities of need and enjoyment in eschatological terms? Once again the tension is between desire as an expression of lived experience and desire as a logical structure of interpersonal relations.

In Desiring Subjectivity: Sartre and de Beauvoir (Part III) the account of desire is framed in existential terms—those of Sartre and de Beauvoir. Christina Howells points out that in Sartre desire is incompatible not only with beauty but also with love. Like love, however, desire pursues an impossible ideal: to possess the other as both subject and object, as embodied transcendence. Sartre's phenomenological descriptions of desire are predominantly negative, involving the body as flesh, as contingent, as being-in-itself. The fundamental project of the for-itself is its impossible desire for being, and this is manifest in all modes of desire. *Saint Genet* provides clues for a better understanding of these questions, especially in its inversion of Kantian ethics. Desire in Sartre is the paradoxical reconciliation of subject and object, love and desire that is our ultimate aim—not the failed synthesis that he had outlined in *Being and Nothingness* but rather a still point of fragile (and impossible) equilibrium. This impossible desire would make the transcendental desire of Kant or even Hegel or Husserl a real, existing phenomenon (were it not impossible). Sartrian desire always falls on the side of the desiring subject and never overcomes the dichotomy inscribed in the impossible dream.

Eleanore Holveck's reading stresses the role of Simone de Beauvoir's, "ethics of ambiguity" in understanding female sexuality as basically incompatible with the Sartrian view. She rejects psychoanalytic readings of de Beauvoir's notion of female sexuality and links it more to the Hegelian tradition. And perhaps this very ambiguity of experience reformulates the "impossible desire" in Sartre. In de Beauvoir's notion of ambiguity, the very dilemma of desire between the psychoanalytic (Freudian) version and the dialectical, transcendental (Hegelian) version is particularly evident.

Reading Feminine Desire: Irigaray (Part IV) takes the question of female sexuality and reads it in the terms offered by Luce Irigaray as "a different relation to the transcendental." For Irigaray, according to Simon Walter, the concept of *specularization* is an important figure in the nonacknowledgment of sexual difference. The constituted otherness of woman has been subsumed into a discourse of masculine sameness. The only representations of women possible within this economy are duplication, opposition, or insertion. The masculine has spoken the universal on behalf of woman by erasing her from discursive history. In Hegel and Heidegger, the relation of Being to non-Being implicitly relegated woman to the position of nothingness in an ontological hierarchy; psychoanalysis, in its description of linguistic signification, makes this identification complete by excluding woman from the circulation of phallic meaning. The explicit sexualization of discourse is not simply a reactive development in metaphysics. Woman becomes visible in her absence, disrupting and instigating the rereading of the whole of the discursive history of subjectivity.

10

According to Dorothy Leland, Irigaray provides an inadequate "account" of the gendering of desire, partly because of her Lacanian tendency to ignore the social institutions and practices that contribute to this process. Leland's literalist-based complaint about Irigaray's discourse on feminine desire transfers to its strategic construal. If Irigaray is not giving an account of the gendering of desire, then she should not be criticized for failing to link this process to historically and culturally specific social relations. But her texts conceptualize this process as bound to the psychoanalytic tales she deconstructs. The "effect" at least at the level of image and symbol, is to leave women where Freud and Lacan have consigned them, relegated to the realm of the ahistorical, transcultural other, endowed with a "supplementary *jouissance*" that lies beyond the symbolic, linguistically constituted, phallically oriented world of men.

In **Writing Desire: Barthes and Derrida** (Part V) Robert Solomon explores how Roland Barthes writes desire through the genre of the "lover's discourse." Desire is written in Barthes's text in a putatively "impersonal" way—offering a dictionary/encyclopedic format that yields only an "arbitrary" list of love words and phrases. In many respects, Barthes's *A Lover's Discourse* is a rejection of an entire tradition of philosophizing about love, but its charm is its personal, even confessional nature. He claims that his work is impersonal ("there is no question here of a history"), but Solomon suggests that we should take this too as part of the writerly lover's discourse, one of those proclamations that we would expect from Barthes as part of his effort to "discourage the temptation to meaning." Hence Solomon invokes Barthes's own "impersonal," "lexical" mode of writing in order to show (discursively) how love and desire are acutely personal despite Barthes's semiological claims to the contrary.

By contrast, Nancy Holland offers an account of Jacques Derrida's discourses of desire across the thirty years of his highly productive career. She shows that at least two different discourses of desire are at work in Derrida's writings. The first, "male" discourse is discussed in the context of three essays in *Writing and Difference* (1967); the second, "female" discourse is discussed in the context of *Cinders* (1980) and *Memoirs of the Blind* (1990). The conclusion drawn from these texts is that while the "male" discourse allows for the possibility of a feminist understanding of the play of desire in traditional philosophical discourse, the "female" discourse in Derrida does not. The necessity of this paradox is examined in the light of the more general problem of the exclusion of female desire from the phallogocentric tradition.

Productive Desire: Deleuze and Guattari (Part VI) concludes the volume with a consideration of Gilles Deleuze's philosophy of desire in the context of the history of philosophy. Alan Schrift claims that the whole history of philosophy conceives of desire as a "lack in the object." Gilles Deleuze, however, explicitly associates the view of desire as lack with Freudian psychoanalysis and offers an alternative notion of desire as productive. Schrift shows how Deleuze draws upon Spinoza's *conatus* and Nietzsche's "will to power" for his account of productive desire in order to present an "other" discourse of desire in the history of philosophy—one freed from the constraints imposed by the ideology of lack.

Correspondingly, Dorothea Olkowski situates Deleuze's writings in relation to theories of the body and desire in recent feminist philosophy. She argues that Deleuze and Guattari's account of the body and desire does not establish a precultural eros, as some feminists claim. Focusing in particular on *Nietzsche and Philosophy* and *Anti-Oedipus* (by Deleuze and Guattari), Olkowski argues for a conception of positive desire that is not connected in any way to the Platonic schema of "man" as lacking being and therefore limiting human productive activity. She questions Oedipal constructions of the body and desire as hierarchical and exploitative. She further demonstrates how, for Deleuze and Guattari, the body (understood broadly as chemical, physical, biological, and social) is the force that undermines such constructions so that productive desire can once again open up human creative and political freedom.

Acknowledgments

There is joy in bringing this volume to its conclusion—much pleasure in working with our various contributors and developing together an account of desire in contemporary continental philosophy in relation to the history of Western thought. A comprehensive account would not have been possible, but certainly the broad outlines as well as many crucial specificities concerning contemporary theories of desire have been articulated in these pages. I am especially grateful to all of our contributors, who have provided their various interpretations and understandings of desire today. And to the members of the Continental Philosophy editorial staff, I must admit once again that this project would not have seen the light of day without them—and certainly not without the intellectual enjoyment we share in producing these volumes. Michael Sanders has taken the lead in helping to coordinate and maintain all aspects of the Continental Philosophy series. I am extremely grateful to him for all his extraordinary abilities, insights, and labors. Jim Keller provided expert help in making sure that the electronic version is properly entered and precisely engineered. His good spirit and commitment to this project is always appreciated. As he has for many years now, Norman Bussiere keeps us all on equilibrium, persistently and perspicuously scouting out any trace of copyediting, concordance, or syntactical error. His generosity and goodwill are a delight to us all.

We are pleased to include once again photographs by James R. Watson, associate editor, providing some visual shape and interpretation to the grouping of the essays included here. The process of selection has been a collective one and we hope that the reader will find them appropriate. Once again our bibliographer, Hélène Volat, has produced a helpful bibliography—as she has since the inception of the Continental Philosophy project. The intelligent and valuable contribution of other associate editors, such as Forrest Williams and Wilhelm Wurzer, is greatly appreciated. And the many anonymous readers and evaluators of the essays that make up this volume play a major role in helping to maintain quality in all the books in this series. Most of the essays have been rewritten and edited many times to achieve the highest standard of writing. The other assistant editors, such as James Hatley, Brian Seitz, James Clarke, and Gary Aylesworth, continue to be actively involved in our work. At Routledge, once again, I would like to thank its president, Colin Jones, for his commitment to this whole project, Marie Leahy for keeping us in the limelight, and Gayatri Patnaik for keeping us on track. The subsequent Continental Philosophy volumes on Lyotard and on Foucault are nearing completion. We hope that readers will look forward to them with anticipation. We also hope that the present volume will provide a sorely needed insight into the role of desire, as it has become a topic of pressing interest in the current political, social, intellectual, philosophical, and artistic contexts of the fin-de-siècle twentieth century.

PART I
EROTIC PRACTICES/EROTIC TRANSGRESSIONS

Chapter 1

ALETHEIA, POIESIS, AND EROS: TRUTH AND UNTRUTH IN THE POETIC CONSTRUCTION OF LOVE

M. C. Dillon

Never seek to tell thy love, Love that never told can be.
—William Blake

What's love got to do with it? What's love but a second-hand emotion?

—Tina Turner

I.

Does the telling of love constitute love? Or does love always elude the attempt to capture it in words? Is the history of love a history of narrative forms? If we understand *poiesis* to designate the generation of a narrative that, once espoused by a community, becomes a social form, then is love nothing more—and nothing less—than a poetic construct?

The attitudes regarding erotic love reported in Plato's *Symposium* presuppose a legitimacy of the love for boys, if the boys one loves have reached an age "when they begin to acquire some mind—a growth associated with that of down on their chins."[1] Foucault suggests that although this relationship with boys was regarded as "problematic" among the upper classes at the time, if "it comprised . . . the elements that would form the basis of a transformation of this love into a definitive and socially valuable tie, that of *philia*," it could be regarded as "morally honorable."[2] Contrast this with our culture, which, although it is beginning to legitimize homosexual relationships, regards sexual relations with pubescent children as criminal whether these relations actually involve penetration or not.

17

Stendhal reports that courts of love were convened in France in the last decade of the twelfth century. At one of these courts, held in 1174, the Countess of Champagne, answering the question posed by a troubadour whether true love can exist between married persons, judged that it could not. Stendhal goes on to recount the thirty-one articles comprising the "Code of Love for the Twelfth Century" as set forth in the works of André the Chaplain. The article given the preeminence of first place on the list states that "the plea of marriage is not a legitimate defense against love."[3] Our culture has developed more lenient attitudes toward adultery than those dramatized by Nathaniel Hawthorne in *The Scarlet Letter,* but it is arguable that the revelation of adulterous liaisons in the lives of such notable figures as Kennedy, King, and Clinton detracted from their public stature and that for us the plea of love is not a legitimate defense against charges of adultery. And we are more inclined to regard love as the only legitimate motive for marriage than to conceive marriage and love as incompatible.

Just as the definitions of love evolving through the historical vicissitudes of one culture contradict each other, so are there contradictions across cultures. Feminists in our culture who espouse a doctrine of radical tolerance in the name of multiculturalism are nonetheless disposed to undertake militant action against the practice of clitoridectomy in other cultures. In our culture the pleasure to be obtained from stimulation of the clitoris is held to be essential for a woman to experience genuine erotic love; in some other cultures that pleasure is held to constitute a danger for abiding love relations (as it was by Freud in an earlier phase of our own history).

These contradictions in the conception and practice of erotic love reinforce the postmodern case for nominalism and conventionalism, that is, for the standpoint that there is no reality corresponding to the name "true love" and that this designation is more like an honorific applied to the social construct that happens to be privileged in a given place at a given time. If one asks about the genealogy of the construct, postmodern thought offers a series of replies. The quest for the origins of a normative construct is misconceived (1) because origins are inaccessible, (2) because norms imply *tele,* which reside as much in an inaccessible future as they do in an inaccessible past, and (3) because it is more accurate to regard genealogical accounts as narratives—that is, as chains of signifiers—than as chains of causes. If one subsumes narrative under the general heading of *poiesis,* then love is a social construct produced by language itself, rather than by the individual poet who happens to be its conduit.

Language spoke this way through Sappho:

> my feelings for you, my beautiful ones,
> will not change.[4]

And this way through Ovid:

> Helen . . .
> Weeps at the old bitch staring from her mirror.
> And who would rape her once or twice now?
> Time and Old Age eat all the world away—
> Black-toothed and slow, they seem to feast forever
> As all things disappear in time, in death.[5]

Why does language contradict itself when speaking through different poets at different times in different places? If it is intrinsic to the language of our passing era to differentiate the world through systems of binary opposition, that is, to generate contradictions, and if the generation of contradictions is the mark of the absurd, then what are we to learn from our poets? What is the truth here?

What is the truth about love? Is it true that love is a social construct grounded in the speaking of language that produces absurdity? If truth itself is but one pole of an absurdity-producing binary opposition, what are we to make of the assertion that love is a social construct grounded in the speaking of language that produces absurdity?

II.

If the quality of one's life is affected by the manner in which one loves, by the narrative one enacts, then how might one choose— if one can choose—among the many narratives competing for our devotion? Or, finding little or no promise in the field of competition, how might one invoke language to speak in another way?

Something happens to human bodies at adolescence. Granting Freud the point that infants are sexual, it is nonetheless true that a qualitative change in human sexuality takes place during puberty and adolescence. We may also grant to Freud and the host of psychologists—behavioral, experimental, developmental, humanistic, and so on—who follow him on this issue the point that we tend to recapitulate the models imprinted upon us in infancy; still, it remains true that during adolescence we rebel. That rebellion may indeed amount to a recapitulation in the negative mode, but it may also take on new forms: Every celibate was conceived, and, to the distress of sociobiological theory, an unbroken chain of heterosexual reproduction can produce an individual who decides that he or she is exclusively homosexual. Theories based on the model of imprinting and recapitulation may reflect the backward-looking structure of causal explanation more than the data to be explained. Causes are retrospective, but motives are prospective in that they are pointed toward a future ideal. Is there, then, a promising prospect to be found—or made—by changelings in search of sexual identity and erotic love?

If we live at the end of the era of onto-theological metaphysics, ambivalently tossing through the wake of the second death of our god of love—if we are ready to exorcize not the demon in the flesh but the demonization of the flesh—then perhaps we are ready to embrace the flesh that makes words rather than merely incarnates a word already spoken.

Kierkegaard wrote words to the effect that no man ever wrote poetry to the woman he got. I know that to be empirically false, but I think it is empirically true that no one ever wrote a love poem before the age of puberty. What happens at puberty? Floods of testosterone and estrogen. Conspicuous secondary sexual characteristics develop—breasts and reedy voices, accompanied by pimples—which, through the phenomenon Sartre called "the look," produce the self-alienating, self-generating capacity for reflective thought. Reflection, in turn, produces the mother of all binary oppositions: shame and lust. And the agon between shame and lust (i.e., the pleasure-pain of sexual desire) portends the history of post-Socratic *eros*.

Denis de Rougemont was not the first to comment on the fact that romantic love, still the model of love for our time, was a product of Christian culture, but his genealogy of romance is the most compelling account I know. What does this have to do with adolescence and the poetic construction of love? De Rougemont argues that "all European poetry has come out of the Provençal poetry written in the twelfth century by the troubadours of Languedoc" (*LW*, 75), that this poetry is the proximal origin of romantic love, that romantic lovers "love love more than the object of love" (*LW*, 50), that the love they love feeds on prohibition, and that "this obstruction is what passion really wants—its true object" (*LW*, 42).[6] Romantic love loves love, loves the emotional turbulence, and above all, loves the ideal projected upon the love object, an ideal that reflects the immanent fantasy of the lover rather than the transcendent reality of the beloved.

Departing somewhat from de Rougemont, I would add that the Christian transformation of *eros* into *agape* is predicated on the demonization of sexuality, incipient in Socratism, that provides the frisson-generating obstacle definitive of romantic love. Romantic love feeds on the unknown otherness or transcendence of the prohibited object and loses its passion once the prohibition is lifted. This is why Bataille regards the religious experience of the sacred as essential to erotic love.[7] The sacred is the source of the taboo, and the taboo is the source of the fascination: Erotic love thrives in the ambivalent space created by taboo, where the physically close love object is rendered metaphysically remote by the consecrating prohibition.

Taboo and prohibition do not create sexual desire—animals manifest desire—but they do qualify it in the way that generates romanticism or eroticism. This is the truth of constructivism: If prohibition is a social phenomenon—the creation of a *nomos* through an act of *logos,* perhaps an invocation of Lacan's *nom du père*—then the peculiar nature of the taboo will generate an erotic ideal commensurate with the prohibition. The lability of sexual objectification through the structure Freud identified as transference is well known: There may or may not be a general progression from mouth to anus to genitals, but it is clear that sexual interest can shift focus through a wide range of partial objects or fetishes, be they body parts (feet, breasts) or objects associated with them (shoes, brassieres, lingerie in general). There is a connection between fixation on partial objects and specific prohibitions—where the female breast is not hidden through the motive of shame we call modesty, it does not seem to become a fetish—but there are aspects of this connection that necessarily elude constructivist explanations.

III.

Anatomically speaking, the organs of reproduction among mammals are also sometimes associated with the organs of excretion. Human waste is sometimes a vehicle of disease, but human waste has also been eroticized and fetishized: de Sade delights in giving accounts of coprophagy, and there is a genre of erotic depiction associated with toilet functions known as "water sports." The restriction of sexual behavior to potentially reproductive acts is not the only source of the perversions and prohibitions attributed by Foucault to Freud. Sanctions are also generated from concerns about health and from increasing empirical knowledge about such dangers as blood-to-blood or semen-to-blood contact and the ingestion of feces.[8] Empirical fact has a bearing upon prohibition and hence an explanatory role in the understanding of erotic desire or love. Love is certainly not reducible to biology, but neither is it reducible to *poiesis.*

De Rougemont asserts that "happy love has no history—in European literature" (*LW,* 52). This is at best trivially true, that is, true only if one sanctifies the term *literature* and therefore refuses to apply it to such forms as Harlequin romance novels. Shakespeare was closer to the mark with Lysander's observation in *A Midsummer Night's Dream* that "the course of true love never did run smooth" (1.1.132). Does the bump, the obstacle, the prohibition generate the truth of love? Does it test the truth of love? Or is it just somehow true that love always encounters obstacles?

The family is both a social unit and a natural unit among mammals. The rule of exogamy also straddles the distinction between the social and the natural. If one tries, as did Aquinas, to specify the norms governing sexuality, marriage, and the family under the heading of natural law, one eventually confronts difficulties arising from the oxymoronic character of "natural law."[9] Law, as etymologists tend to agree, is something that is laid down in a social or linguistic act, and the natural order is usually conceived as transcending human institution.[10] Without providing the treatment this issue requires, let me just stipulate here that although human institutions are founded upon such natural givens as gravity and the biology of reproduction, nature allows for multiple determination and does not univocally demand one kind of institutionalization to the exclusion of all others. Rather, it delimits the range of possible and probable forms of institution. Royal families, for example, tend to die out at a rate that is proportional to the degree of enforced incestuous proximity.[11] In short, there is a primacy to natural origins, but a circumscribed plurality of social forms founded upon them.

Regardless how broad the scope of the family and how loose the sanctions upon the law of exogamy, the two structures engender some degree of violence in the process of mate selection or love. There is necessarily a breaking of old social forms and a creation of new ones, be they abiding families or transient affairs. That is one of the reasons for ritualization and attendant prohibitions. Whether

it is strife between the Montagues and the Capulets or values of mis-
cegenation in the heritage of an Alabama high school principal, the
existing social order is disrupted by the novel formation generated
by erotic liaison. Since social orders tend to be self-conserving,
lovers have obstacles to overcome. To love is to disrupt.

Disruption occurs for the sake of a new union: another binary
opposition. Like others, this one is resolvable through the circularity of repetition, as was dramatized in the ancient Greek phallic
plays: the young man's phallus supervenes over the old man's
phallic order, the bride is taken, and the cycle begins again. This
is ritualization, socialization: the generation of institutions that
minimize violence through codification and repetition. Thus
love is intrinsically ritualized under social forms; although these
forms vary, there are constants and limits dictated, ultimately, by
pragmatic constraint and the related constraint upon imagination.
Here is the domain of erotic *poiesis*.

IV.

Ich bin von Kopf bis Fuss auf Liebe eingestellt.
                                        —Marlene Dietrich

Here also is the domain of adolescence, the lived body, and truth.
No erotic *poiesis* arises before adolescence because the floods of
estrogen and testosterone are needed to fill the poet's pen. Eros
and desire may indeed have filled the infant's soul. But the
shame, born of reflexivity, needed to internalize the sanctions
and externalize the object of desire does not come upon the
scene until the hormones flow and the secondary sexual characteristics emerge to provoke the disgusting, enticing, erotically
interested look.

Changelings disrupt the social fabric simply by changing,
becom-ing sexual. The rites of passage associated with adolescence are constructions that vary from culture to culture. We send
our changelings to school, preferably boarding school, summer
camp, or boot camp, to be initiated into the practices that have to
be mastered to gain adult autonomy and readmission to the
social order. Other cultures send their adolescents into the jun-
gle or forest or desert for other modes of initiation, but a functional isomorphism in these rituals is apparent across cultures.

23

Infants and adults are socially stable in comparison to changelings. Changelings destabilize and threaten social order; they are banished until they learn how to behave. And there is always a specialized caste—call them shamans, priests, teachers, drill instructors—charged with inculcating the society's basic dogmas in its youth and training them to acceptable practice. Beneath the variable social construction, the natural process motivates the institutional deployment of power and can serve as one of its measures.[12]

Changelings disrupt the social order, which restores itself through the institution of norms. The regulations coagulate around such myths or poetic constructions as natural law. Natural law ties sex to reproduction through institutionalizing love in marriage and the family, whose own norms are structured by the telos of propagating the species. As they exercise the sexual autonomy demanded of them by their hormones, our culture's changelings remind us daily that poetic forms failing to accommodate natural measures survive only in mutation. We are now teaching our youth how they might love without invoking the nemesis of unwanted progeny and disease.

Aquinas taught that true love is possible only when consecrated by marriage. Twelfth-century courts of love taught the opposite: that true love is impossible within the confines of marriage. Our culture is living through the chaos generated by the contradiction embodied in this binary opposition. Contemporary eros loves the prohibited object because it is prohibited, thus contemporary eros thrives on dissatisfaction. Is *this* true love? Does the truth about desire live in the *jouissance* of deferring the union that would spell its death?[13]

Merleau-Ponty designated as "profound" the following remark made by Malraux about modern painters: "Although not one of them spoke of truth, all, faced with the works of their adversaries, spoke of imposture."[14] Something like this may also apply here. Despite our reluctance to define "true love" for all times, given its intimate connection with the processes of becoming, we are not quite so hesitant to identify inauthenticity in the erotic domain. The project of seduction depends upon deceit. Don Giovanni masks his identity from Donna Anna, Donna Elvira, and, one assumes, the remaining thousand and one conquests he made in Spain alone. The masking was essential to the project of seduction because it protected him from having to fulfill his promises of undying love. Let Don Giovanni be as innocent as Kierkegaard said he was, let him believe every promise in the moment he makes it; the inauthenticity is simply doubled, the lie to himself merely facilitating the lie to the lady.[15]

There may be no single great truth to be unveiled about love, no divinity who embodies an immutable "true love," but I believe finite, mutable truths intertwined with lies can be articulated in the erotic domain. Let me conclude with the thought that has been trying to express itself throughout this essay.

The binary opposition between nature and construction, between biology and *poiesis,* generates mystification just because it is a binary opposition. One does not eliminate binary oppositions, not this one at least, by attempting to reduce one of the terms to the other, i.e., by privileging the linguistic structure and refusing to consider the biological structure. One might rather develop the aspect of *aletheia* that Heidegger describes in terms of *Gelassenheit*—letting-be or listening—and associates with freedom.[16] Coupled with letting-be as its indissoluble correlate is a form of forgetfulness Heidegger designates as insistence, a projection upon beings, including the beings that are other persons, of categories that allow them to serve our purposes and that reduce them to instruments overlooked in the process of utilization.[17]

Romantic love, the poetic construct that still defines love in our era, does not let the being who is loved be, but insists upon projecting upon the love-object an ideality constructed by our own muses and poets. One overlooks the flesh-and-blood person in the mode of forgetfulness known as transcendental constitution. Marriage is a threat to romance because the propinquity of one spouse forces upon the other an awareness of the person's reality as a living body. The clutter in the bathroom obtrudes upon the vision illumined by candles. Demands and purposes compete with the insistence of the projected ideal.

Contemporary romantic love is essentially inauthentic insofar as the poetic construction collides with the desire to be loved for oneself. If the only form love can take is provided by poetic construction, then there is no love beyond romance. The alternative is to write one's own poem to the person whose life and body has intertwined with one's own in a manner that reveals and enhances both. If the little death is inseparable from the big one at the end, if the love that intensifies the one assuages the pain of the other, that may actually be a natural fact enriched by a poetic vision.

Chapter 2

BATAILLE'S EROTICISM, NOW: FROM TRANSGRESSION TO INSIDIOUS SORCERY

Marc J. LaFountain

> The BELOVED has become the only force in this
> world in dissolution that has kept the power to bring
> us back to fervent life.
> —G. Bataille, "The Sorcerer's Apprentice"

Foucault suggested that transgression, quickened by Bataille's "promising ashes," will find the space of its language and the illumination of its being almost entirely in the future.[1] That future is *now,* and Bataille's eroticism must be reconsidered in the light of this moment in which I write: Bataille's "eroticism" within the space of transgression and the discourse of desire.

Transgression has been insidiously successful at inciting a condition of *non-savoir* in contemporary human existence. Because of transgression's capacity to shatter and fragment, to affirm loss and sacrifice, and to embrace the impossible, I am required to "test the extremity of its loss" (*LC,* 43). In that this loss is an exhausting and inexhaustible "spiral" or "flashing of lightning" (*LC,* 35), it is crucial to consider its movement. To do this is to engage in the "recognition" of unrecognizable negativity at the "current end of history" that Stoekl advised we pursue.[2]

In situating Bataille's eroticism in relation to death, excess, and writing, Foucault noted that "modern sexuality" has emerged as a force that extends beyond animality toward Absence. This acknowledgment of histories recommends we consider what history Bataille's eroticism evokes now: the death of the social as (dis)figured in ways consistent with, but yet beyond, what Bataille inscribed. "Death of the social" refers to Bataille's notion of "communication."[3] For him, communication must both suffer and be the ecstasy of death. He tracked this death of the social both anthropologically (through studies of archaic rituals and modern sociopolitical formations) and philosophically (through the mutilation of the subject and its writing).

However, the death of the social suffers yet another death that Bataille himself could not have anticipated, an impossibility most insidious. While Foucault asks what Bataille's transgression "might mean at the heart of a system of thought" (*LC*, 49), I ask what it means at the heart of a system of communication. I shall approach the philosophical question concerning eroticism, as did Bataille, in a fashion that passes through the space of sociology.[4] The erotic-sexual body is transfigured as and *con-fused* with the erotic-textual body, resulting in a simulated eroticism whose meanings need to be considered now. Here, sexuality extends beyond animality toward Absence and the glare of questions about "loss" and insidiousness torment luminously.

For Bataille, eroticism is not necessarily restricted to an exclusive focus on physical bodies. His concern was as much with a particular space of intimacy and destiny of which bodies can be the site. As sites, orgasmic bodies are significant, as rendered in his erotic novels and his studies of the "sacred" at the Collège de Sociologie. Nonetheless, I shall focus on the philosophical status of the body as the site of the erotic. Eroticism is for Bataille a certain continuity between bodies, but the issue is the pinnacle that this continuity opens. For Bataille, eroticism, like poetry, leads to "truth" and to the "real," both of which are "impossible." Herein lies the sense of Absence to which Foucault alluded. In contemporary history, the erotic body now includes and is inhabited by the text and the reader/writer. Together they form an erotic couple that poses new questions about just what "the BELOVED" could be *now*.[5]

I.

Communication figures prominently in Bataille's work as the site where humans work out their "destiny": an overcoming of the dissociative features of a servility grounded in production, accumulation, preservation, and utility. Life, Bataille asserts in "The Sorcerer's Apprentice," is "that which escapes servitude" (*SA*, 21) by seeking a "unity of the elements composing it" (*SA*, 18). This unity, however, inspired by an "avid and powerful will to be" (*SA*, 20), expresses the "fundamental right of man . . . to signify

27

nothing."[6] In expenditure, humans experience the "wholeness" of "existence," for to exist is to dispense with utilitarian projects and engage the "violent dynamic that has no other object than the return to a lost totality" (SA, 23). Such encounters open the "interior experience" of wholeness and belong to the realm of the sacred and the erotic. Their "truth" is known only as a consequence of a set of accidents (SA, 20).

But destiny is an aleatory figure, and its fulfillment is possible only by including the unincludable. To include the unincludable is to gather what transgresses limits of propriety and property, to contest limitation by affirming the impossible. Bataille proposes "heterology" to include that which is repulsive or "obscene"—that which is useless, negative, wasteful, excessive.[7] Heterology celebrates a "general economy." Excess beyond use can only be lost.[8] To be whole, to experience existence, is to seek excess, to lose oneself in it, to be tortured by its rapturous overflow—the work of the sorcerer's apprentice.

The practice of sorcery is the repetitious practice of liberating desire. Desire seeks no satisfaction but affirms humans by being the sign of destiny at the end of history. Much as Sartre and Merleau-Ponty condemned us to freedom and meaning, respectively, Bataille "condemns" us to transgression. Only by destroying ourselves, only in death, can we rid ourselves of satisfaction and steep ourselves in the free accidental play of desire, but to do so is to reiterate the death of God and the death of the God-simulacrum: the subject.

Desire, useless and excessive, is the practice of death and transgression, and for Bataille it is associated with eroticism. While sexuality travels with eroticism, eroticism is more an "assenting to life up to the point of death" (DS, 11) than an "act." "Acts" are despicable, for they "stifle" passion and affectivity and subjugate them to servility (SA, 17). Eroticism is a revolt, not an exercise of power, but a tumultuous upheaval of limitation, which Bataille named "sovereignty." Eroticism is a meaningless loss— a "transcending [of] the development of means . . . escape . . . release . . . acrobatics (in the worst sense of the word)."[9] But escape is toward the "impossible," whose extreme limit "assumes laughter, ecstasy, terrified approach towards death" (IE, 39). What is terrifyingly ecstatic, and comic, is the specter of non-savoir and its graphic blindness. At the extreme limit, "I see what knowledge was hiding up to that point, but if I see, I know. Indeed I know, but non-knowledge again lays bare what I have known . . . (without possible end)" (IE, 52). Infinite egress.

Non-savoir is anguish and disquietude, pleasurable catastrophe. "As if foreign to man, ecstasy arises from him, ignorant of the concern of which it was the object . . . for concern, it is nonsense; for the eagerness to know, it is non-knowledge (*IE*, 60). In the moment of *non-savoir,* no repose or appropriation, no comfortable possession is possible, only affliction and supplication, for "I am open, yawning gap, to the unintelligible sky and everything in me rushes forth, is reconciled in a final irreconciliation" (*IE*, 59). Eroticism is a disheveled joy, a dismemberment of I and we by a luscious madness. "Communication," beyond dissociative, discontinuous communication, is social interaction.

Eroticism is a revolt against a thinking that privileges the space of the subject. The subject that knows, idealizes, and acts pragmatically is lacerated; its embodiment in the world of everyday affairs is rendered a fanatical dance that finds it "necessary to become completely other, or to cease being" (*VE*, 179). Subject and self are no longer stable sources of meaning and productivity, but instead become accidents, "nomads." Only in the dissolution of the subject do we know that "consciousness is the ecstatic discovery of human destiny" (*SA*, 19). Not an originator or a proprietor, but a fissure, an opening "where you would like to grasp your timeless substance, [there] you encounter only a slipping, only the poorly coordinated play of your perishable elements" (*IE*, 94). The acrobatics that eroticism makes of knowledge and utility are also a sundering of language.

Transgressed by the overabundant totality of inner experience, language inevitably expends itself in an effort to say what it cannot. Bataille reveled, tormented, in the accident-prone, faltering, slipping nature of language. Language is an opening, a space of sacrifice and excess, a space where a destructive fusion occurs—a theater or altar at which meaning and signification are made and become their own victims. Similarly, in religious ceremonies, members of a community fuse in a consensual ritual of violence and destruction where individuals are torn from their social order and plunged into an "intimacy" and "communication" that is both death and plentitude. Here we find a "death of the social," for in death's expenditure, the community mutilates and obliterates itself in a glorious effusion that exceeds all reason and meaning and can only be known in frenzied laughter and crying. The "social," conventionally figured as production and coherence, is sacrificed in favor of a delirious derangement that surpasses meaning. Waste and negativity flow from within the community.

Likewise, language is an entourage of signs consensually joined for purposes of productivity and utility. But from within language, and at its extreme limits, it too is torn asunder in its attempts to extend its utility into the realm of that which is its own "destiny": an exorbitant, inclusive totality that is impossible.

Language becomes transgressive when sovereign, revealing discursive language to be a blindness. But when discursivity becomes sovereign it "prolongs the obsessive magic of spectacles, whether comic or tragic" (R, 67). Sovereign language, an excursion into the dark light of *non-savoir,* is an intimacy and communication that destroys sociality and reassembles it in a frightening and enlightening "sociality" named eroticism. Because nonsovereign discourse is blind to "mute, elusive, ungraspable" destiny, it can only neglect it. Undercut by "vague inner movements, which depend on no object and have no intent . . . [and] are not warranted by anything definable . . . [it] is dispossessed, can say nothing, is limited to stealing these states from attention" (IE, 14). A sovereign discourse of desire, however, "contests" and opens what is hidden and delayed. "Every human being not going to the limit is the servant or the enemy of man" (IE, 39–40). Transgression, then, is "a spirit of contestation . . . within us . . . a necessity for constant exchange, for frenzies following upon bursts of energy, for agitation, at times burning, feverish, at others icy, for a questioning undertaken endlessly in a new direction" (IE, 181).

Eroticism arises in contestation, for I (we) give myself (ourselves) as gift to the other in an intimacy that can only destroy me and us. Eroticism is the anguish and ecstasy of a violent fall, the impossibility of "my" or "our" being—the joyful, teary "little death" accompanying the extreme pleasure of "total" communication ("Pleasure is so close to ruinous waste that we refer to the moment of climax as a 'little death'" [DS, 170]). Eroticism is play, fissure, ungraspable effervescence and an "exuberance of life . . . even in death" (DS, 11). In Cixous's words, it is

> the voice which opens my eyes, its light opens my mouth, makes me shout. And I am born from it. . . . There is a link between this kind of star and the eruption of my soul. Thus it spreads in the air that makes it move, and from the mixture of its beams and my breath is born a field made of stars' blood and panting.[10]

Eroticism is a catastrophically anguishing and ecstatic experience of time and space "unhinged" (IE, 73–74). Again Cixous: "Whirl, the celestial canopy spreads its milky rivers, I succumb, I

roll a long, long time numb in the waves of my own flesh unfurl-
ing over the earth" (*S*, 21–22).

II.

Eroticism is indeed bound up in orgasmic bodies, but even more
so for Bataille in the impossibilities of death, excess, and continuity. Humans live though multiple deaths, and here I want to
explore the problematic of the death of the death of the social,
where transgression turns on itself and becomes insidious.
Among the deaths humans can live are what I might first call the
"big" death: the actual death of the living body, the irrevocable
spurt of blood, the scream, the whimpering assent or silent resignation accompanying expiration. Such a death may be embedded
in sacrificial rituals and festivals characteristic of archaic societies where people communally experience the radiance of a dark
sun beyond their knowing. Here the sacred, the orgiastic, and death
conspire to make humans whole and fulfill their destiny. But big
death also takes the form of fascist, criminal, sadistic, and other
acts. Desolation, nihilism, and eroticism became wrenchingly
problematic issues for Bataille's politics.

Because Bataille himself trembled at the prospect of big death,
it was crucial to move to arenas where it could be symbolically
experienced, or could be experienced as a "little" death. This is
Bataille's concession against wanton torrents of "absolute" negativity. Although Bataille maintained that life "has the simplicity of
an ax stroke" (*SA*, 18), there were only certain strokes he would
sanction. To assent to big death in modernity is to risk sustaining
de Sade's murderous aberration (*DS*, 18–19).

With the *Acephale* group, Bataille launched into a series of
Nietzschean revelries and subversions that valorized the risk, loss,
and sacrifice of the individual. The very notion of "*acephalic* man"
celebrated, for instance, in the "The Practice of Joy Before Death"
was an ax stroke that doubly severed the individual from him/
herself and dismembered the social by inserting in its worldly communion a transgressive negativity (e.g., "The Obelisk"). This individualism promoted a "useful uselessness" with its attacks on
fascism, whereas Bataille's earlier *Contre-Attaque* stance fell dan-
gerously close to a useless uselessness associated with fascist violence and sacrifice. Here, "the individual"—in political, social, and
philosophical domains—is stripped naked and sacrificed. A discontinuity is thus established. But without some other continuity,

as provided in eroticism, this would be but isolation and desolation. Nonetheless, this stripping naked is a "decisive action" (*DS,* 19).

Taken into the domain of writing, this violence and denuding were evident in *Inner Experience, Guilty,* and *The Impossible.* These texts are lacerated, and language is made to stumble and fall. Pushed to the margins that expose the limits of language—its very impossibility—transgression disfigures the linguistic production of meaning. The author is condemned to automutilation and autoeroticism. Sentences, powerless to grasp anything but their failure and their effort of contestation (*IE,* 15), utterly futile, nonetheless permit their own "useless noise to die out" (*IE,* 181). Without such "obstinacy," as Klossowski referred to Bataille's writing, there is no descent into the night of existence or climb to its "pinnacle" (*DS,* 275). With "slipping words," writing makes us familiar with a "helpless foolishness" that conceals intensities, and through these words, we approach the extreme limit—"the only point through which man escapes his limited stupidity, but at the same time in order to sink into it" (*IE,* 39). Sacrifice, an "infinite foolishness" that assumes laughter, ecstasy, terror, error, nausea, unceasing agitation, and degradation, is the only release from a "despicable destiny" (*IE,* 40) grounded in knowledge and sense. Communication, desire, and writing compel by an immensity I do not know, yet in knowing it, I am destroyed. Again Cixous: "I move between the cloths of this furnishing air, which forces me to sculpted gestures" (*S,* 79–80).

In that writing is a convulsive site where eroticism overcomes discontinuity in the "impossible" movement of continuity. Bataille focused on the sovereignty of poetic and erotic (for many, "pornographic") writing. While different from each other, "poetry leads to the same place as all forms of eroticism" (*DS,* 25)—truth. But truth is only attained in the "the extremism of desire and death," for "only death and desire have the force that oppresses, that takes one's breath away."[11] A violence accompanies truth, and that is its impossibility. The work of life (destiny) is to oppose utility with violent pleasure and horror. But "we are never within our right in preferring seduction: Truth has rights over us" (*I,* 10). These "rights" (a "declaration of the rights of humans") consist in abandonment to desire—an avid will to be, to signify nothing, to destroy self-preservation, to seek excess and extremity. Only in their practice is it possible to silence the nostalgia for continuity, a continuity eroticism's disequilibrium intimates (*DS,* 12–18). The truth of eroticism is the impossibility of our being that is predicated on a death of the social ("the real") that folds back on itself and accomplishes a continuity that itself is a death of the social. "Intimacy" and "communication" involve fissure as well as consummation. Bataille demands and finds the impossible in poetry as well as in sexual encounters. "True poetry is outside laws. . . . I approach poetry: but only to miss it" (*I,* 158–59). Poetry, like erotic sexual encounters, is a space in which we contest the impossible, consisting in little other than forgetting the truth of the rights it imposes on us "only by accepting disappearance" (*I,* 10).

Sexual encounters, as erotic deflagrations, mark a "convulsion that involves the whole movement of beings." This "convulsion goes from death's disappearance to that voluptuous rage which, perhaps, is the meaning of disappearance" (*I,* 10). But erotic writing, like the "hatred" of poetry (*I,* 10), is not just ignominious or lugubrious. It is also an exalted event, for it reminds us that thought and writing are not separate from desire, from the body, but are in fact coterminous with passion and the body, as are the "truth" of death and desire. And just as the body of writing is forced into a frenzy that disrupts its coherence, so too do the bodies of "I" and "we" disappear, screaming and crying, into an abyss, united beyond any fusion they could ever say or use: "You could not become the mirror of a heartrending reality if you did not have to be broken" (*IE,* 96). The "little death," whether in Bataille's sense or in Barthes's "pleasure of the text," is a preferred *simulacrum* of death. I underscore simulacrum to differentiate it from symbolization, for the latter bears the aura of mimesis and representation Bataille so despised. Bataille would accept this difference based on his own substitution of a deleterious repetition for mimesis: "The fall of the 'return' is FINAL" (*VE,* 220). But can we now know the difference between simulated and symbolized death? If we did not know the difference, we would lose sight of the extreme limit (impossibility) without ever knowing it had been lost. This would be sorcery's insidious turn.

Another disappearance and violence opens as the spiral of transgression turns back on itself *now.* This "now" is important for another convulsiveness, also erotic, situated in the space of writing *after* the instantiation of transgression by Bataille. Recall Foucault's comment that the plentitude of transgression's "scattered signs" and "language" will appear in the future, which only echoes Bataille's claim that "one day" impossibility "may" become clearer (*I,* 10). According to Bataille's double interest in language and anthropology, "signs" are social as well as linguistic, and "semiotics" extends into the organization of human affairs and arrangements (cf. Barthes, Kristeva, Deleuze) as well as into linguistic orders. This requires that we recognize that social being and linguistic being are conjoined in the movement of transgression. This must be brought to the fore in considering "the extremity of the loss" incurred in transgression.

The social world (and writing) requires a certain order based on utility, productivity, and signification. It necessarily depends upon identification and systematization, requiring a sense of personal order (e.g., sanity, coherence). Bataille would suggest that this ordering, in its own way, is similar to reproduction in nature—it creates discontinuity, or discontinuous beings. "Between one being and another, there is a gulf, a discontinuity" (DS, 12) that stands as a death of the social. At the core of community and communication is a cleft between what is marginalized/excluded and what is included and closed in the name of identity and coherence. A death of the social at the very beginning of life is alluded to by Bataille's recognition of a "nostalgia" and "yearning" that torment our "random and ephemeral individuality" (DS, 15).

Because discontinuity is the death of the social, a nostalgic "obsession with a primal continuity" (DS, 15) emerges as eroticism whose "whole business . . . is to destroy the self-contained character of the participants as they are in their normal lives" (DS, 17). Here eroticism's agitation as an exhausting, abysmal continuity "in-sites" a death in the death of the social, a continuity with everything, hence excess (a "general economy") beyond use or signification in death. Whether in physical, emotional, or religious forms, "the concern is to *substitute* for individual isolated discontinuity a feeling of profound continuity" (DS, 15, emphasis added). But this death of the death of the social is itself a death of the social, for at the heart of a continuity that requires social interaction as a condition of communication is another "communication" and "intimacy" that sacrifices and destroys the very unity that ended discontinuity. Thus, while eroticism brings about sovereignty, it nevertheless *requires* the notion that social interaction is indispensable as *the limit* through which "communication" is achieved. Social interaction is "the stabilized order of isolated appearances [that] is necessary to the anguished consciousness of the torrential floods which carry it away (IE, 95) . . . we can discover only *in others* how it is that the light exuberance of things has us at its disposal" (IE, 97, emphasis Bataille's). Bataille could not avoid writing when silence would have seemed appropriate because writing was a necessary "betrayal" that could open the catastrophic "pinnacle" (IE, 66–68) of exhausting totality: destiny.[12] Social interaction is unavoidable as a betrayal that opens to this destiny. Social interaction, which makes of you and me "in the vast flow of things only a stopping point favoring a resurgence" (*IE*, 95), is a semiotic order akin to writing. It marks the limits, the "fragile walls," of one's isolation that serve to "reflect for an instant the flash of those universes in the heart of which you never cease to be lost" (*IE*, 95). Eroticism is a death of the death of the social, which also defines the movement of the space of desire.

As transgression spirals *now*, we may speak of yet another death inscribed within the death of the social. The problem of the impossible, the extreme limit and *non-savoir* that anguished Bataille, torments this very writing, and already I, it, and *we* become warped. Because *now*, within the "labyrinth" (*IE*, 81), I detect something else set in, in-sited, insidious, within the opening of destiny. Within the widening of includability opens another gap: a possible unincludable. Its very possibility marks a turn of transgression toward insidiousness.

In the movement from big death toward little death, transgression has settled now on textual violence and sacrifice. As writers, we practice intently the subversion of teleology, dialectics, representation, idealism, and a host of other formations we take as servilities (deaths) to be exceeded. In doing this have we, unlike Bataille, restricted our eroticism to a proper (property) preservation of philosophizing that excludes poetry and novels from our writing? Dedicated to our tactic, have we become overly obsessed with excessive writing such that an insidious excess has canceled destiny's excessiveness? We have, of course, made of philosophy and poetics a literature, and in that sense we have permitted Bataille's claim that "philosophy [is] on the same level as life . . . [and is] no longer a phenomenon of circumstances alien to fear and desire. . . . A man in life's grip [is] obviously dealing with questions of philosophy as if he were in a stranglehold. In this, philosophy [is] . . . reduced to literature."[13] Have we perhaps mutilated eroticism, making of it a textual matter in which sexuality, as a texture of sociality, has tumbled into the fissures of our writing? I suggest we have substituted (*DS*, 15) the textual for the social, and this amounts to an insidious turn: a simulating and canceling of the sociality of the "burning intensity" whose thickness relates one person to another. Even Bataille suggested that symbolic communication is a condition against which expenditure operates, and without actual interaction, there is a danger of a freedom or loss that is little more than "rhetorical."[14]

Have we confused the sacrifice of communication (which worldly communication accomplishes) with the sacrifice of communication that stems from "excessive writing"? Here the question is about excessiveness as a servile dedication to writing for certain purposes, for example, efficient, productive knowledge within the academy (*savoir*) versus excessiveness as sovereignty and eroticism (*non-savoir*). If the former holds, we have parodied eroticism in favor of a "timid attachment . . . a laughable error . . . dwindled existence . . . an absurd little turning in on itself" (*IE*, 95). When questioned by Blanchot about the possibility of pursuing inner experience as if he were the "last man," Bataille indicated that doing so would mean he could not "escape" and would, *without others*, be "thrown back into myself . . . empty, indifferent" and would "remain before infinite annihilation" (*IE*, 61). Sovereignty is possible "for others," through others, and because of others. Others are not hell; they are instead the condition of sacrifice, anguish, and communication. Actual social interaction, whether as ritual religious sacrifice or erotic encounter, is the communication in which I am destroyed. "I felt myself to be in solidarity with the existence which fell before me in Nothingness. . . . It must be communicated from one man to another . . . inscribing its point of night in the luminous order of things" (*IE*, 194).

Let us approach this by returning to Bataille's problematic of the relationship of isolation (and madness) and linguistic transgression. Transgression's "projectless project" (*IE*, 46) is inner experience, and nondiscursive writing is capable of sovereignty. Bataille, as Richman observed, insists on the "isolation of the act of writing." The "written product . . . will induce communication at its most significant level" (*R*, 74). For the author, and for the reader who also experiences "communication" and "intimacy" through writing (*IE*, 94), something internal becomes external. Without externalization and dramatization, without a "coincidence of wills," we would never move beyond our immediate, isolated, suffering selves (*R*, 72). In commenting on Nietzsche's writing as a means of liberating the individual, Bataille offers that excessive individualism borders on tragic and unintelligible privatization, on madness. Instead he seeks "a burning intensity as the condition of the relation to another" that avoids "a futile, empty expenditure" (*VI*, 12–13). Sovereignty, through writing, must then address—via a rupture—a rapture that announces death, and thus fulfillment, through "superabundance" and "plethoric disorder" (*DS*, 101, 104). But does the self-referentiality of the text cast the writer (or reader) and text as a simulated erotic couple that destroys the very interaction that is vital to being the limit of an excess that is "animated, passing from one to another in love, in tragic scenes, in movements of fervor" (*IE*, 94)? As writers, we are fervent about our textuality. But if it is our constant partner, haven't we substituted it for that sociality that can *only* be found in our lovers's arms?

The problem, then, is that at the end of history now, when big death has moved to the theater of little death, and literature has become the "heir to religion" (*DS*, 87), how do we live in the communicative context of everyday life, in the sociality that is the condition of the "sociality" of abysmal continuity? When the sacrifice is a text that becomes the site of a theater or drama reduced to a final episode where the human or animal victim acts alone until death (*DS*, 87), has transgression folded back on itself in a fashion Bataille did not imagine? That is, in the substitution of the text as the site of the sacrifice of object and author, how do we know that this dramatization, which Bataille so obviously took as a *symbolic* substitute, is not in fact a simulation? How do we avoid the tragedy of interpretation and know whether in fact it replaces anything or achieves nothing (i.e., excessiveness and death)? Of course, this is the problem of *non-savoir* Bataille himself so ardently embraced. But because we cannot know this now, because another impossibility has been in-sited, transgression has become insidious.

The supreme moment of eroticism is the ecstatically disgorged silence exceeding and following the rupture of signification and sense. "But language does not vanish. . . . How should one reach the heights if language did not point the way?" (*DS*, 275). Since "language" is not just a semiotics or an institution of words, but simultaneously a semiotics of interaction and exchange, sociality neither should nor can vanish. Transgression, as death, desire, is the "game" or "play" (*DS*, 275) that inscribes in both language *and* sociality a destruction of discontinuity that dissimulates continuity in favor of a yearned-for continuity.

Insidiousness parodies or inverts the dissimulation, confusing the role of silence in such a way as to place it within the sphere of the sociality that is necessary to "reach the heights." Does this rending condemn us to a writing and reading alone, an autoeroticism, that is tantamount to an erasure of sociality—thereby a canceling of the "whole business of eroticism"? Are we making of eroticism, as writing, an end, a knowledge, and in so doing substituting our own blind spot for Hegel's (*IE*, 111), thus eclipsing the radiant luminosity of the dark of night? Is transgressive writing useless uselessness or useful uselessness? Can we tell the difference now? Has that which constitutes "non-logical difference"

(*VE*, 129) been effaced, and with it the improbable conjunction of the possible and the impossible? Has another impossible been sited? These are terrifying questions, and herein lies their insidious force. They *do* impose now.

Bataille leaned heavily (e.g., *DS*, 36) on what Stoekl has considered an "advanced dialectic," born of the impossibility of neither integrating negativity nor of doing away with its betrayals.[15] Stoekl also suggested that in taking up this "utopian" advance, which both embraces and subverts a dialectical operation, "we incessantly betray our own methodology (and thus we betray Bataille)" (*PWM*, 131). I would add that insidious writing amounts to a betrayal. To take substitution as symbolization rather than simulation is to take it that writing *about* eroticism, which doubles *as* eroticism (i.e., writing erotically), is sufficient to fulfill an avid will to be and is sufficient to fulfill the conditions of a "burning intensity as the condition of *relation* to another." It appears Bataille understood this problem, for in *The History of Eroticism* he offered that the erotic couple, as *social* individuals, is a possible basis for a new social order.[16] Offered, however, in the same text (*HE*, 163) is the notion of a "private eroticism" (e.g., writing as an individual practice). Nevertheless, to consider symbolization without considering simulation is to constitute an inversion of the problem of eroticism as the *end of discontinuity!* Here we find embedded in Bataille's exclamation "I am myself war" something other than the impossibility of holding together Nietzschean and Hegelian proclivities (e.g., *VE*, xxiii; *PWM*, xv). Perhaps Bataille knew well that the move from big death to little death to writing carried with it a "trickery" (*VE*, 224, figure 16). Is this trickery emerging insidiously?

A question is thus raised about the possibility of something exterior to and in excess of Bataille's general economy of "nonlogical difference." Because this emerges as an impossibility, Bataille's transgressive writing ironically fulfills its destiny of sovereignty and expenditure. What is particularly important for the notion of insidiousness is that this insidiousness in our writing is a question, and we are anguished now to know whether or not we are perpetuating a discontinuity whose trajectory is desolation or one whose fractures and fissures are the ecstatically agonized cries and tears of individuals fulfilled and overcome. My questioning is not a move in the direction of Habermas's "communicative action" or Baudrillard's "fatal strategy" or Manfred Frank's critique of neostructuralism. The question vexing us now is whether or not our eroticism is an "art of disappearance," a void into which "we" fall while Bataille himself is "forgotten."[17] Does the production of absence and negativity double as an "art of disappearance" where the (auto)eroticism of excessive individuality simulates both the sacred and sensuous sociality? Richman quietly raised this specter with her comment that one aspect of the project of *Inner Experience* was to "*simulate* ecstasy" (*R*, 70, emphasis added). In her treatment of transgressive writing she offers that simulated ecstasy can achieve sovereignty vis-à-vis the institution of language (*R*, 72–75). What then becomes of the extreme limit of eroticism and its effort to vivify the "total man" (*VI*, 429)? Resituating isolation, via the insidious turn of eroticism, repositions the limits of communication and intimacy.

If transgressive writing is an "advanced dialectic," as Bataille suggested, where the "Hegelian nature of this operation . . . corresponds with the dialectical phase described by the untranslatable German *aufheben*: to transcend without suppressing" (*DS*, 36), then is insidious writing an "advanced transgression"? Or is it outside transgression? This is not a matter of nihilism or cynicism, or even "guilt" (*PWM*, 130). Neither is it a Bataillean reaction to the "world in dissolution," nor the scream of one experiencing the violence of a fall to wholeness. Rather it is a question concerning the effacement of the difference between the two. Transgressive writing is a form of mutilation and fracture. Whether an advanced transgressiveness or some other impossible, the spiral into the future problematizes language, sexuality, sociality, and eroticism. Is Bataille's suggestion that this impossibility and the "meaning of disappearance" (*I*, 10) might one day become "clearer" actually trans(ex)piring now?

Concluding her own reading of Bataille, Richman suggested the challenge of Bataille is to future readers who are "called upon to propose yet another reading" (*R*, 153). I agree with her echoing of Bataille's claim that literature reorients human relations. Thus, is Bataille's eroticism something to be assented to or resisted now? Has he succeeded in generating a "utopia" (*PWM*, xi–xix) where "non-logical difference" marks our existence? Is transgression a seduction that can only betray us as we betray it? If so, what is the limit of the betrayal?

Bataille incessantly wrote of "tears and laughter" when discussing the irruption of the sacred in our existence. We need to ask whether these "tears" are the emanations of eros's ravishing rupture, that is, tormented joyous liquidations and excretions of "the eye" (pineal or solar), or whether they are just rips and gashes that make of laughter the derision of a very black humor. This *non-savoir* is further complicated in that "tears" is a difference that cannot be written but can only be said. Because eroticism's new theater (writing, reading) has been substituted for and simulates "lovers in bed" (*SA*, 18), we are no longer compresent and cannot say it. We can "liberate language" and we can write transgressively to incite eroticism textually, but are we erotic sexually anymore? We may remember what Bataille meant by "the beloved," but do we know anymore what is "beloved" for us? This is not to miss the point of transgressive writing and bow down to the "puerility of reason," but rather it is to "test the measure of the loss."[18] Nor is it to miss the point about the significance of nondiscursive, fractured writing, but rather to question whether or not a transgression of the text's semiotics precipitates an insidious sociality that folds back on and cancels the social. Were this the case, we perhaps would have a writing that is dead, an "absurd little turning in on itself" (*IE*, 95) that simulates the "living myth" of the sorcery of that which we do not know is an effect of the sorcery we practice.

Do we affirm Bataille, then? Yes, but only if he is read against himself, and here I concur with Shaviro's "echolalic" contestation of Bataille.[19] Affirmation is possible if we acknowledge that insidiousness is another dissolution not previously recognized and that it does form an extreme limit that requires surpassing. This would vivify Bataille's claim that "on the most fundamental level there are transitions from continuous to discontinuous or from discontinuous to continuous" (*DS*, 15). Then again, in the same breath, a failure occurs if we infuse discontinuity with a terrible negativity that excludes transition and metamorphosis, substituting an isolation impervious to the play of accident. We must continue to distinguish between "destruction" and "annihilation."[20] "Continuity is what we are after, *but* generally *only if* that continuity which the death of discontinuous beings can alone establish is not the victor *in the long run*" (*DS*, 19, emphasis added). Here is where *savoir* and *non-savoir* continue without possible end (*IE*, 52). If "existence" is communication, and communication sacrifice, then "the one who sacrifices is himself affected by the blow he strikes. He succumbs and loses himself with his victim . . . in . . . an incompleted world . . . incompletable and forever unintelligible" (*IE*, 153). We must distinguish in eroticism whether or not "with his victim" suggests the materiality (mood, flesh) of the sensuous "beloved other" or the materiality of a text's simulated beloved other: "Only the lovers' accord, like the agreement of players, creates the living reality, yet undefined, of correspondences" (*SA*, 20).

40

If "what there is of tragedy and deep loss within a being, that 'blinding miracle,' can be encountered now only in bed" (*SA*, 18), then perhaps to raise the question of insidious writing means only that we need to ponder the extreme limits of textual existence. Perhaps we are to consider the degree to which eroticism, as writing, makes an *impossibility* out of the "accidents that give an avid, powerful will to be the response it desires" (*SA*, 20). Where there are no accidents, there is no risk or vulnerability or opening but only closure and servility. Perhaps our simulations and substitutions are but "cowardly gestures" (*VE*, 69) that, like sacrificial mutilation used for expiation and propitiation, only make victims and destroy heterogeneity and change instead of promoting the self-transformation that throws one suddenly outside oneself (*VE*, 70). Is our eroticism, destabilized by a disfigured sociality, the self-mocking dissolution and parody of an "agitated caressing hand [that] is not seeking an entry, a hold, or a secret; it is only departing from the point of encounter, getting lost, describing a space in which it can lose itself"?[21]

If eroticism is a "projectless project," then just what is its uselessness? And what is, now, the measure of its loss?

PART II
DESIRE FOR THE OTHER:
LEVINAS

Chapter 3

THE (NON)LOGIC OF DESIRE AND WAR: HEGEL AND LEVINAS

Brian Schroeder

Ever since Alexandre Kojève's celebrated lectures on Hegel in the 1930s, European (especially French) and continental philosophers have often focused their attention on the theme of *desire* and, like Kojève, have often relied heavily on Hegel's analysis of desire in the *Phenomenology of Spirit,* even to the point of presenting it as the heart of the Hegelian project.[1] While the attention given to the *Phenomenology* can and has been justified (particularly given the concerns of existential phenomenology and Western Marxism), in order to understand the Hegelian enterprise as a whole, the earlier *Phenomenology* must be interpreted through the categories of the later *Science of Logic.*[2] Hegel himself stresses this in the opening passages of the introduction to the *Logic,* where he states that the dialectic of the *Phenomenology* is no different from that of the *Logic.* However, as Jean Hyppolite points out, the relation between these cornerstone texts of Hegel's philosophy is far from being definitively resolved.[3] The present essay eschews this debate, but proposes an unorthodox reading of the "logic" of desire from the perspective of the *Science of Logic* in an effort to more fully understand its structure as presented in the *Phenomenology of Spirit.*

This essay will examine the theme of desire, its logical and religious structures, and its relation to the most extreme form of interpersonal violence—war—by assessing Hegel's philosophy through that of Emmanuel Levinas, who radically reconceives the relation between intersubjectivity and desire.[4] On Hegel's reading, desire (*Begierde*) assumes an essentially negative function in that it fills a lack or void between the subject and object, between the self and its other, while for Levinas, Desire (*désir*) is that modality of subjective being that brings us into a genuine relationship with otherness while preserving the Other's alterity.[5]

What are the differences and similarities between their respective positions? How is Levinas's philosophy influenced by Hegel's, and in what respects does it represent a significant departure and advance from it? Does the negativity, that is, otherness, that desire negates in its movement as Spirit render the relation with the Other obsolete, or does it bring one into a genuine relation with the Other?[6] What is the role that desire plays in the promotion and/or overcoming of the violence that is war?

I.

In Hegel's philosophy, Spirit (*Geist*), the movement of History toward its self-actualization as Freedom, is the recognition of what is already given to consciousness in the immediacy of sense certainty. As the process and goal of absolute knowing, Spirit is not the imposition of any new thought-determinations (*Gedankenbestimmungen*); its *formal* truth content is always already fully present, even in its initial undisclosedness. Hegel maintains the essentially paradoxical position that, on the one hand, the Absolute is sheer self-immediacy (selfsameness) and, on the other, that it is self-differentiation (self-sundering and returning from otherness). The "power of the negative," as contradiction itself, both compels (via desire) and propels (via negation) the dialectic: it is "the principle of all self-movement" (*WL* II, 496, 835), the "*void* as the principle of motion" (*PhG*, 32, 21).

The *telos* of Spirit is but its return via mediation to its beginning. For Hegel, the question of the infinite is inseparable from the status of *Grund* and of the teleology of Spirit. Hegelian logic claims superiority over traditional or formal logic in that formal logic does not begin from a critical, presuppositionless standpoint. Formal logic asserts the permanent diremption of the terms "infinite" and "finite." In Hegel's logic, the question of origin is that of the end and vice versa. Circularity is exalted as the "true" or affirmative infinity (*Unendlichkeit*) (*WL* I, 138, 149; II, 504, 842).

What is the relation between the concepts of infinity and alterity? What is the relation of this question to the origin (*archè*) of violence and war? And what is the role of desire in determining these questions?

The infinite of dialectical logic (*Vernunft*) differs from the infinite of formal logic (*Verstand*), which is only a "finitized infinite" (*WL* I, 125/137). The understanding (*Verstand*) is confined to a bad concept of infinity because it perpetually questions and criticizes the notion of the unity of the infinite and the finite. As such, the understanding continually oscillates between the two determinations of the moments of unity and separation without reconciliation.

The supersession (*Aufheben*) of the infinite as the affirmative negation of the infinite and of the finite as a unitary process, claims Hegel, is the "genuine" infinite. As the negation of the negation (finitude), the infinite is becoming; it is the self-overcoming of limited being. This is the realization of Spirit as freedom. The infinite does not stand as completed and superior to finitude as "beyond being" (*epekeina tes ousías*) in the Platonic sense of the term.[7] Being is the infinite becoming of finite being. The finite and the infinite stand in a relation of qualitative determinate difference to each other while, at the same time, negating and transcending their difference or limitation and thus passing over into itself (*an sich*), that is, becoming infinite. Infinity is "the indeterminate void, the beyond of the finite" (*WL* I, 128, 139).

The question is the status of "the beyond" (*das Jenseits*). Since the infinite is characterized as a circle, then there is no beyond, no radical difference. The finite and the infinite are connected by the very negation that separates and distinguishes them from each other. Each term acts as the limitation of the other. But at the same time, each term dissociates itself from the other as its limit, as its nonbeing, and "as qualitatively separate from it, posits it as another being outside it" (*WL* I, 129, 140).

The continual oscillation of the finite and the infinite constitutes the "spurious" or "bad" infinite for Hegel (*WL* I, 128, 139). Trying to avoid the mere alternation of terms, he claims that the connection between the finite and the infinite is external but essential. Each term needs the other in order to be what it is. The true infinite is thus a "finite infinite" and an "*infinitized finite*" (*WL* I, 133–34, 144–45). Infinity reveals itself to consciousness as finitude; it is only the self-transcendence of the finite, and as such, the affirmative negative. The finite is the infinitely finite. The infinite and the finite are the same (*WL* I, 136, 147), an observation made nearly four hundred years earlier by Nicolas Cusanus.

The universal substance in absolute idealism is realized as "subject" since "in the negative unity of the Idea [*Idee*] the Infinite overlaps [*übergreift*] and includes the finite, thought overlaps being, subjectivity overlaps objectivity."[8] The infinite return of consciousness to itself mediated by otherness demonstrates the priority that is assigned to the subject, that is, to selfsameness. Subject is the truth of Substance and so transcends [*übergreift*] what is just the object, though the difference between subject and object is maintained in the unity of the Idea. Subject is the relation of the Idea to consciousness, of the world (*Welt*) as ideal, as subjective and objective unity. The parameters for understanding the trajectory of intersubjective desire and the relation between war and peace are determined within this move.

The Idea (*Idee*) manifests itself to consciousness as the concept (*Begriff*). This is taken up in the *Phenomenology of Spirit,* which is preeminently concerned with the relation between concepts. The aim of Spirit, the transformation of consciousness into self-consciousness, is achieved only after all the possible shapes that "natural" consciousness can assume have been exhausted. This occurs in the move to "philosophical" consciousness, which takes immediate natural consciousness as its object. Natural consciousness is deficient in that it is aware only of the immediacy of its own existence. It takes as its object those things that are outside itself. Philosophical consciousness, on the other hand, takes the concept (or itself *qua* thing or substance) for its object. Seeking knowledge of knowledge, it aims to close the gap between the *an sich* (in-itself, being, truth) and the *für sich* (for-itself, knowing). This is accomplished via the acquisition of the *adequate* concept, the thought-determination that knows no other than itself: Totality.

In Hegelian dialectics, otherness has no meaning apart from its relation with sameness and vice versa. This holds true for every dialectical opposition. While each dyadic term is distinct and knowable as such, its truth value lies in the holistic relation that it has with its opposite. Absolute knowing is the process of consciousness arriving at this truth since "everything turns on grasping and expressing the True, not only as *Substance,* but equally as *Subject*" (*PhG,* 19, 10). In the *Phenomenology* and in the *Logic* the problem of otherness is reconciled in the dialectics of the *Aufhebung.* Substance is realized as Subject only by virtue of its having been mediated by the object of its reflection, that is, by alterity.

II.

Hegel asserts that freedom, and presumably peace, are possible only if some sort of transcendental subjectivity, an "absolute knowing," is realizable. The subjectivity that comes to know itself as freedom is political subjecthood. Spirit (*Geist*) is the actualization of citizenry in the homogenous State. The universal citizen is not only the cornerstone of community; it is the (non)face of Spirit as well. Self-consciousness is manifest as the totality of social relations. The *telos* of Spirit, aside from being the recognition that the individual existent has no meaning apart from the collective social totality and that history is the unfolding of freedom, is also the realization by consciousness of what Parmenides of Elea espoused so long ago, namely, that being and thinking are virtually indistinguishable in their relational unity.

So just how other is the Other? Is there a truly genuine other in Hegel's thought? To be "other" is to be by its very definition *other than,* just as consciousness is *consciousness of,* at least in its Husserlian formulation. Absolute alterity is other than the concept or thought of otherness and not just the polar opposite of the concept of the same. Yet Hegel maintains that universality is simple selfsameness mediated by alterity. In other words, self-consciousness consists in being recognized as self-consciousness by another self-consciousness. But is this a recognition by a truly other, or is it merely a self-recognition by the same?

The assertion of the equiprimordiality of each term of every dialectical opposition renders the Absolute as Totality. This totality, Hegel repeatedly states, is the identity of identity and difference, the unity of unity and multiplicity, the sameness of sameness and otherness. The synthesizing activity of the *Aufhebung* (negation, preservation, supersession) always returns to the beginning, to the sheer immediacy of identity present in and to natural consciousness, that is, of sense certainty. The totality is identical with itself (and thus with its other) from the beginning. Philosophical consciousness is the recognition of this simple yet complex point.

The concept of the *Aufhebung* is the cornerstone of Hegel's thought; however, it denies the full status of the Other as other insofar as the supersession is actually a self-mediation of consciousness by its own alterity of thought. Hegel admits this, though he holds that it does not preclude the integrity of the other in its alterity (or of the Other in her alterity?).

Does the concept of the *Aufhebung* conceal a latent *metaviolence* upon which all other violence is predicated? If so, then as the absolute move of the absolute Idea, this condemns historical progress to the impetus of a necessary violence or conflict. So what founds the violence of history? Is it the commencement of

49

the relation with the Other (*l'autrui*) through speech action? Is it the negation of the other (*l'autre*) as a necessary dialectical stage in the self-realization of Spirit? Or is there a pretemporal originary violence that precedes any concrete historical violence, a violence whose essence lies in the logic of the Idea?

Violence, by Hegel's own admission, is unavoidable in the historical progression of Spirit. The concept itself contains the seed of violence insofar as it is primordially selfsame and always returns to itself as such. This is the focus of Levinas's critique of Hegel's variant of idealism.[9] What is violence if not that which is directed toward the suppression or the negation of that which is other? If desire, as the manifestation of the power of the negative, is that which overcomes the separation between self and other, between the for-itself and the in-itself, is it not the very movement of violence? Here is questioned the claim of preserving the integrity of the difference of the other. Does Hegelian philosophy constitute an actual recognition of alterity at all?

The epistemological and metaphysical circularity of the concept reveals itself as a form of conceptual "imperialism." Violence is done to the Other not in the sense of negating the other (which is actually only an *auto*negation), but in that the Other is not recognized as being genuinely other. Consciousness's quest for recognition reveals itself as a narcissistic longing and self-fulfilling aggrandizement.

The apocalyptic vision of Spirit rests on the establishment of the total, universal State. Toward this one goal, posited as freedom itself, all becoming is subject. Is this the actual meaning of the famous dictum "Substance is Subject"? Does subject truly denote subjectivity? Is the judgment that properly belongs to ethics that of history? These questions rest essentially on the status of the Absolute, of the Infinite. On Hegel's interpretation, infinity is equiprimordial with the finite. The two terms cannot be thought separately, as they derive meaning from their dialectical relation with each other; but the two terms are also fundamentally different from the very outset. Is it possible, then, to assert an adequate correlation between a fundamentally *a*historical term (the idea of infinity) and a term that is steeped in historicality (finitude)? The alleged equiprimordiality of the two terms is the question here. Hegel's objection to the Infinite as proposed by Levinas would be that "in the very act of keeping the infinite pure and aloof from the finite, the infinite is only made finite" (*WL* I, 125, 137).

Is infinity present in history *as* history, or is it *trans*historical? If the latter is the case, does this imply a noninvolved, nonpraxical theory of politics, or even the impossibility of such a project? On the metaphysical level, the question is that of the status of infinity. Epistemologically, is infinity recoverable in its totality as an object for thought? Or does the very impossibility of such a closure—on one level, meaninglessness itself—convey a signification whose meaning is ethical and perfect, as Levinas purports? If there is no real distinction between the finite and the infinite, as Hegel claims, then is he not correct in arguing for the inevitable perfection of history as politics?

III.

Levinas maintains that Western philosophy (a tautology) is dominated by the "concept of totality," which "suspends morality" and renders in its "visage of being" the very advent of the violence that is war.[10] In opposition to this totalizing ontology that has dominated since Aristotle, he posits a redefined notion of "metaphysics" as the nontheoretical ethical or social relation.[11] This relation is characterized as the movement of Desire toward and for the infinitely other, which is to say the Other. Metaphysics is the relation of consciousness with a prior term absolutely exterior to it, a term prelinguistic and preconceptual. Hegel and Levinas are united in the essentially Greek position that holds to the code-termination of metaphysical and political concepts. But the definition of "metaphysics" as the nonconceptual mode of relation with the other in all its manifestations shifts the ancient complicity to that between "ontology" and politics. Metaphysics, the nontheoretical movement of Desire characterized as speech (dialectic in the Platonic sense) and not vision (Hegelian dialectic; phenomenology as ontology), is ethics. The opposition of ethics and politics opens *Totality and Infinity* and underscores its entire reading. Philosophy's task is to avoid "being duped by morality," that is, to avoid conflating ethics and politics. Is that not to deny, though, the very intersection of ideas that will bring peace? Is not the very separation of these fundamental terms the root of violence? What is the danger of such a union?

"Political society," says Levinas, "appears as a plurality that expresses the multiplicity of the articulation of a system" (*TI,* 239, 216). The respect for, and maintenance of, plurality constitutes the essence of the ethical relation, since with the introduction of the "third party" justice enters the world. Plurality is alterity itself; the metaphysical One is social (historical) multiplicity. Here

51

Levinas appears to repeat the position of the *Phenomenology.* But in the *Logic,* plurality is an inessential moment that does not designate the other and hence is not accorded a full measure of reality. Plurality "appears not as an otherness, but as a determination completely external to the one" (*WL* I, 159, 168). Social plurality, the stuff of ethics, is subsumed in Hegel's system under the thematic of universal citizenry.

The origin and function of politics is necessary and inescapable. Neither Hegel nor Levinas would deny this. However, if politics is opposed to ethics, if freedom is superordinate to justice, does this not deny the preontological signification of the "face-to-face," the very relation that opens the possibility, not only of political discourse, but of all discourse? Levinas claims that the face-to-face relation escapes comprehension by either formal or dialectical logic. Such reason manifests itself in the ontological concept of unity, "an ancient privilege . . . affirmed from Parmenides to Spinoza and Hegel" (*TI*, 105, 102). Formal or traditional logic is based on the law of noncontradiction, whereas dialectical logic is understood as the coordination or interrelation of terms into a comprehensible totality. Dialectical logic purports to maintain the separation and identity of each term in the relation while simultaneously asserting the mutual coidentity of each term. Dialectical logic does not merely negate the truth content of formal logic; it surpasses (*aufgehoben*) the ability of formal logic to affirm the wholeness of the relation. In the final analysis, though, on Levinas's reading, both formal and dialectical logic are inadequate or deficient in their attempt to grasp the nature of alterity; they are logics of the *same.*

The unity that is the legacy of Western ontology is manifest as two similar yet separate movements of thought. The first, says Levinas, is the "way of the same," and the second is the "ontology of totality." They are not synonymous. The question here is whether Hegel effects a move in his system from the former term to the latter. If so, this move is the origin and locus of the violence of the concept that, according to Levinas, grounds concrete intersubjective violence. To use the language of the *Phenomenology,* this movement would be that of desire (*Begierde*), the modality of becoming that closes the gap between the for-itself and the in-itself, thereby supplying consciousness with the necessary adequate concept (totality) requisite for the transition to self-consciousness and then Spirit.

Though implicated in the very ontological structure that fosters war, the logic that belongs to sameness is decidedly different from the dominating concept of totality that "engenders war at its most primordial level." The logic of the same does not found the violence of war.[12] War actually "destroys the identity of the same" rather than ensuring its survival (*TI*, 6, 21).

War presupposes the transcendence that the face signifies; it is actually founded on the same structure that makes peace a possibility (*TI*, 245, 222). In both war and peace, there is a refusal of the totalizing structure of the State as law-giving community. War is not the entering into the totality; it is the willful rejection of the totality (community) by the I-ego—though not a rejection of relationship, says Levinas, "since in war the adversaries seek out one another." In war the self seeks to transcend the totality as separate, that is, by claiming to be infinite. This is the origin of violence, claims Levinas. In attempting to recover infinity as a concept for consciousness, the Other is in turn conceptualized as an object, thus denying the basis for any true mutual recognition to occur. Hegelian recognition is therefore essentially solipsistic. Peace, on the other hand, rejects the totality as a means of unification. To be ethical, the whole, can only be a differential social multiplicity, in which case it is also a refusal of the sameness of totality.

According to Levinas, subjectivity is the way of the same; he presents his philosophy as a "defense of subjectivity" (*TI*, 11, 26). This is not to promote the way of the same (freedom) as the highest of ideals, the tendency of Western thinking from Socrates to Hegel. There is a prior, more elevated position with regard to the Other that precedes freedom—the unconditional responsibility of *justice*.

IV.

Hegelian metaphysics defines the Absolute as the simultaneously total and infinite. The two terms are not mutually exclusive—the fault of previous metaphysical forms, according to Hegel. The opposite term of infinity is finitude, and not totality. This difference in interpretation is the focus of Levinas's criticism: Infinity is accessible to consciousness because it is temporally present in a nontheoretical manner; infinity is revealed in the face of the Other and is produced within consciousness as the idea (not concept) of infinity. The collapse of infinity and finitude into a speculative unity betrays the transcendence that infinity implies and so constitutes the initial intersubjective violence. The idea of the

Infinite "overflows" or surpasses the form of its concept, thus signifying the irreducible difference or distance that exists within
being between the same (*le Même*) and the other (*l'Autre*). "The
distance that separates *ideatum* and idea here constitutes the content of the *ideatum* itself. . . . The transcendent is the sole *ideatum*
of which there can only be an idea within us; it is infinitely
removed from its idea, that is, exterior, because it is infinite" (*TI*,
40–41, 49). The question is whether consciousness is able to
comprehend, and not merely apprehend, infinity.

If the absolute totality is the universal simple selfsameness of
identity and difference, if infinity and totality are mutually inclusive, then does this mean that infinity essentially belongs to the
order of the same and does not present itself to thought as its
other? That is, if infinity is the thought that thought itself cannot
contain (Spirit is, after all, only real in its actualization in historical self-consciousness—a finitude), is the Infinite alterity itself
and not the same? Or are the two terms truly reciprocal and the
above questions true and false simultaneously?

In the *Science of Logic*, reciprocity is understood in terms of
the causal nexus. The parts and the whole of the Idea are code-
termining. This principle applies also to the nature of the State
and the functions of the social totality. The infinite circularity of
cause and effect repeals the infinite regress of the past and constitutes the true infinite as a self-determining totality. Reciprocal
cause and effect does not mean that the effect is also the cause
of the cause; it means that in every causal relation each term
acts as both cause and effect for other relational terms. The
causal reciprocity is the element of necessity in Hegelian dialectics. Without such reciprocity, absolute knowing would be an
impossibility.

Are reciprocity and symmetry synonymous terms? The teleology of Spirit reveals an asymmetry of terms in that the subject/self
is accorded a privileged position with regard to the object/other.
Levinas maintains that the ethical relation is "asymmetrical." If
this is indeed the case, then Hegel's violence consists of a *double*
violence: not only is the fundamental asymmetry of terms denied
in an alleged totality of meaning, but the asymmetry is weighted
in favor of a preponderance of the subject (to invert Adorno's
phrase).[13] The violence of totality lies in its *simulated order*—as
primordial and as ground, that is, as the same.

On Levinas's account, the reciprocity that is founded and
necessitated both logically and existentially (and for Hegel, the
terms are not contradictory) between the terms "subject-self"

and "object-other" does not contain the symmetry that dialectical thought supposes it does. The constitution of intersubjectivity
does not lie in the mere mutual recognition of self and other, a
relation predicated upon a presumed identity of terms. Subjectivity is not a mutually shared experience; if it were, it would no
longer be subjective, unique. The essence of subjectivity lies in
the promotion and maintenance of distance or separation that
exists between the self and the Other. Desire is the mode of relation between the self and the Other that ensures this separation;
it is not the adequate concept or the means to that concept that
closes the distance.

Still, Hegel and Levinas are united in their conviction that the
meaning of subjectivity lies in intersubjectivity. According to
Kojève's interpretation of Hegel, "satisfied" subjecthood is possible only by way of citizenship in the universal homogeneous
State (which is yet to be realized concretely), and the essence of
subjectivity and intersubjectivity lies in the dialectic of lordship
and bondage.[14] In such a political State desire would be placated
through universal recognition by the Other, that is, by other citi-
zens. The question is whether Hegel is able to accomplish this;
and if unable, where must thought move in order to overcome
violence and engage in a positive relation with alterity?

In the *Phenomenology,* desire ends in the action, the work (*die
Arbeit*), of mutual recognition and forgiveness. Desire (*Begierde*)
is a negation in that it wishes to fill a lack or void. This gap is
being-for-another and is the origin of the "thingish I" of desire.
Once the subject (self) appropriates the object (other), the desire
is eradicated and the self becomes complacent.

> Desire has reserved to itself the pure negating of the object and
> thereby its unalloyed feeling of self. But that is the reason why this
> satisfaction is itself only a fleeting one, for it lacks the side of objec-
> tivity and permanence. Work, on the other hand, is desire held in
> check, fleetingness staved off; in other words, work forms and
> shapes the thing. (*PhG*, 148, 118)

To this, Kojève maintains that the only way the alterity of the
object can avoid extinction is to replace the desire for the object
with the desire for another desire that is not consumable. This
desire is within the self and, since the other is merely another
self, within the other as well. The dialectic of desire, which culminates in mutual forgiveness, is a double process.

The violence that shows itself in war is able to be overcome, if
not actually, then at least theoretically in the Hegelian framework.

Transcendence occurs in and through the reciprocal action of confession and forgiveness.[15] Since this dialectic must be enacted in order to be fully manifest, it appears that Hegel has finally reconciled the divisive dualism between action and thought and between the self and the other. Is Hegel's philosophy violent insofar as "the System" is predicated upon the concept of totality, which, even though it resembles the way of the same, is not identical with it and thus gives rise to war at its most foundational level, that of the concept? The logic of the same is an internal logic; violence arises in its externalization as the ontology of totality.[16] How, then, is the metaphysical asymmetry of the ethical relation to be maintained along with the reciprocity requisite for the legal working of justice?[17] This is the problem facing the legal and political application of Levinas's social (religious) ethics.

V.

On Levinas's interpretation, Hegel lacks an adequate (or rather, a *non*adequate) understanding of alterity. What he construes as "other" is actually a projection of selfsameness onto the object of reflection on the part of consciousness. The Hegelian concept of the other does not signify an irreducible otherness, that is, irreducible to the concept of the same. This absolute irreducible alterity Levinas terms the Infinite; but Hegel considers such an infinity spurious, recalling the impossible infinite regress rejected by an earlier Aristotelian-substance metaphysics.

Seeking to be free of the confining syntax of Hegelian metaphysics, this movement beyond the totality is *non*-negative. Infinity does not confine itself outside the totality of being as in a vacuum or as a mere concept; rather, infinity is found in the face of the Other (*le visage d'autrui*), "reflected within the totality and history, within experience" (*TI*, 7, 23). Infinity is a surplus in the sense that the Platonic Good is a plentitude. This surplus or ethical transcendence is metaphysical Desire, the manifestation and expression of the excess that the absolute goodness of otherness signifies. Desire (*désir*) is not to be described negatively, nor is it to be construed as a purely positive movement (*TI*, 32, 42). Here is a split with speculative (*begreifende*) dialectics. In Spirit's quest for recognition, desire (*Begierde*) is a negative movement, since in order for Spirit to become certain of itself, it must negate its alterity. However, Hegelian desire does not respect the Other as other; its impetus is actually that of need (*besoin*).

Desire (*désir*) maintains the radical separation that exists between the same and other without fusing into a rational unity or logic. The metaphysical relation with the Other (Desire as transcendence) occurs without the benefit of an intermediary. The luminous concept of mediation is replaced in the Levinasian analysis by that of "proximity,"[18] a position that maintains the separation of subject and object, of self and Other, without compromising the integrity of the relation or theoretically encapsulating it, since it is enigmatic.[19]

Levinasian Desire is the movement toward the other that simultaneously maintains the distance or separation between the self and the Other. Hegelian desire culminates in the act of forgiveness in which the Other is allowed to go free as different, as distinct, as separate. Is there an actual and radical distinction between Levinasian Desire, as the maintenance of the alterity of the Other, and Hegelian desire, which realizes itself precisely in the action of forgiveness in which the Other is established as other? Or is it merely the teleology of the dialectic to which Levinas refers, in which the difference of the other is superseded by the notion of citizenry in the State?

The distinction between *désir* and *besoin* in *Totality and Infinity* is operative in the sense that Hegelian desire (*Begierde*) is actually need (*besoin*) insofar as it seeks to fulfill or satiate itself in a total way. Hegelian desire implies a sense of lack, a separation that must be overcome or bridged in the self-other, subject-object relation. This occurs in the intersubjective relation in the moment of reconciliation, the moment of mutual and self-forgiveness after the initial clash or conflict for recognition takes place in the famous dialectic of lordship and bondage in the *Phenomenology of Spirit*.

Desire is a movement toward the Other that does not strive to bring the Other into any comprehension on the part of the self-same consciousness. The Other is desired precisely because the Other *is* other and not for any self-interested motive. The Other will always remain outside of the self's conception of her or him. This non-negative movement of Desire does not originate from the selfsame; it originates from the Other. The Other calls upon the self to respond to the face; and the face, in turn, calls one's subjective freedom, one's domesticity, one's at-homeness, into question. The movement of metaphysical Desire that is solicited by the Other is a movement that commences with the I. "Alterity is possible only starting from *me*" (*TI*, 29, 40). Desire, therefore, is nonteleological in the sense that it does not attempt

to draw the Other within the totalizing domain of selfsame consciousness. Desire is a reaching out toward the Other in a way
that more than just lets the Other be (as, for example, in the
Heideggerian notion of *Gelassenheit*). This is Desire interpreted
as *transcendence.*

Metaphysical desire, the Desire for the absolutely other, for the
Good, is transcendence in the very sense that Plato understands
it. One does not desire the Good as one does an object; the
guardian rulers in the Platonic republic relinquish this negative
type of desire in the face of which the Good takes flight. The Other
signifies the goodness of Desire in a concrete sense, the desire to
let the other be different. Desire is the allowance and maintenance of individual and cultural integrity and diversity without
reducing the marginal, the exterior, to the apparatus of economic, cultural, political, social, or ecclesiastical machinery.
Transcendence, as the movement of Desire, is the celebration of
difference and radical separation. Transcendence is profoundly
ethical for Levinas; that is its meaning. Ethical transcendence is
praxis, the unity of the political and the ethical. Desire as transcendence does not assume the form of ego-transcendence, as it
does, for instance, in Husserl and Sartre.

Dialectical metaphysics does not allow for an ethical critique
of politics in the same manner that it does not allow for a religious critique of philosophical theology. No thinker has shown as
forcefully as Hegel that theology and philosophy are essentially
the same project: the subordination of (ethical) transcendence
to the concept thought. Ethical transcendence (Desire) is the
refusal of the ontotheological viewpoint that radical exteriority is
subject to totality. In this sense, transcendence *is* infinity, that is,
the impossibility of encompassing or totalizing alterity. The non-
theological nature of transcendence is genuine *a-theism.* This is
opposed to Kojève, who maintains that Hegel's alleged *a-theism,*
for example, results from not positing a "beyond" outside the
totality of existence. For Levinas, though, *a-theism* is neither the
affirmation of the purely immanent nor pejorative in meaning;
a-theism represents an independent position prior to affirmative
or negative predication.

The opposition of religion and politics is meant to serve as a
relational modality that does not reduce the self and the Other to
moments in a collective totality. Democratic politics rests on the
primacy of reciprocal recognition (equality). It attempts to ensure
happiness by reconciling the personal freedom of the I with the
freedom of the Other; but "the distance that separates happiness

from desire separates politics from religion" (*TI*, 58, 64). Desire is not the fulfillment or satisfaction of the ego. Happiness is not commensurate with Desire but with need. Again, the status of infinity is the crucial point to bear in mind. Since the absolutely other is meaningful only in the face of the Other, infinity remains irreducible to selfsame consciousness.

VI.

Perhaps the most profound expression of Desire in Levinas's thinking is to be found in his account of *eros,* delineated in the third section of *Totality and Infinity. Eros* is not desire in the sense that the two shall become one, a totality; rather, one desires the beloved precisely because the beloved is different from the self. Desire is perpetually aroused, as it were, since the Other is the embodiment of surprise. Even the sexual union, coitus, the supreme erotic act, does not produce a union or totality of the being of the self and the Other, though it may produce a third. This is the wonder of fecundity: that the parents are able to produce beings that, though a part of them, are nevertheless completely independent from them in their will. In fecundity the originary relationship between the same and the other, that is, *a-theism,* is perpetually renewed and reenacted as "an ipseity, in the fundamental phenomenon of enjoyment. One can call *a-theism* this separation so complete that the separated being maintains itself in existence all by itself, without participating in the Being from which it is separated" (*TI,* 52, 58). Putting it in terms of the relation to the absolutely other, Levinas continues:

> By *a-theism* we thus understand a position prior to both the negation and the affirmation of the divine, the breaking with participation by which the I posits itself as the same and as I. It is certainly a great glory for the creator to have set up a being capable of atheism, a being which, without having been *causa sui*, has an independent view and word and is at home with itself. (*TI*, 52, 58–59)

Levinas's *a-theism* signifies not the disbelief in the divine but rather the *a-theistic will,* the wonder of the truly unique and subjective creating will, a notion to which Nietzsche has contributed much. Religion and *a-theism* go hand in hand for Levinas. The absolutely other nowise resembles for Levinas the theistic deity of ontotheological metaphysics. The Levinasian Desire for God, for the Invisible, the absolutely other, *pace* Sartre's notion of "bad faith," is not commensurate with a desire for unity with the divine, for the collapse of individuated subjectivity into a collective or transcendental subjectivity. Subjectivity is what it is precisely because it is *not* the eternally Infinite; subjectivity is the *trace* of the Infinite present in the face. The eternal is infinitely separate from the temporal; eternality and temporality do not form a totality, as they do in Hegel, who in a sense self-baptizes human consciousness as divine consciousness.

The idea of infinity is the idea of metaphysics, of "religion" in Levinas's construal of the term. Infinity a *revealed* idea, though not in the sense of natural religion. Neither a concept nor an object, infinity is the movement of Desire itself. Desire is the language that bridges the distance or separation between self and other. The self and the Other are *paradoxically* absolutely separated and absolutely proximate to each other. This is the "miracle" of finite, a-theistic existence. Jacques Derrida recognizes the paradoxical structure of Desire in Levinas: "Despite his anti-Kierkegaardian protests, Levinas here returns to the themes of *Fear and Trembling:* the movement of desire can be what it is only paradoxically, as the renunciation of desire."[20] In Derrida's all-too-Hegelian reading, this paradox is a problem to be overcome; but Levinas is fully cognizant of this, in that the paradoxical ambiguity of Desire infinitely resists the totalization of dialectical thinking, a totalization that ultimately vanquishes or subsumes the alterity of the infinitely other—the Other.

Levinas's conception of infinity is to be construed not as synonymous with the concept (*Begriff*) nor as resembling the Idea (*Idee*). The idea of infinity contains no precoded logic of which it is the seed. Its "logos" is nonteleological, nongrounding, and nontotalizing. Its signification lies precisely in its inability to be comprehended. The idea of infinity is nonconstituted and makes possible the nonviolent, passive receptivity of relationships between free individuals. Such an infinity, Hegel would assert, is only an empty and abstract concept. Genuine or true infinity is able to be interiorized (*erinnern*), superseding (*aufgehoben*) the distance or separation between its form and content. Accordingly, Levinas's conception of Desire as the desire for the Infinite would be dismissed as spurious by Hegel inasmuch as he would interpret such a conception of infinity as the mere positing of the infinite over against the finite.

Still, Levinas claims that the infinite exceeds the totality of finite existence, "overflows the thought that thinks it [*déborde la pensée qui le pense*]" (*TI,* 10, 25). The question for both Hegel and Levinas is the presence of infinity within the context of history and, more specifically, the mode in which it is manifest. Hegel thinks that infinity presents itself to consciousness as the highest of concepts (*Begriffe*), synonymous with the concept of totality. Levinas maintains that infinity is present to thought as that "idea" that thought itself can*not* contain. In Hegelian dialectics, the conflation of subject and object, self and Other, into a unitary theoretical structure (*Begriff*) is the objectification and subsequent elevation of subjectivity as a transcendent ideal. This results in, on Levinas's reading, the self-proclaimed sovereignty of the subject as Spirit revealed as the violent imperialism of *theoria*, the trajectory of Western ontology and politics as a whole. The subordination of infinity to the concept thought prioritizes the subject (*ego cogitans*) and minimizes the function or status of the object (other). Infinity thought as absolutely separated alterity assigns a certain (negative? non-? pre-?) dialectical primacy to the object over that of the subject.

Infinity is not an object, or a concept; it is found in the face of the Other, the desired, which arouses the movement of Desire, "a measure through the very impossibility of measure" (*TI*, 56, 62). Desire originates from its object; need arises from the subject. The Other is desired precisely because it transcends every category of thought. Need (*besoin*), on the other hand, implies a lack or deficiency on the part of the selfsame. The object of Desire, the infinitely other, is unattainable by possession. Desire does not seek to fill the void of the soul, as does need. There is no emptiness or lack to which Desire is correlate; Desire is the movement toward the Infinite, a response to the other as Other.

VII.

Given Levinas's analysis of the (non)logic of Desire, the realization of Spirit, historically actualized in the formation of community through the concrete act of forgiveness on the part of the self, appears to be not the formation of community but just the opposite: Spirit is actually the denial of true communion with the Other. The road to autonomy is paved with the blood of the Other; Spirit is a theodicy. To be in communion is not to be "one" in any transcendent or quasimystical sense, nor is it subjection to the greater will of the State. It is the ability to accept the radical difference of the other and to coexist in spite of the infinite distance or separation that will always remain between the same and other.

To be is to be economically; it is to exist within a complex web of relations. Economy implies tension and, at times, violence. To be in relation is to be confronted by another face. But is this engagement initially and invariably conflictual? Is the "face-to-face" possible noneconomically? Peace would be this solution. However, if peace is a relation with that is beyond the totality of the logic of desire and war, then is it a relation at all? The locating of war as a relation outside the totality would amount to the same criticism. And who would deny that war is a reality? Peace is only accomplishable by beings capable of war. On some levels, violence is, arguably, if not justifiable, at least sometimes necessary. As Nietzsche so poignantly reminds us, creation and destruction go hand in hand. But does this not merely repeat what has been Hegel's position all along?

Chapter 4

INSCRIBING THE "SITES" OF DESIRE IN LEVINAS

Bettina G. Bergo

και ε συνεστηεσεται απασα ε συλλυπεσεται.
—Plato, *The Republic*

The theme of desire emerges early in Levinas's work. From the outset, it names the impetus to transcendence that ensures to prereflexive subjectivity an openness of structure both to the world and to the other human being. Of itself, this is not a remarkable claim for desire, nor is it a particularly arresting strategy to avoid the charges of solipsism that have often been leveled against phenomenological projects. Indeed, the notion of desire functions in an analogous fashion in psychoanalytic theories of the subject and in much of French philosophy influenced by Kojève's reading of Hegel. In both cases, desire refers not to the acts or choices of a subject who, like a rational arbiter, experiences urges, assigns them value, or calculates their priority in a Platonic manner. Desire denotes instead a precognitive movement that, as the difference between urges and their expression, undercuts the binary distinctions of subject and object, passivity and activity. Thus for a post-Hegelian thinker such as Jacques Lacan, desire arises in the submission of urges and needs to the law of their expression in a symbolic code. A subject, then, arises not first as a sovereign, or an active principle of meaning creation; it arises as itself subject *to* the movement of need and the implacable law structuring need's expression. This subject is active neither in regard to its needs nor in respect to the form in which these are communicated. It is not itself an *archè*, but is produced as a result of the difference between the force of need and the possibilities of need's communication. If desire points to the irreducible noncorrespondence between need and law, expression and its code, then the subject is the passive site of the desire born from their problematic conjunction.[1]

The notion of desire serves as a partial (nondialectical) mediation in post-Kantian philosophies that focus upon relations between incommensurables (self and other, self and world, "experience" and expression). Desire expresses the difference between disparate terms or events in such a way that none of them is reduced, or sublimated, to a single constituent element (whether "subjective" or "objective"). Neither is the relationship between such terms or events deprived of an efficacy peculiar to itself. For Levinas, as for phenomenology and for the thought born of semiotics, the relation in question concerns alterities both human and mundane. From his earliest original works (1935–1947), Levinas aligned desire (initially expressed as the internally diversified complex of urges or needs) with a transcendence operative at two levels. First, a corporeal desire is coextensive with the fugacious transcendence entailed by sensuous enjoyment. Second, a "metaphysical" desire produces a transcendence of a different sort.

Desire and transcendence represent the paradoxical cornerstones of Levinas's philosophical project. Paradoxical is their *rapprochement* here, for if the logics of desire in philosophies after Hegel establish mediations that are neither a part of an unfolding dialectic nor fully binding on the terms thus approximated, these logics tend to undercut as much the abstract identity of the idealists' subject as they do the priority of the thinking ego before "its" world of objects. Thus, like much of the phenomenology, as well as the "new thinking" of the twentieth century, Levinas's work participates in a sustained effort to move past the formalism of German idealism toward an enlarged empiricism adequate to "life" (and intersubjectivity) in its actuality.[2] For Levinas, a true return to the *primum vivere* required, as for Heidegger, a description and conceptualization of affect and sensibility. Both philosophers believed there could be no integral thematization of life and world if the affectivity through which one is open to exteriority is held separate from comprehension. This was precisely the error committed by the neo-Kantians' epistemological interpretation of the first *Critique*. It was also a clear tendency in all but Husserl's last phenomenology owing to the priority he ascribed to the conceptual reconstruction of the structure of intentional life. For this reason, in his dissertation, devoted to Husserl's theory of intuition (1930), Levinas paid explicit homage to Heidegger's step beyond the intellectualism of Husserlian phenomenology (stating nevertheless that Heidegger was only making explicit themes already evinced by his teacher) toward the richness of concrete life. However, Levinas sought subsequently to push his own hermeneutic of prereflexive subjectivity beyond Heidegger's by breaking the connection Heidegger established between ontic comprehension and the affective *Stimmungen,* or moods, through which prerepresentational subjectivity accedes to the world. In order to make this break definitive, Levinas attempted to conceive a primordial subjectivity that did not first find itself dwelling alongside the entities in its world.

Levinas's extension of the Husserlian *Rückfrage* called for the elaboration of a spatiality and temporality that presupposed neither the duality of interiority and exteriority nor an ecstatic temporal structure whose metaphoric core was being continually "ahead of itself." Levinas hoped, moreover—in thus pushing back the analysis of the self behind subject-object dichotomies *and* prior to suppositions of a world or site in which the self first finds itself—to bring to light a *transcendence* not rooted in futural projections at the expense of the present moment. Thus he set about to open what he argued was Heidegger's closed circuit of immanence and comprehension to an intersubjectivity grounded not upon active understanding, but on a being-together with the other arising from passivity and desire. If transcendence could be conceived in this way, like an atemporal ecstasy, Levinas would presumably avoid assimilating the other as alter ego or as part of the "they." He could then circumvent the reduction of the other's significance for the same in a Heideggerian-like project of holding oneself open to one's most personal and absolute possibility, death.

No adequate discussion of desire in Levinas should overlook his contribution to a reconceptualization of subjective spatiality and temporality, since it is precisely as a result of his rethinking of the space and time constitutive of the "proto"-subject, or "self," that Levinas can criticize Heidegger's *Dasein* and his *In-der-Welt-sein.* Thus only by rethinking spatiality and temporality can Levinas step behind the Heideggerian ontico-ontological architectonic without returning to a Kantian metaphysics of subjectivity. In highlighting this reconceptualization, the body of this essay will consist of four parts. It will deal with: (1) Levinas's account of desire in *De l'évasion, De l'existence à l'existant,* and *Le temps et l'autre,* in the period from 1935 to 1947; (2) the innovations introduced by *Totality and Infinity* (1961); (3) the pervasive ontological language of *Totality and Infinity* and the difficulties this language poses for notions of desire; and (4) how, in his last great work, *Otherwise Than Being or Beyond Essence* (1972), Levinas's conception of desire loses ground to a sensuous vulnerability—refracting any egological or temporal synthesis, and suggesting a phenomenological unconscious. I will conclude with a consideration of the implications of such an "unconscious" and of the difficulties that beset Levinas's notion of vulnerability—one that neither desire nor the preintentional openness to exteriority can surmount.

I. Transcendence, Desire, and Spatiality in Levinas's Early Writing

> Affectivity or Desire—[understood as] disinterested, wherein plurality, in the form of social proximity does not have to assemble itself into the unity of the One— no longer signifies a simple privation of coincidence, [or] a lack of unity. [It is rather the] excellence of love, of sociality, of the "fear for the others," and of responsibility for the others, which is not my anguish over my own death.... Transcendence would no longer be a failed immanence. In sociality it would have ... the excellence proper to spirit ... perfection, or the Good.
> —Levinas, *Transcendance et intelligibilité*

De l'évasion

In an essay crowned by the Belgian Royal Academy but underappreciated by English-speaking readers, Bernard Forthomme characterized Levinas's philosophy through *Otherwise Than Being* as "*une philosophie de la transcendance.*"[3] The qualification is justified: transcendence and desire, transcendence as a certain desire, are the *via regia* that Levinas will take to pass beyond idealist formalisms and the sway of Heideggerian immanence and finitude in his approach to space and time. Any discussion of Levinasian desire and spatiality must come to terms with his criticism of conceptions of transcendence, for transcendence is so often taken for an adventure of immanence, an ecstasy of a consciousness, or an *unio mystica*.

66

From the time of *De l'évasion* (1935) through *Totality and Infinity* (1961), Levinas proposes a transcendence that as an interruption of subjective immanence in its selfsameness is pure affect (initially as "need to escape being" and later as "metaphysical Desire").[4] In *De l'évasion,* transcendence denotes the need that arises not from an existential deficiency or ["a nostalgia for Being" (*DE,* 83)] but from our immediate presence to ourselves in affectivity. Thanks to its moments of fulfillment in the present time of pleasure, the subject emerges from being. Affect or pleasure is not a sign of this transcendence, it is transcendence itself. The transcendence of pleasure is the subject's true spatiality, its "internal structure of self-positing" (*DE,* 73, 75); as a "sort of dead weight at the bottom of our being." Prior to any being-out-ahead-of-oneself, the affective tones of pleasure, shame, and nausea ("the pure experience of pure being") delimit our relation to being. "The experience of pure being," Levinas writes, "is at the same time the experience of its internal antagonism and of the evasion that imposes itself" (*DE,* 90).[5] Through affectivity, Levinas profiles a "life" and a Being quite different from what Heidegger brought to light in *Dasein*'s self-constancy as care (*BT,* 369 ff.). In Heidegger's schema, the evasion of being corresponds only to derived affects—such as "wishing, addiction, and urge" (*BT,* 227). These derived states must be analytically (and existentially) surpassed; their common root in anxiety before self and world must be disclosed and comprehended as *Dasein's* "Being-free for" its highest potentiality for being (*BT,* 228 ff.). Thus in Heidegger's resolute self-projection toward the existent's own ending, the present loses what is for Levinas its structural primordiality. Such a projection is precisely the false transcendence of a "missed immanence" (*immanence manquée*).

De l'évasion insists that subjectivity is the interiority of an "autonomous person" (*DE,* 70), not a "*lieu-tenant*" of being. It describes the space-time of the subject as a restless yearning and suffering *in the present,* for its condition is to be tied to its world and "caught in the incomprehensible machinery [*engrenage*] of the universal order" (*DE,* 70). In a move that deliberately blurs Heidegger's distinction between the "being-in" of entities in world space and the being-in proper to *Dasein,* Levinas argues that this interiority is the "very immobility of our presence." Our existential condition does not consist in a leap toward the ontological; rather it is the weight and seriousness of our here and now, our bondage to the present. This bondage frames both the solipsism of prereflective subjectivity and "its" urge to "excend."

For Heidegger, *Dasein*'s spatiality is derived from its being-in, and its being-in signifies a dwelling alongside the world. *De l'éva-sion* subverts this dwelling alongside. It does so not by denying our familiarity with or concern for the world, but rather by suggesting that in our ontic finitude a limit is found. A desire to cross the limit or get out of being "appears as the internal structure of [the] fact of positing oneself" (*DE*, 75). The subject strains against what becomes the *burden* of its position; in self-positing it desires to break out of itself *qua* here and now. Therefore, finitude—whether we consider it as spatial or temporal—aspires to free itself of itself and so poses the question of infinitude, or what Levinas also calls the Eternal.

For Levinas, solipsism—the "very immobility of our presence," and the "impossibility of stepping out of the game" (*DE*, 70)—is the ground both of suffering and of the desire for evasion. Existence is turned in on itself, and our condition proves oppressively in-sistent. At this point, a displacement of the ontological difference—indeed, a displacement that looks like its obfuscation—is inevitable for two reasons. First, our attempts to escape from Being are *not* a fall from authenticity. Second, to be tied to Being means to be tied just as much to our everyday history, our particular spatiotemporal situation. It is impossible to maintain anything like Heidegger's distinction between an "ordinary understanding of history" (*Historisch*), grasped by a self "lost in the 'they,' "[6] and *Dasein*'s resolute "historizing" (*Geschichtlichkeit; BT*, 431 ff.).[7]

Existence and Existents

Begun before 1938 and published around the same time as *Time and the Other* (1948), *Existence and Existents* foreshadows the analyses of "Separation as Life" in *Totality and Infinity*.[8] The pathos of consciousness as desire and as struggle against itself and against its immersion in being is explored in the light of the emergence of the subject as localization and position. In *Existence and Existents*, the falling into and emergence from sleep constitute the spatiality that is the very condition of consciousness. Levinas writes, "It is starting from rest, from position, from this unique relationship with the site, that consciousness comes. Position is not added to consciousness like an act that it would decide; it is starting from position, from an immobility, that [consciousness] comes to itself. It is an engagement in being which consists in holding oneself precisely in the non-engagement of sleep. [Consciousness] 'has' a base, it 'has' a site. [This is] the sole 'having' that might not be encumbering, but which is its *condition*: consciousness *is* here" (*DEAE*, 120, my trans., Engl., 70). To avoid our confusing such an engagement in being with willing, Levinas adds that this "is not . . . a fact of consciousness, nor a thought, nor a sentiment, nor a volition, but the position [itself] of consciousness . . . [in which] the subject posits itself as a subject" (*DEAE*, 120, my trans., Engl., 70).

In *Existence and Existents*, this "condition" deepens the investigations into need, pleasure, shame, and nausea begun in *De l'évasion*. This particular relation to a site becomes the original interiority and substantiality of the subject, something Levinas calls the "hypostasis." Levinas opens the hypostasis by underscoring its utter fragility, rooted in its sensuous vulnerability. Consciousness is dissolved and flies from itself in the wake of emotion and sensation, "which [are] more than a knowledge" (*DEAE*, 123, my trans., Engl., 72). Quite possibly with the analytic of *Dasein* in mind, Levinas writes, "Emotion places not existence, but the subjectivity of the subject in question; it keeps [the subject] from gathering itself, from reacting, from being someone. . . . Emotion is a manner of holding oneself while losing the basis" (*DEAE*, 121, my trans., Engl., 71). Correlatively, the body *qua* material being is not just a possession; the body as sensation is me. "I *am* my pain, my respiration, my organs" (*DEAE*, 123, my trans., emphasis added, Engl., 72). But if the base falls out when emotion "grips" me, if I *am* my pathos, I do *not* exist, *qua* subject, in the mode of an adverb the way *Dasein* does. I am—as a substantive because I *am* position—and not the *manner* [merely] by which [one] is engaged in existence" (*DEAE*, 123, emphasis added). Here again, the Levinasian subject is evinced as folded upon itself, that is, as interiority that retreats or lapses into itself, but it is also, as stance and emotion, radically open to exteriority.

The interiority-exteriority of the hypostasis is corporeal before being representational. Prior to positing or understanding anything, it *is* stance and position itself. The hypostasis crowns the double reduction that evolves over the course of Levinas's early essays: the formal, disembodied, or intellectualist consciousness (Kantian or Husserlian,) *and* the being-there that understands and presupposes the world in which it dwells.[9] The significance of this incarnate spatio-temporality is developed fully in *Totality and Infinity*.

II. Transcendence, Desire, and Spatiality in *Totality and Infinity*

A critical remark by Levinas in 1947, once again in regard to *Dasein*, indicates the stakes of his logic and the difficulty of carrying out his project.[10] Levinas must think transcendence on the basis of a sensibility that is simultaneously immanent—and productive of its own prediscursive excess of meaning.[11] Levinas conceives of desire and the call of radical alterity as ethical, without committing himself to so much as a rudimentary logic of inside versus outside; that

> Heidegger's concern, wholly illumined by comprehension (even if comprehension gives itself as concern), is already determined by the "within-without" structure which characterizes light. Without being knowledge, Heidegger's temporality is an ecstasy, "being out of itself." Not transcendence of theory, but already a stepping out from interiority toward an exteriority. (*DEAE*, 138–39, my trans., Engl., 81)[12]

This remark should give us pause, for it is vital that interiority *not* be set down as merely antithetical to exteriority. *Totality and Infinity* must *not* be understood as presenting simply novel interpretations of interiority and alterity as radical exteriority. If we approach the work in this way, the immanentized alterity found in *Otherwise than Being or Beyond Essence* appears like an invention *ex nihilo*. Instead, Levinas's project approaches desire throughout by way of a deformalization of time, where time is conceived as other than duration or a transcendence that is "out ahead of itself." It deformalizes space as positing *and* as being-in-the-world. In the place of these formal constituents, Levinas explores a subjectivity that arises unconsciously from itself in an instant *before* dwelling alongside the world concernfully.

Totality and Infinity integrates Levinas's earlier descriptions of spatiotemporality as our sensuous corporeity. However, it deemphasizes certain figures (or modes of being) that color the earlier works, such as shame and nausea (*De l'évasion*), laziness and fatigue (*De l'existence à l'existant*). Moreover, Levinas shifts his conception of alterity. In *Totality and Infinity,* he no longer conceives the feminine other as the model of alterity, as he had done in *Time and the Other.*[13] Instead, he integrates desire and feminine alterity into a schema whose logic unfolds with the emergence of the subject. Just as we have no mastery of our physico-psychic beginnings outside of limited memory (*TI,* 27), our consciousness comes to "be" not *ex nihilo* but as the contraction into ourselves that is need, enjoyment, and suffering.[14]

The genesis of interiority, as contraction, proceeds neither according to a linear logic nor in the guise of a dialectic of before and after. Rather, it passes through various metaphoric levels of experience (e.g., the plenitude of need, openness of desire, excess of enjoyment, dwelling, eros, fecundity, filiality), opening them respectively to various modalities of the "good." Thus need and enjoyment open to the good in being, while eros opens to the good of fecundity, and the desire for the other person opens to the ethical good of responsibility and justice. Although they have an analogous structure and deploy what Levinas argues is a non-normative hierarchy, these levels intersect one another without sharing a relationship of causality (*TI,* 189). For this reason, *Totality and Infinity* effects a *rapprochement* between the emergence of *ethical* subjectivity—as non-erotic desire for the other—and the *moral* significance of being a lover, father, son, or brother. And here, where one might suspect a biologistic reduction, Levinas is at his most spiritual. He articulates the emergence of subjectivity as awakening, enjoyment, and assuming being's weight with the possibility of an unperceived ethical "time" innervating the larger temporality of history and society. Metaphysical desire "is" its own temporality because it does not endure, but repeats itself. It is essentially objectless and so escapes conation and intentionality and their correlative "temporalities." Nevertheless, metaphysical desire intersects historical time. Thus the lovers intuit the openness of the future through fecundity, which gives meaning to eros. In his turn, the son discovers the height of ethical election by one greater than he, his father. He also comes to know the pluralism *in nuce* in the community of brothers, all of them chosen by the father. These "experiences" are all, in their respective experiential modes, aspects of the spatial and temporal separation of an I who is thus capable of desiring and receiving the other across the interval created by its own existence in several "time sites" (*TI,* 260 ff.). This separation allows Levinas to bind an ontic desire to a metaphysical—better, an eschatological—one, and redefine transcendence starting from their interconnection. Ultimately, *Totality and Infinity* refers to these crossed registers as "resurrection" (*TI*, 260).[15]

Totality and Infinity describes the emergence of subjectivity in the self-gathering of sensuous enjoyment or "love of life" (*TI*, 122).[16] This emergence suggests the transcendence and plenitude of corporeal need or need-desire that *is* us. In need is produced an ontic goodness.[17] Ontic goodness—because it is in no sense an "inauthentic" good—is doubled and surpassed by another good that arises out of our *desire for* and encounter with the unassimilable alterity of the face. At this other level, the "Good" ("Desire for the Other"), which Levinas scruples to conjoin with the ontic, must again be dissociated from things as better than ontic: It is "meta-physical desire" and "transcendence." Metaphysical desire becomes generosity and justice; it alone "puts in question the world possessed" (*TI*, 28 ff.; 172–73).

In this regard, Levinas writes, "We here enter the order of Desire and the order of relations irreducible to those governing totality. The contradiction between the free interiority and the exteriority that should limit it is reconciled in the man open to teaching" (*TI*, 180; cf. also *OB*, 118–21). Therefore, upon reconstruction, the tension between these two orders of desire admits a certain sublimation. Phenomenological reconstruction constrains the phenomenal itself. Metaphysical desire *precedes* need in the temporality peculiar to our being—whose unity, he argues, does not depend entirely on memory. Starting from the "ontic" experiences of awakening, stance, and enjoyment, we discover a strange temporal hiatus in our experience of responsibility to the other. Yet this hiatus—wherein our physical enjoyments appear to us like a usurpation in the face of the one to whom we spontaneously offer an account of ourselves—is itself our ethical origin. The spatiotemporality of need-desire is opened *by* an exteriority (the face) that lies between appearing and a sheer performative efficacy. Thus the first deformalization of space-time, as sensuous enjoyment and distance from brute being, is itself interrupted and transcended, thanks to the coming of the other.

This approach is always already accompanied by an extraordinary desire. It does not negate the truth of the spatiotemporal deformalization. Instead, it does something more remarkable, providing the "form," or possibility, of all openness. The reconstruction of the genesis of ethical life as desire and transcendence seeks to show that metaphysical desire precedes need-desire in the order of existence, but not of logic. It precedes the ontic need-desire because only through the former do we accede to thought and memory. The interruption provoked by the face inaugurates true reflection. Levinas writes:

> That there could be a chronological order distinct from the "logical" order . . . that there could several moments in the progression, that there is a progression—here is separation. For by virtue of time this being is not *yet*—which does not make it the same as nothingness, but maintains it at a distance from itself. It is not all at once. Even its cause, *older than itself,* is still to come [to its consciousness]. The cause of being is thought or known by its effect *as though* it were posterior to its effect. . . . This illusion [i.e., the "as though"] is not gratuitous, it constitutes a positive event. The posteriority of the anterior—a logically absurd inversion—is only produced . . . by memory or by thought. But the "unlikely" phenomenon of memory or of thought must be interpreted as a revolution in being. (*TI,* 54, trans. modified, emphasis added)

The unlikely phenomena of memory and thought arise first in metaphysical desire, which is expressed as apology for self and as speaking to the human other. There would be no such apology if the coming of the other did not interrupt enjoyment, if the other did not affect us, precisely at the level of our sensibility, of our skin, as a call and an injunction. Here, where there is no longer any "sinking one's teeth into being," an "uncharted future [opens] before me" (*TI,* 150). The ontic, and my pleasure in it, is transformed into a giving of self and things.

Totality and Infinity thus deformalizes the spatiotemporality of nascent subjectivity by framing it as an ontic need-desire. However, it completes the circuit of its logic with a certain deformalization of another spatiality: that of intersubjectivity, which belongs to the primordial "dis-order" of metaphysical desire. On one hand, then, individuation through sensuous happiness singularized the I whose concept ("ipseity") stands outside of both bio-logics and socio-logics (*TI,* 153). On the other hand, however, within the space of intersubjectivity the plurality of I's—in their incommensurable spatiotemporalities—retain their respective secrecy and ex-orbitance with regard to being. This disparity makes possible a social plurality that is more than rhetorical. As such it is also the possibility, and the evanescent "form," of utopia as disinterested desire and the distance from ontic drives.[18]

III. *Otherwise Than Being or Beyond Essence* and the "Site" of Obsession, Recurrence, and Substitution

> Desire is absolute if the desiring being is mortal and the Desired invisible. (*TI*, 34)

> The subject called incarnate does not result from a materialization, an entry into space and into relations of contact and money which would have been realized by a consciousness. (*OB*, 77)

The critical requirements of rethinking *Dasein*'s spatiotemporality, its modes of being, can be achieved by establishing a tie between Desire and need at the origin of the self,[19] overdetermined the language of Levinas's *Totality and Infinity*.[20] The ontological language of *Totality and Infinity* is due to the philosophical interlocutors explicitly and implicitly present in that work.[21] This language is also the result of a sustained effort to hold at bay the immense threat of psychologism.[22] Nevertheless, the dual openness of the "subject" in *Totality and Infinity* to both the better-than-being of enjoyment and to the "transascendence" (*TI*, 35) of metaphysical desire, or responsibility, created the impression of a hierarchical ascent *within* ontology, even as it set about to step outside of being itself.[23]

Otherwise Than Being deepens the intuition already present in *Totality and Infinity* that need and Desire point toward a "site" that is neither the pure immanence of an idealistic subjectivity nor the pure exteriority of alterity. Without evacuating the onticometaphysical ambivalence of the Good, without denying that the Other is unencompassed by thought, without abandoning the *significance* of the trope of fraternity, *Otherwise Than Being* returns to the subject and to Husserl's investigations into passive synthesis. It does so in order to situate the ethical difference in and as the "psyche."

The original site of this "ethical difference," is fissioned subjectivity. One commentator has deemed this subjectivity a "phenomenological unconscious."[24] If by this term we mean the pre- or paraintentionality of sensuous existence and its peculiar way of signifying, then the designation appears worth examining. According to *Otherwise Than Being*, this paraintentionality, signifying without word or symbol on the inner side of intuition, is what Husserl failed to investigate in his phenomenological psychology and in his exploration of time consciousness. Husserl therefore missed the structure of the subject at the level of passive synthesis.[25] "Subjectivity" is not first a synthesis, even if spontaneous and passive. Transcendental apperception, as a continuous operation of the unification of consciousness, is only secondarily the *archè* of the subject. This is because the deduction of a unified, self-positing subjectivity proceeds from an inadequate exploration of embodiment as vulnerability. Certainly Husserl's "doxic thesis" is true: Sensation is in fact always on the verge of turning into an intuition (*OB*, 76). But "on the verge" is neither an equation nor an equivalence. If we give up intentionality as the lens through which we view subjectivity, we discover a *residuum* that does not pass into a theme (*OB*, 67–68). This *residuum* is not phenomenal; neither is it like the Heideggerian openness or disclosure (*OB*, 67). It is, Levinas argues, "a body animated by a soul" (*OB*, 67–68), a vulnerability in which inside and outside are together. This vulnerability, like a wound or raw flesh, signifies in a way that is unlike the "sense" of knowledge or representation. If such a signification is self-contradictory, we must remember that a reduction more radical than Husserl's transcendental *épochè* has opened the dimension of sensuous life that precedes the ordering, or the quadrature, of interior-exterior, before-after—indeed, of I and other.

Language at this level moves between phenomenological description and a poetics of the unthinkable. Vulnerability to and desire for the other are "proximity," but not in the sense of spatial contiguity. Levinas qualifies proximity as the "other-in-me" (*OB*, 69) and as the "same for and by the other" (*OB*, 69), but we understand that he means this without reference to the logic—or physics—of container-contained, form-matter.

The theme of the posteriority of the anterior is developed with a different focus. Exposed by my skin, which *is* me, in proximity I am as if driven back behind the unified selfhood or *cogito*. I do not have the time in this instant or interval to conceive or represent this being-driven-back. So it is meaningless to qualify this as the effect or action of the other; it is likewise meaningless to surround this other with predicates of position. This proximity has no ego, no pilot; it comes to pass as gasping. An analogy with Heidegger's "experience" of falling tied to anguish is not wholly inappropriate. We see a multiplication of tropes denoting trembling, opening and closing, implosion and expansion. Levinas speaks of the systole and diastole of the heartbeat (*OB*, 109), of inspiration, the touching and being touched of the caress (*OB*, 76), of panting (*OB*, 115), and of maternity (*OB*, 68 ff.). Here, "on the hither side of the zero point which marks the absence of protection"

(*OB*, 75), "proximity is narrower and more constrictive than" the space of "contiguity"; and because memory cannot provide sensuous vulnerability with an image or explanatory event, proximity is also "older than every past present" (*OB*, 76).

What, then, has become of need and Desire, of love of life? What has become of communication and learning, of the other as orphan *and* my master? It is as though a reduction had been performed not only on Husserl's subjectivity but on many of Levinas's own themes from *Totality and Infinity*. Desire, whether erotic or metaphysical, is produced because sensibility, as vulnerability to the (effect of the) other, signifies as for-the-other. Indeed, Levinas goes so far as to declare libido dependent upon proximity and eros the child of proximity and substitution (*OB*, 192 n. 27).[26] There is not space enough here to explore this claim, much less the complex significance of the opening and closing, the diastasis, of sensibility as for-the-other.[27] Certainly the logic of the "posteriority of the anterior" has been fully developed, but the amphibology, or the displacement of the ontological difference toward an ethical one, is made possible by the twofold quality of sensibility in proximity: on the one hand, it is the "dispossession, the contraction, in which the ego . . . immolates itself" (*OB*, 118), and on the other, it is the opening-out in election and the speaking of the "hostage" who utters "After you, sir" (*OB*, 117).[28] This duality is neither two positions nor two times. It is like a circulation without beginning or end (*PI*, 226, 243 ff.).

IV. Remarks on Transcendence and Intersubjectivity

At the level of protosubjectivity, contraction and opening are not difficult to conceive. However, the passage to phenomenality, thematization, and sociality is more enigmatic, because the binaries of ontico-metaphysical desire, and mediation of eros and fecundity are given up. If we can speak at all of a "space" of intersubjectivity in *Otherwise Than Being*, we may consider this metaphorical space as deployed by five moving loci: the self, the other, the "there-is," the infinite ("illeity"; cf. *OB*, 123), and the "third party."

The last two are related—almost in the way the tropes of the brothers and the father expressed relation in *Totality and Infinity*. Levinas writes, "Consciousness is born as the presence of a third party. It is in the measure that it proceeds from [the third party] that it is still disinterestedness. Consciousness is the entry of the third party, a permanent entry, into the intimacy of the face to face" (*OB*, 160). As consciousness is born, as we receive through it the "origin of an origin" (*OB*, 160), the nature of signification passes from obsession and substitution to the intentional and the rational. The event of the third party as the Other's other is a kind of miracle: It signifies the possibility of a measure on earth. The measure, as miraculous in its sense as the passage of proximity into saying, also reflects the outside-of-being of infinity (*OB*, 156). It shows that being and history can be open to what initially has neither their time nor their space. Yet being itself now reappears as chaos and *gravitas*. It is the *there is,* capable of suffocating us *and* of conferring its "weight" upon our actions toward others (*OB*, 162–65). A degenerative tendency in being pulls downward what is said and done, just as the Good passes through it. This is the spatiality deployed in the limitation of proximity and substitution by the third party: the indefinite, ever recommencing move to sociality and to a system of general signification.

I am speaking of these loci as tendencies, forces. All these terms are abusive and tempt us to ask, "What is their milieu?" and "What makes them move?" To pose these questions would be to seek a cosmo-*logy* (or at least a sociology) in Levinas in the sense of an account of an encompassing order and an account of the moral and socio-political universe. Yet we can no more fix the structure of the field of forces that "opens" between the fissured subject, the other, the infinite, and the third party than we can ask here what cosmology Levinas would write. Still, the self as hostage bears a responsibility whose repetition and increase, whose lack of conceptual boundaries, make us think it is bearing all of creation in immanence (*OB*, 125). So we might begin by speaking of a "xenocentric" cosmos, where the stranger within me is the impossible Archimedean point in an order become uncanny. The egoless self of vulnerability—whether synonymous with or more radical than metaphysical desire—is the open site that is weaker than being, yet which cannot but assume (by *kenosis* and expiation) its charge.

This phenomenological unconscious displaces a Desire that remained perhaps too close to intentionality. It overcomes the empirical and dialectical aspects of the need-Desire duality, without trying to argue against their intersection. The exacerbation of subjectivity as agonistic transcendence in immanence—and as transcendence in sociality—might be called *Otherwise Than Being*'s psychoanalysis of "prophetism." Yet I suspect that for Levinas a concept such as the "phenomenological unconscious" too quickly unites a neurophysiology of drives and a symbolic symptomatology—to the detriment of the meaning of ethics and transcendence as he conceives these. Whether we understand being-for-the-other as the signification of vulnerability or as metaphysical desire, it must lead to elsewhere than being; it must short-circuit the will or thrust of existing. In what follows, I will nevertheless ask whether such a concept might not begin to address an important criticism leveled against *Otherwise Than Being*.

V. Critical Questions in the Guise of a Conclusion

Let us evince some of the questions inaugurated by this critique. In the first place, what can we conclude about Levinas's logic, which stakes itself upon the meta-rational (hence ethical) claim that ontology, as existence and violence (and their signification), is exceeded or transcended by meaning itself? Why is this a question at all, since such a logic is perplexingly open? It has been suggested that in the absence of mediations—whether they be evanescent, like a subject's historical "knowledge," or factical, like social institutions and mores—Levinasian Desire is continually betrayed, but in a sense to which Levinas's thought itself has not done justice. Accordingly, it would be betrayed by the violence ineluctable in the thinking of the other, which comes about thanks to the contemporaneousness of the third party and the other.

The third party brings about an opening out of the "structure" of responsibility, toward sociality and justice. But does this opening itself not contain the violence necessary to and implicit in the limitation of infinite responsibility, without which no Saying can be said? Can Levinas argue that de facto sociality and justice entail violence simply because of a tendency to disorder intrinsic to what-is? Can he designate the zero degree of being, that is, the 'there is', as the (ontic) reason for historical, worldly violence, and separate this violence from the violences of responsibility and the third party? If so, in what sense does the chaos of the ontological account for the irreducible violence amongst people and within the practices of language and even justice?

Citing passages from Levinas's essays "The Pact" and "The Ego and Totality," one such critic, Gillian Rose, first emphasizes a claim relatively underrepresented in Levinas's thought: "If I recognize the wrong I did you, I can, even by my act of repentance, injure the third person."[29] And she suggests, "This seems to acknowledge that the *meaning* of confession and forgiveness may be *inverted* in their unintended consequences" (*TBM,* 262). Additional citations from Levinas justify her subsequent discomfiture before this philosophy. She writes, in respect to Levinas's declaration: "'Who is closest to me? Who is the Other? Perhaps something has already occurred between them. We must investigate carefully. Legal justice is required. There is need for a state. This seems to acknowledge the possible inversion of even acute responsibility for the other, neither intimate nor neighbor, out of the contingencies of history, which may, nevertheless, be comprehended, and which give rise to this perplexity of the face to face. It implies that historical knowledge must precede any assumption of 'responsibility'" (*TBM,* 262).

I do not believe the argument need be pushed that far; historical knowledge need not precede, absolutely, the assumption of responsibility. That much said, historical knowledge *accompanies* responsibility. And, for Levinas, it does so in a way that is fundamentally unstable. The third party, he is wont to say, looks at me in the eyes of the other; two levels of desire, then, must cross each other in the encounter with the Other.[30] The perplexity of the face-to-face relationship is that of the movement between these two levels and the question of how the obsessive metaphysical Desire *becomes* worldly. In other words, how can something like Levinas's "Saying" be maintained as without content, yet also signify an excess of meaning *and,* thanks to a "miracle" called the third party, condition and overflow what is said? It is as if two logics struggled within the Levinasian ethical moment for a certain preeminence and, while crossing each other, neither shared common terms nor admitted *rapprochement* by way of mediations.

Rose is one of the few commentators to pursue this polemically. She does so using Levinas's own texts through the thought of Kierkegaard and Rilke, among others.[31] She writes, "Without legitimate knowledge or representation, this wisdom [of love, or responsibility], which would alert us to the incipient 'Stalinism' [the expression comes from the essay of Levinas she is addressing here] of our *principled generosity* and teach us instead a perfect equity, can only appear itself as a 'disengaged' prescription—holy and without any purchase on 'the real world.'"[32]

For our purposes the question must be stated more broadly than this, for even the notion of the "real world" involves us in a logic of representation *or* love, engagement *or* detachment, against which Levinas has attempted to work. If it is not his intention to separate these terms, the question remains about the enactment of Desire and the passage of the "wisdom of love" into intentionality. Even without an elaborate historical knowledge, how could the oscillation between infinite responsibility and the third party inaugurate action or reflection, indeed be sayable *without* turning into "principled generosity" or a prescriptive narrative? It is not hard to imagine that responsibility can be discovered reflectively, as "prior" to other forms of desire and the more mundane transcendences such as enjoyment. But what could inaugurate the oscillation between the other and the third party that limits, even "rationalizes" the very incipience of reason and language in responsibility? How does an athematic, prelexical, and sensuous "knowledge" open into Saying both as the gesture of generosity *and* as the rationality of social intercourse? Is the metaphorical heart of this prereflexive knowledge not, as psychoanalysis suggests, an unthinkable response to the desire of the other? Such a response would not entail the conscious recognition of the other's desire, but it would demand a certain approximation between the "desires," or their mediation. Although the third party limits logically the infinite responsibility, it does not mediate, cognitively or temporally, the relationship of the I and the Other—for the third party appears contemporaneously with the Other, yet cannot lay claim to its ethical priority. For this reason we must ask Rose's questions: What is it that holds together, for the self, the discontinuity to which Levinas's text bears ardent witness, between other and *socius* (or third party)? And what could ensure their concomitant separation *and* continuity under the sign of the Good, whether as responsibility or justice? The answers lies with two related ideas, standing at the limit of Levinas's thought: repetition and obsession.

The logic of *Otherwise Than Being* makes use of the notion of repetition at three levels. First, the existential structure of corporeal pleasure and need gives rise to, and is driven by, the possibility of repetition. Pleasure and need, like metaphysical Desire, are never fulfilled. Rather they are characterized by sensuous excess and suffering. Second, repetition at the level of erotic desire lies outside of intentionality. It arises and "takes form" as a fantasy (the implicit promise of "fecundity") that inverts the order of ethical investiture. This erotic inversion of the ethical scheme of transcendence, viewed outside of fecundity, suggests something like a "good" versus a "bad" alterity. Repetition takes place as a plethora of "drives," but also as generosity and giving, which have a validity or authenticity different from ontic eros.

Finally, since it cannot ever be satisfied, metaphysical Desire exemplifies repetition. It is produced as the obsessive inadequacy between subject and other. Indeed, its "telos" (to the extent that it *has* a finality) self-destructs and opens beyond itself as pure gratuity. But how would contentless form open beyond itself? Levinas writes, "[Its] formal characteristic, to be other, makes up its content (*TI*, 35). The distinction that putatively sets *this* Desire apart from all other forms of desire and transcendence therefore lies in the impossibility of having a content.

If this is to be called "desire"—or indeed (proto-) "religion," as Levinas says—it is because the prereflexive structures of need and erotic desire serve as an incomplete analogy with metaphysical Desire (*TI*, 40).[33] Repetition becomes something like a *tertium communis* governing this analogy, oscillating between its quotidian enactment (at the level of need and enjoyment) and an obsessional repetition whose "source" is both outside the self and within the self. Levinas calls this obsessional repetition true transcendence, or "transascendence" (*TI*, 35). Interrupted by the other, the self of obsession and recurrence is "in relation" with an immanent signification: It is altered by an "event" that could not have happened, because it is not factical. In this "relation," the self *becomes a sign*—indeed, a sign par excellence that gives, or a sign that is a giving. Levinas is explicit: Metaphysical Desire (or "Substitution," to use the language of *Otherwise Than Being or Beyond Essence*) "is signification" (*OB*, 13). But let us recall an earlier question: What is it about the (nonphenomenal) third party that also ensures the possibility of responsibility and signification?

The violence of the other in the same (obsession, expiation, "systole") is doubled by the violence of the same self, opening in responsibility and "sincerity." This opening is altered by the third party so that measure and reason can interrupt infinite responsibility. But is this a violence (to the relation with the other, and so to the self) that rectifies the violence in Being and history? Such a notion of violence has lost its polemical value for an ethics stretched between an eschatology (of interruption and the perhaps violent, demand for justice) and an irenics of the State (the "production" of goodness in Desire). And what is it "to do violence" to a subject already broken *for the other*? The excessiveness of nascent meaning in the Levinasian schema has the peculiar effect of sapping the meaning of concepts such as "violence," "love," and "peace," because it undercuts the semantic tensions that make their very definition possible. Levinas's logic—though it is quite deliberately a paralogic—strains the plurality it posited (self-other-third) to the breaking point, because "desire" denotes a multiplicity of events for a self (Desire) and for a subject (desire, need, enjoyment). Given the radical dissymmetry of the Same and the Other, nothing can be said of the desire of the other. What, then, may be said *to* the desire of the other? In a logic of transcendental bracketing, this question appears moot. But here a notion of a phenomenological unconscious would be of great value. And what if this unconscious were ethical?

PART III
DESIRING SUBJECTIVITY:
SARTRE AND DE BEAUVOIR

Chapter 5

SARTRE: DESIRING THE IMPOSSIBLE

Christina Howells

"The beauty of a woman kills our desire for her."[1] Sartre's separation of imagination and perception is radical; he situates the aesthetic firmly in the imaginary realm and desire in that of the real. The paradoxical notion that beauty kills desire disturbs our assumptions about desire and prepares us for the later analyses that envisage desire as irremediably doomed to failure.

In *Being and Nothingness* there are two major sections on desire. The first, which constitutes part of the chapter devoted to "Concrete Relations with Others," is entitled "Second Attitude Toward Others: Indifference, Desire, Hatred, Sadism" and is concerned with sexual desire as a manifestation of being-for-others. As figured in the first section, desire is implicated in the conflict and struggle for power in all human relations. The second section is to be found near the end of the book, in the examination of the cardinal categories of human reality: having, doing, and being. Desire is considered in the chapter devoted to "Being" and "Doing," under the two headings of existential psychoanalysis and of possession. Here the sexual nature of desire is hardly significant, but its metaphysical implications are vast. The concrete, psychological tenor of the earlier discussion of sexual desire tends to occlude the more fundamental issues raised in the later section, though the latter is ultimately necessary for an understanding of the former. Both sections suffer from being overly familiar, frequently summarized but rarely reexamined. I will propose a fresh reading that will attempt to explore some of their more surprising implications.

The broad plan of *Being and Nothingness* is tripartite: to interrogate the relations of the *for-itself* of consciousness with the *in-itself* of all non-conscious being, to consider such relations in the presence of the "other," and finally to sketch out a metaphysical theory of being in general. The *for-itself* nihilates

85

the *in-itself,* which it both flees and pursues (*EN,* 428–29.) This ambivalent movement, described by Sartre as *fuite vers,* flight toward, shows the *for-itself*'s double aim—to escape fixity and stasis and remain free, while achieving the security and permanence embodied in the being of the *in-itself.* The *in-itself* is thus both a lure and a threat, with all the seductions of stability and all the horrors of sclerotic immobility. The *for-itself* cannot be neutral with respect to the *in-itself.* Its nihilating activity is not freely chosen; it is a destiny. Consciousness cannot but nihilate being; it is "condemned to be free" (*EN,* 515). The presence of another consciousness further diminishes the room for the *for-itself* to manoeuver. Its flight and pursuit are no longer situated in a perpetual elsewhere. Beyond the reach of the *in-itself,* they become themselves *in-itself,* irremediably fixed from outside as an objective characteristic of consciousness, condemned in a further sense to be free (*EN,* 429). The *for-itself* has two options in the face of the threat posed by the other. One is that it can try to overcome the objectivity and being that have been imposed on it by attempting to regain its position as subject and reduce the *for-itself* of the other to an object in its turn. Alternatively, it can attempt to harness the freedom of the other and use it to ground its own being, which would thereby remain free while being its own foundation. If the free transcendence of the other could be recuperated in support of the freely chosen being of the *for-itself,* the *in-itself* would be mastered and controlled. No longer an object of flight or pursuit, it would be possessed. These two options are radically incompatible. Sartre makes it clear that they do not constitute a dialectic. They can never be synthesized, and they present an inescapable and certainly vicious circle. What is more, they can be identified with desire and love, respectively.

Desire, then, is incompatible not only with beauty but also with love. Sartre's position is not as inimical to intuition and experience as it might appear. He is referring to fundamental attitudes of consciousness—we may desire a beautiful woman (or man), but not while we are taking up an imaginary attitude toward her (or him) and contemplating her as an aesthetic object. Similarly, we may love and desire the same person, but not at the same time: Love and desire are different attitudes that have at their root a basic polar opposition.

Desire, Sartre argues, arises from the failure of love, and vice versa (*EN,* 448). And love is bound to fail. When I love, I want the other to love me freely in return, but I do not want the insecurity his freedom entails. The freedom of the other endangers me. In love, I am at the mercy of the loved one. Rather than grounding myself in freedom, I lose my freedom in alienation to another subject. Love is an attempt to assimilate the alterity of the other, to possess the other *as* free, to be both self and other, to be like God. This is an impossible ideal. It is an ideal that seems likely to slide downward toward masochism if I accept my status as object for the other's subjectivity. Yet even this position is untenable, as I am never truly able to give up my freedom. The alternative position is that of desire. Love fails me by reducing me to an object. So I reassert my subjecthood and attempt to meet the other on an equal basis—to confront him freely as a free being, to look him steadily in the eye. But this is precisely what I cannot do, at least not without reducing him in his turn to an object (the object of my look) who cannot look at me. His freedom is once again out of my reach. The pursuit of synthesis—the aim of reconciling subject and object, the quest for a mode of being that would be both *pour soi* and *en soi*—is doomed to endless *tourniquets,* to an unholy whirligig of conflictual relations of power.

But what has this to do with desire? Desire, for Sartre, is intentional (in Husserl's sense). It is a mode of consciousness, like imagination or perception, directed toward an object. Indeed, it is a primary (*originelle*) mode (*EN*, 451), fundamental, not contingent. Sartre is taking a stand here against the opposed camps of empirical psychologists, on the one hand, and "existential philosophers" (*EN*, 451) such as Heidegger on the other. Both conspire to reduce desire to a matter of physiology—to mere "instinct," which falls within the realm of biology rather than philosophy. Sexual desire is, for Sartre, a fundamental aspect of human existence. In describing desire as a mode of consciousness, he is also implicitly rejecting the Freudian model of desire as emanating from the unconscious. "Who desires?" he asks. I do: *"C'est moi"* (*EN*, 455). (We might note that Sartre's formulation does not pose the problems attributed to it by a recent critic who believes that Sartre's assertion of the originally non-thetic nature of desire makes its subject "pre-personal."[2] Of course, the ego does not desire, for the ego is a construct. But it is still the conscious—if not the *self*-conscious—subject.) Desire may be defined by its transcendent object. Desire is not desire for pleasure, for sexual intercourse, or for orgasm. These are its end but not its aim. They are secondary objects that habit, convention, or fatigue may cause us to confuse with the primary object of desire— the other. And desire pursues not *just* the body of the other, but the "body and soul"—the conscious, corporeal being (*EN*, 455), the spirit incarnate. Desire is precisely the desire to possess the other as both subject and object, *for-itself* and *in-itself*, as embodied transcendence (*EN*, 463). Like love, it pursues an impossible ideal (*EN*, 463).

But before exploring further the implications of this view of desire as impossible, we will examine Sartre's phenomenological descriptions of the experience of desire, for these inform his literary texts and have retained the attention of many commentators. Sartre's descriptions of the desiring consciousness seem loaded with negative connotations: Desire compromises the *for-itself*, and it is a fall into complicity with the body; in desire, consciousness becomes *empâtée*, opaque, *pâteux*, heavy, swooning (*pâmée*), and vertiginous. In a word, consciousness becomes bodily. And what it seeks is a similar incarnation of the other's consciousness. Its quest is the appropriation of the other as flesh—as contingency, as facticity, as matter: the body as *en soi*—not as agent, as instrument, as active, intentional, and goal-directed. Purposeful activity (such as aesthetic contemplation) masks the flesh—the grace of a ballet dancer, argues Sartre, clothes her. And the obscene reverse of grace, the hapless indignity of the body revealed as partially out of control, the wobbling buttocks or breasts, are still part of the truth of the flesh, but the truth of the flesh perceived without desire (*EN*, 472). Grace and beauty may kill desire, but flesh on its own is not sufficient to arouse it. One man's eroticism is another man's disgust. My body will excite you only if you already desire or wish to desire me. Consciousness chooses to desire (*EN*, 460). And it attempts to arouse the desire of the other through the caress, for example, which reveals the body to itself as passive, as surface, and as desirable flesh.

This phenomenological account contains within itself the key to the inevitable failure of desire. Flesh and agency are incompatible. If I become too fully flesh, I lose my subjecthood, I identify with my body, and I become once again an object in another form of masochism. Pleasure entails the death of desire, not just because orgasm brings desire temporarily to an end, but because pleasure may become not the product but the object of desire. This diverts desire from its true end in the other. Conversely, when I deliberately try to arouse the desire of the other, I revert from flesh to bodily agency. I become a subject; the other becomes an object. The reciprocal incarnation of desire is broken. I approach sadism; my hand—or my penis—becomes a *tool*.

Sartre's fiction also displays several exemplary instances of the failure of desire. Finding much evidence of true desire in any of Sartre's literary works is difficult. This failure seems consonant with Sartre's literature as revealing a variety of modes of inauthentic behavior and relations. In *La Nausée,* desire is never an intentional consciousness directed toward another person; it is always diverted toward the secondary aims of pleasure or domination. Roquentin's sex with the *patronne* of the Café Mably is a matter of convenience, merely *politesse*—he desires not her but sexual release, and the disappointment he feels when she is not available is experienced primarily as a disagreeable tickling sensation in his penis, which quickly leads to nausea (*OR,* 25).[3] Later he is vicariously excited by a newspaper report of a young girl's rape and murder. Roquentin feels no desire for the "other" as embodied consciousness, but experiences only a sadistic fantasy of control and violence directed at her dead flesh, as he gives himself up to imaginary sexual stimulation. Lulu, in *Intimité,* is aware of the potential sadism of sex and finds the transformation from body to flesh too threatening to allow herself to enjoy it. She is aroused by fantasies of other women, by undressing in front of her young brother, and by masturbation—situations over which she retains full command. With men she is frigid, terrified of being possessed and of losing control. She hates especially men who are sexually experienced, *"qui savent faire"* (*OR,* 306) and who make her feel as though her body is an instrument on which they can play.

In *The Age of Reason* the focus is again on desire for the secondary objects of pleasure or control. Mathieu, we suspect, like the "average man" of *Being and Nothingness,* "through mental laziness and conformism conceives of no other end for his desire than that of ejaculation" (*EN,* 454). This partly explains why he remains with Marcelle, whom he no longer loves. Even his desire for her body has become precarious. He claims to be attracted to her "soft, buttery flesh," but is ruefully aware of its excess fat and strange odors. She can still give him pleasure, but his real desire is for his enigmatic student Ivich, whom he longs to understand and possess. To seduce Ivich, on the other hand, would serve as a means to an end—invading her intimacy, her hostile independence, and *knowing* her. But Mathieu resists the sexual nature of his desire because of an implicit awareness of its power to distract him from Ivich as conscious subject, and a fear that it will lead to dependence, boredom, and banality, as it did with Marcelle:

"It isn't true," he said to himself determinedly, "I don't desire her, I have never desired her." But he knew that he was going to desire her: It always finishes like that. I'll look at her legs and her breasts and then, one day. . . he suddenly saw Marcelle stretched out on the bed, entirely naked, her eyes closed: He hated Marcelle. (*OR,* 462)

Boris, like Lulu, fears desire because of the loss of lucidity it involves. At the point of no return in a sexual encounter with Lola he fights ineffectually against orgasm:

Soon she groaned, and Boris said to himself, "That's it. I'm going to pass out." A thick wave of desire spread from his loins to the nape of his neck. "I don't want to," Boris thought, gritting his teeth. But he suddenly felt as though he was being lifted up by his neck, like a rabbit, he let himself go on Lola's body and was reduced to a flushed whirl of sensual pleasure. (*OR,* 429)

All the characters slip into one or another of the pitfalls of desire: its diversion into pleasure, desire for the flesh without true subjectivity, domination, fear of domination, or self-protective frigidity. Desire appears like a quagmire or a dangerous ocean where the desiring subject is shipwrecked on the reefs (*écueils*) of either the Scylla of sadism or the Charybdis of masochism (*EN,* 475). Sartre's characters lose their physical excitement in the attempt to arouse and control the other or lose sight of the other in their own sexual arousal.

But who or what is to blame for these shipwrecks? Is it the inauthentic characters who fail in desire as they fail in love and politics, or other vital spheres of the human situation? Or is desire itself fundamentally flawed—an inauthentic mode of relations with others that is irremediably steeped in conflict and in the struggle for power? Is desire simply a bad thing, a conflation of the sexual urge with the will to dominate or be dominated? Is desire a way of relating to others that would be outmoded in an unalienated, postcapitalist society? Is desire outmoded even within the "ethics of deliverance and salvation," hinted at in a famous footnote?[4] First appearances to the contrary, the answer seems to be "no." On the one hand, my desire is a "*conduite d'envoûtement,*" a magical attempt to compensate for my inability *really* to possess the other, by ensnaring his freedom in his flesh (*EN,* 463). On the other hand, desire pursues an impossible but nonetheless fundamental goal: "to possess the transcendence of the other as pure transcendence and yet as body" (*EN,* 463). The *tourniquets* of desire are inevitable since "we could take a consistent attitude toward the other only if he were *simultaneously* revealed to us as subject and as object . . . which is, in principle, impossible" (*EN*, 479). The other is "*insaisissable*": elusive, protean, fleeing me when I seek him and possessing me when I flee. Sartre sees even the Kantian precept of taking the freedom of the other as an unconditioned end as a form of alienation of the other, an attempt to transcend his transcendence (*EN*, 479). Desire in fact desires for the other what it desires for itself and also desires what the other desires. Its failure arises not from its inauthenticity, nor from its enmeshment in power, but from the nature of human reality at its most basic level. Desire desires the other as in-itself-for-itself. The other, similarly, desires to be in-itself-for-itself. This is the original useless passion (*EN*, 708). The second of the two sections of *Being and Nothingness* devoted to desire makes this clearer.

All desire, Sartre contends, be it for a woman, for the world, or for God, has a similar structure, root, and meaning. All desire, however distorted and partial, refers back to the totality of the subject's "*élan vers l'être*" (*EN*, 650), his "impulse toward being"—back to his original relation to himself, to the world, and to the other. The fundamental project of the for-itself is to realize its desire for being (*EN*, 651). This desire is manifest in the multifarious attitudes of the human situation—jealousy, avarice, the love of art, cowardice, courage, and so on. Being-in-itself is the object of this original desire. The project of the for-itself is to be in-itself as is manifest in all modes of desire. "The for-itself has the project of being, as for-itself, a being which is what it is" (*EN*, 653). Sartre calls this desire the "desire to be God" (*EN*, 654). This form of desire underlies the myriad forms of its concrete manifestations and its transcendent objects. This "desire to be" is the very "lack of being" that constitutes human freedom (*EN*, 655). Sartre contrasts this with what he sees as the reductive and biological Freudian notion of the libido (*EN*, 659).

But Sartre does not simply state that every desire is an expression of the desire to *be*. He follows this up with a phenomenological description and analysis of different forms of desire to show how this may be understood in concrete terms. Initially desire may seem divisible according to the three cardinal categories of having, being, and doing. I may desire to *possess* an object, to *be* someone, or to *do* something. However, he argues, the desire to do is reducible, it is a means to an end: that of possession. In some cases this is clear—I make a walking stick from a branch in order to *have* a walking stick. Other activities might seem less appropriative: scientific research, sport, or artistic creation, for example. But knowledge, physical activity, and aesthetic production are all modes of relating to and ultimately of possessing the world. All desire tends to consume its object, so possession cannot in fact ever slake desire. I cannot have my cake and eat it (*EN*, 668). We have already looked at the consequences of this in the realm of sexual desire.

The relation between desire and possession poses certain problems. Sartre's ontology has shown that desire is the desire to be, and it is characterized by a free lack of being. But also desire is desire to have, a form of appropriation. Desire thus seems doubly determined: on the one hand, a quest for the ideal and impossible state of in-itself-for-itself, on the other, an appropriative relation with a concrete and contingent object. Is this a case of overdetermination? Are the two characteristics compatible? Sartre's discussion of possession shows that, once again, its inbuilt *failure* renders desire ultimately reducible to a desire for being. Possession leaves its object intact if it does not destroy it; my appropriation of it does not affect the painting, garden, or book. The relation of the for-itself to the in-itself leaves the latter totally untouched. However passionate my desire to possess something, the desired will always remain at heart separate from me and unaffected in itself by my desire. Possession is in this sense magical rather than real (*EN*, 681). Like emotion, possession is a way of changing the world that leaves the world just as it was, while disturbing only my project toward it. Possession may give me the illusion of projecting myself onto the world around me, but this relationship is symbolic and ideal. Possession is not a once-and-for-all affair; it is the work of a lifetime and remains incomplete at my death. Destruction or consumption may be the extreme form of reaction to my realization of the unreal nature of possession—if my house is in ashes, no one else can ever possess it, but neither can I. All our attempts at possession are attempts to constitute ourselves as founding the world and thereby founding ourselves. But the in-itself does not need the for-itself in order to be. And the for-itself lacks the being it needs to be its own foundation. Possession is a mediation of the desire to be in-itself-for-itself, but it enjoys no better chance of success than does desire. It is another form of useless passion (*EN*, 708).

The failure of desire depends not merely on the failure of all human relations—they are trapped in the eternal struggle for power described by Hegel and other philosophers of conflict—but on a deeper failure: that of the human project in its most original and most metaphysical form. This means that desire may be illuminated by analyses that seem at first sight not to concern it. One such analysis appears in the tantalizing two-page passage "Moral perspectives," which closes *Being and Nothingness.* Here Sartre speculates all too briefly on untheorized existential self-analysis as a "means of deliverance and salvation" (*EN,* 721) and on the possibility of freedom taking *itself* as its own aim and highest value. This would entail freedom choosing rather than fleeing its "lack of being" and the riven nature of consciousness:

> A freedom which wills itself as freedom, is in effect a being-which-is-not-what-it-is and which-is-what-it-is-not who chooses, as an ideal mode of being, being-what-it-is-not and not-being-what-it-is. It chooses then not to *possess* itself but to flee itself, not to coincide with itself, but always to be at a distance from itself. . . . Is it a matter of bad faith or another fundamental attitude? And can one *live* this new aspect of being? (*EN,* 722)

Saint Genet may provide hints for an answer to these paradoxical questions.

Genet's position as scapegoat, object of society's scorn and revulsion, seems at first perhaps to promise more material for reflection on power and conflict than on the self-assumption of freedom. Similarly, his homosexuality and cult of violence might be adduced as extreme examples of Sartre's descriptions of the sadomasochistic *tourniquets* of love and desire. A foundling child, fostered by a Morvan peasant couple, the young Genet is surprised from behind while stealing from the family who gave him a home. Labeled a thief, Genet internalizes society's contempt for him and his status as object within it; he makes himself into the image of evil that has been shown to him in the mirror of society's hostile eyes. He becomes a thief, an outcast, and a passive homosexual, constantly affirming his own domination by the other. He also becomes a writer. I have discussed the details of this story elsewhere, and its outline is in any case familiar.[5] In the context of desire what is important is not so much the intimate detail of Genet's sexual behavior and fantasies but the unexpected reversal of evaluation given in Sartre's concluding chapter: "Please use Genet properly."

Sartre decides to "betray" Genet's aim of contaminating the bourgeois reader with his bile by turning the tables on him and using his principle of "*qui perd gagne,*" loser wins, to show not so much how Genet beats the apparently superior bourgeois at his own sadomasochistic game (winner loses), but how against all

93

his (worst) intentions, Genet teaches us a paradoxical moral lesson. This is where Kant reenters the picture. Kant's categorical imperative has been described in *Being and Nothingness* as alienating the other and in the *Notebooks for an Ethics* as alienating the subject.[6] It is criticized in *Existentialism Is a Humanism* as abstract and impractical, and it is parodied in *Saint Genet* at the point where Sartre defines Genet's position as a mad inversion of Kant's:

> Act in such a way that society always treats you as an object, a means, and never as an end, as a person. Act as if the maxim of each of your acts had to serve as a rule in a den of thieves. (*SG*, 83)[7]

In the face of Genet's perverse program of corruption, Sartre returns to Kant's "impossible" ethics. What Genet's works produce in the reader—by their hostile seduction and their unwelcome invitation to share the subjectivity of a pederast and thief—is a disturbing awareness of the failure of the most basic of human experiences: intersubjective communication and mutual recognition. By showing the subjectivity of the social outcast, not in what it has in common with "us," but in what makes it inalienably "other," Sartre threatens our smug humanism at its base. We are offered the experience of treachery and evil internalized and asked if we can still proclaim our common humanity. Genet's failure, and our failure to engage reciprocally with him, brings us face-to-face with our own human alienation, solitude, and distress. This failure may persuade us to make a last-ditch attempt to achieve the impossible: to reconcile subject and object, if not in the Kantian city of ends (*SG*, 652) then at least in the imaginary.

> If there is still time, in a last attempt, to reconcile object and subject, we must, if only once and in the imaginary, realize that latent solitude that eats away at our acts and thoughts; we spend our time fleeing the objective in the subjective and the subjective in objectivity: This game of hide-and-seek will only cease when we have the courage to go to our extreme limits in both directions at once. Today it is a question of revealing the subject, the guilty one, that monstrous miserable beast that we risk at every moment becoming; Genet offers us the mirror: We must look at ourselves in it. (*SG*, 662)

Genet's failure teaches us the truth of our paradoxical situation. We *must* do precisely what we *cannot* do: see the other as both object and subject simultaneously, *be* both object and subject for the other. This is precisely the aim of desire (and love) described

in *Being and Nothingness*. We are left with the invigorating conclusion that desire shares its impossible ideal with Kantian
ethics. So the ideal may, despite its inevitable failure, reveal the
truth of human relations, the mode of impossible tension, not the
synthesis of two positions of failure (sadism and masochism).
Sartre has already shown their synthesis to be impossible. However, the fragile point between love and desire at which no equilibrium is possible cannot be sustained and is as fugitive as the
present moment. We have a choice, but it is not the choice we
expected. We can pursue our vain desire to be God and lament
our failure to possess the other in his freedom; or, we can learn
the lesson of this failure and celebrate what, for Sartre, makes us
truly human: desiring the impossible.[8]

Chapter 6

SIMONE DE BEAUVOIR'S DESIRE TO EXPRESS *LA JOIE D'EXISTER*

Eleanore Holveck

"Anyone who wants to work on women has to break completely with Freud."[1] Simone de Beauvoir's rejection of Freud, which she stated in various ways during the last decade of her life, has created problems for those of us who consider her to be an important feminist philosopher. On the one hand, contemporary feminists who are seriously interested in Lacan and Derrida consider de Beauvoir's philosophy to be as outdated and as irrelevant as its source, Sartre's *Being and Nothingness.* This is unfortunate, since it means that feminists influenced by two of our greatest contemporary women philosophers, Julia Kristeva and Luce Irigaray, tend to ignore de Beauvoir. On the other hand, when some feminist literary critics deconstruct de Beauvoir's fiction or autobiography, they often argue that her denial of the unconscious and her support for Sartre's masculinist theory of individual freedom are based in her own repressed desires.[2] De Beauvoir herself regretted that she had not developed an extensive critique of Freud. On her seventieth birthday she told Alice Schwarzer that she would have liked to have written a work on female sexuality by giving an honest account of her own sexual experience. She would thus have grounded a psychoanalysis in a feminist and not Freudian perspective. At seventy, however, she felt that she was too old for this task.[3]

Philosophically at stake here is a satisfactory account of human desire, inclination, or libido. I will outline de Beauvoir's position on desire, beginning with her first published novel, *L'invitée,* translated as *She Came to Stay.* The novel in which de Beauvoir struggled with Hegel is an excellent starting point for illuminating differences and similarities between various feminists, since contemporary women who have been influenced by Lacan, Derrida, and Foucault can trace their lineage back to Kojève's lectures on Hegel at the École Normale in the 1930s. After discussing desire in *L'invitée,* I will indicate further developments in de Beauvoir's *Ethics of Ambiguity,* her essay on Brigitte Bardot, and several other works. By examing where their differences lie, feminists grounded in different philosophical points of view might begin to notice their similarities.

In *L'invitée,* Françoise, a thirty-year-old writer, at first hides her jealousy of Xavière, a younger friend, who is in love with Pierre, the theater director with whom Françoise lives.[4] Xavière wants Pierre all to herself, but she is not initially successful, because Françoise slyly agrees to Pierre's suggestion that they form a *ménage à trois.* Xavière consoles herself by bedding down with Gerbert, Pierre's young protégé, but this alienates Pierre, who wants Xavière to live only for him. Françoise, still fearful of losing Pierre and now full of revenge as well, takes Gerbert away from Xavière and, finally, tries to kill her young rival. Simone de Beauvoir took this sordid tale, which might have slithered from the pen of Danielle Steele, and transformed it into a serious philosophical commentary on Hegel and Kant, with references to Husserl, Sartre, and others.

De Beauvoir wrote much of her best philosophy in her fiction. In her 1946 essay "Littérature et métaphysique,"[5] de Beauvoir contended that a metaphysical novel imaginatively re-creates a singular lived situation, which grounds the evidence for a philosophical system. "Just as scientific truth is validated in all the experiences which ground it and which it takes up, so does the work of art envelop the unique experience of which it is the fruit" (*LM,* 95). A metaphysical novelist tests a philosophical theory in her own lived experience, which her writing re-creates. As de Beauvoir wrote: "Existentialism claims to grasp the essence at the heart of existence, and whereas essential descriptions are products of philosophical discourse itself, the novel alone will permit the evocation of the original springing forth of existence in its complete, singular, temporal truth" (*LM,* 102).

De Beauvoir's essay on literature and metaphysics was first presented as a lecture for a class of Gabriel Marcel.[6] Marcel had expressed admiration for *L'invitée,* stating that Xavière was the perfect incarnation of the Other.[7] This ability to portray the philosophical theory of the other studies, in part, why de Beauvoir decided to write primarily fiction and autobiography rather than philosophical essays. She believed she was doing philosophy in fiction, something she also urged Sartre to do. In the film *Sartre by*

Himself, Sartre laughingly recounts that de Beauvoir tried to convince him to give up philosophy and to stick to writing literature.[8]

In Kate and Edward Fullbrooks's *Simone de Beauvoir and Jean-Paul Sartre: The Remaking of a Twentieth-Century Legend, L'invitée* is presented as a metaphysical novel. I disagree, however, with the Fullbrooks's claim that in her novel de Beauvoir "articulates a philosophical system that in its basic structure differs almost not at all from the one found in *Being and Nothingness.*"[9] De Beauvoir wrote a great deal of it in Paris while Sartre was absent in the French army and in a German prison camp—and major sections of the novel were written before *Being and Nothingness,* which in fact uses many examples from her novel. From the very first scene, de Beauvoir's novel is her own commentary on her philosophical predecessors and is strikingly different from Sartre's philosophical writings.

As Françoise and Gerbert work late at night in a small room in the empty theater with the typewriter clicking, the lamp throwing a rosy glow, Françoise thinks, "I am here, my heart is beating" (*SCTS,* 11). The Fullbrooks argue that here is a full-blown philosophy. *L'invitée* demonstrates that consciousness is intentional and prereflective, that is consciousness as nothingness, as non-thetic self-consciousness, is directed to objects such as typewriters and lamps. *"Je suis là"* ("I am here") then expresses the reflection of a consciousness that is aware of itself in space. Sartre, they claim, establishes "that two regions of being, consciousness and things (or, in Sartre's terminology, *being-for-itself* and *being-in-itself*) arise from appearances, but that neither is reducible to the other." The Fullbrooks argue that de Beauvoir's position here is the same as Sartre's ontological argument in *Being and Nothingness.* I do not agree.

As the Fullbrooks note, when Françoise goes outside to sit for a moment on a bench in the darkened city square, the reference to a chestnut tree that might have been in a small provincial town obviously refers to Sartre's *Nausea.* Here de Beauvoir in her first novel salutes Sartre in his first one. De Beauvoir presents Françoise as taking a break from work. It is late at night, and no one else is there (*SCTS,* 108). Françoise on her bench enacts a scene lifted from Husserl's *Cartesian Meditations.*[10] Husserl argued that in straightforward experience—the seeing of a house, for example—consciousness is directed toward its object. Natural reflection on this straightforward act of consciousness yields the Cartesian *ego cogito.* The ego as disinterested onlooker puts the *époché* into effect; this onlooker reveals pure consciousness as the stream of internal time.

Surely de Beauvoir gives us this moment, complete with the examples of Husserl: "All around her the houses were asleep, the theater was asleep. . . . She leaned back against the hard wood of the bench. A quick step echoed on the pavement; a truck rumbled along the avenue. There was nothing but this passing sound . . . there was no Françoise any longer; no one existed any longer, anywhere" (*SCTS*, 12). Husserl's disinterested onlooker, reflecting and bracketing all reference to existing objects and to an existing self, reveals inner time consciousness as pure, streaming intentionality. This is the abstract core of human consciousness; this is not Françoise existing for herself. She has to come back to herself as she goes to fetch Gerbert's scotch.

At first Françoise's love for Pierre bears a striking resemblance to Hegel's conception of Christian love in his early writings. De Beauvoir would have been familiar with these writings since she had been reading Jean Wahl's *Le Malheur de la conscience dans la philosophie de Hegel* (1929).[11] De Beauvoir's letters confirm this.[12] In the fragment "Love," Hegel claimed that love between a man and a woman resolves the opposition between reason, which wills universal law and individual inclination. Lovers can achieve unity because in them "there is no matter; they are a living whole." Love is without shame because "shame enters only through the recollection of the body," which is dependent on matter.[13] Françoise's view of her love for Pierre is clearly described in these early Hegelian terms. "You and I are simply one," says Pierre (*SCTS*, 25). Pierre has "no secret corners, no shame," thinks Francoise (*SCTS*, 26). Into this world of formal, idealized, immaterial love comes Xavière, who is the incarnation of immediate desire. Xavière frequently shuts herself up in her room; she scorns artists who work like civil servants; she insists that drinking a cup of coffee is just as important as writing *Julius Caesar*. In contrast to Xavière, Françoise feels compelled to act dutifully. For Kant, morality is characterized as the conflict between an individual's desire for her own happiness and the will to act according to maxims that could hold good as universal law. Kant discusses desire primarily as *Begehrungsvermogen*, "the desiring capacity," the ability to imagine an object and to become the cause of the actual existence of the object. When Gerbert wants a glass of scotch, Françoise takes steps dutifully to get one, i.e., she walks to Pierre's dressing room, gets his scotch, opens it, and pours whiskey into a glass. For Kant, duty consists in following the moral law for its own sake: one intends to follow the universal with no reference to one's own individual desires. Françoise rejects acting on her sexual desire for Gerbert, because, since she does not love him: she would be using him as a thing to satisfy her own desire. Françoise claims that she is sexually faithful to Pierre not because she is a slave to law, but because she has freely chosen to love, echoing Hegel's position in *The Spirit of Christianity* on the reconciliation of lust and law through love. Love creates a unity that needs no law because love abstracts from all individual matter, all bodies. In *L'Invitée,* Pierre and Françoise have attempted to love each other in this way. No sexual experience between them is ever described; they think perfectly alike. They work together to create an ideal artistic experience: to produce a play entitled *Julius Caesar.* The play is the story of a man, Brutus, who sacrificed his own individual good, a friend whom he loved, in order to promote the good of all.

The confrontation between Françoise and Xavière is a fight to the death for recognition, an enactment of Hegel's master-slave relation. Françoise at first treats Xavière as if the younger woman were a puppet who could act in the plays that Pierre directs and Françoise helps to write. All three would promote each other's happiness equally. However, through Xavière, Françoise comes face-to-face with the Desire of the Other, the *Begierde* of Hegel's *Phenomenology of Spirit,* living, eager desire, a negating activity that wantonly destroys and assimilates what it wants as it reveals the "I." "The I of Desire is an emptiness that receives a real positive content only by negating action that satisfies Desire in destroying, transforming, and 'assimilating' the desired non-I."[17] The physical desire for food, for example, leads to eating, which obliterates and assimilates food. A strictly human desire is the desire to be recognized by the Other's discourse. For example, a slave might grow, process, buy, sell, prepare, or serve food for her master, recognizing his hunger and denying or delaying her own satisfaction, because a slave has access to food only by her master's permission or her master's word. At first Françoise does not incarnate her desire for Gerbert because, since she really loves Pierre first and foremost, Gerbert would be sleeping with Pierre's woman, just as he is drinking Pierre's scotch and writing Pierre's play. Thus Françoise would be using Gerbert as if his existence for her were merely at Pierre's behest.

All her life Françoise has seen herself as an "I," the Kantian *"Ich soll"* or *"Je,"* the Husserlian disinterested onlooker, who thinks and who loves another "I" exactly like herself: Pierre. Throughout the novel, Françoise cannot say the Hegelian "I." She cannot express herself, either in language or in her body. She cannot dance; she cannot even look at herself in the mirror.

Xavière is the first human being Françoise meets who expresses her "I." Xavière does not want Pierre on either Françoise's or Pierre's terms; she wants him on her own terms as the satisfaction of her living desire.

The heart of the novel reveals a Françoise torn between her former Kantian position and Xavière's view, while Pierre does not see the impossibility of reconciling these two. He wants Xavière to acknowledge his relation to Françoise and his career, while loving him completely. But this would mean that Xavière would accept his definition of love and art and the values of fidelity and loyalty. Xavière, however, rejects all these values and lives in the present. She desires Pierre at this moment to be all hers, and she will live, presumably, from moment to moment.

In a last, desperate attempt to prove that lust can be transformed by love, respect, and friendship, and that the emotions can be reconciled with reason, Françoise begins an affair with Gerbert. She sleeps with him during a vacation they take together; she thinks that sex is an embodiment of their love. Pierre shares their happiness; these three can love each other and respect each other's freedom without jealousy. When Xavière finds out about the affair between Françoise and Gerbert, however, she has a totally different explanation. Xavière's story is that Pierre loves her, but, because of Françoise's jealousy, Pierre would have to break off with Françoise in order to live with Xavière; Françoise is forcing Pierre to stay with her out of guilt. Furthermore, Xavière believes that Françoise took Gerbert out of revenge because Françoise knows how much Pierre loves Xavière.

Faced with this picture of herself, Françoise cannot stand it, and, for the first time in her life, she acts in the real world without any idealizations or rational explanations and tries to kill Xavière. Xavière certainly came to stay in Françoise's consciousness; Françoise has accepted her position. At the end of the book Françoise keeps saying, "It is either she or I; it shall be I" (*SCTS*, 3). I would point out the originality of de Beauvoir's interpretation of Kojève. Her two characters do not fit exactly into his master-slave analysis. Rather, one character, Françoise, represents an early neo-Kantian Hegel and the other character, Xavière, represents Kojèvian Desire. The fight for recognition is between Kant and Hegel or between an early and late Hegel.

In *Simone de Beauvoir: The Making of an Intellectual Woman*, Toril Moi gives a psychoanalytic interpretation of *L'invitée*. I will discuss two major points of Moi's analysis. First, Moi compares a scene between Françoise and Gerbert with one of Sartre's examples of bad faith in *Being and Nothingness:* the woman in a café who puts herself in a semi-trance rather than acknowledge her date's taking her hand as his first approach toward their ultimate sexual encounter. Moi argues that Sartre's scene could be described from the woman's point of view as an act of flirtation. In an oppressive, patriarchal society, flirting provides women "with an opportunity to play with the thought of [a sexual] involvement without actually getting involved, and thus without risking the loss of their virginity, honor, reputation, and entire future."[15] Moi compares this flirting to a similar scene between Françoise and Gerbert. On a walking-tour vacation, having dinner in a farmhouse, Françoise tries unsuccessfully to flirt with Gerbert. Moi argues that the failure is due to Françoise's male role; she is older, independent, and powerful. When flirting fails, Françoise declares herself straightforwardly to Gerbert, freely stating her love and desire for him, hoping that he will freely reciprocate. Moi claims that, like a fairy tale, this declaration makes all Françoise's dreams come true; de Beauvoir lapses into romantic clichés.

Perhaps Moi is correct that de Beauvoir writes about Françoise's and Gerbert's affair in romantic clichés. According to Tito Gerassi, de Beauvoir did speak of her actual affair with Jacques Bost as perfect. When she was writing this novel, de Beauvoir's letters verify that she was terrified that Bost, who was in the infantry, would be killed. In the context of the novel the important question is: Does the Françoise-Gerbert affair represent an idealistic Kantian attempt for three people to promote each other's happiness without individual Desire entering the picture? Or is de Beauvoir attempting to found a relationship that is neither Kantian love nor Kojèvian desire? Françoise is not flirting, which is defined as behaving amorously without serious intent; she seriously wants to sleep with Gerbert. She is attempting to get him to declare his intentions first, because without his free consent she will not sleep with him.

In one of the first reviews of Beauvoir's novel, Merleau-Ponty suggested that one of its basic tenets is that real love and real communication might exist. "Communication exists between the moments of my personal time, as between my time and that of other people . . . if I will it . . . if I plunge into the time which both separates and unites us."[16] In the scene where Françoise declares her desire for Gerbert, de Beauvoir's translator describes Françoise as taking "the plunge" across the barn to the place where Gerbert is planning to sleep. Despite both translators' use of the word *plunge,* however, the French is quite different. Merleau-Ponty wrote, *"Si je m'enfonce dans le temps qui nous sépare."*[17] The verb *enfoncer* carries the meaning "to go deep," "to thrust," "to push in," and the reflexive has the sense of "submerging oneself." On the other hand, de Beauvoir wrote that Françoise *"prit son élan"* (*SCTS,* 454–55). The connotation here is "to spring to life," "to take a stance" like an athlete starting to race. While Merleau-Ponty imagines himself thrusting in time with Others, leaving Sartre with a silent, basically inert woman in a café, Françoise springs to life to bridge the space that separates her from Gerbert. De Beauvoir's phrase implies: Here I am or here I come; let us meet and see what happens. In my opinion, de Beauvoir creates a place of her own among these pushy men. Communication happens when I spring freely from my place to meet others who are situated with me, grounding communication in action. Against Toril Moi, I would argue that what de Beauvoir was flirting with was a workable solution to intersubjective communication.

Toril Moi's analysis also concerns the psychological question of how de Beauvoir experienced writing about killing Xavière: "The killing of Xavière cannot be explained by philosophy alone. . . . I find it difficult not to ask *why* Françoise's killing of Xavière represents such a moment of intense psychological investment for de Beauvoir" (*IW,* 96–7). Moi argues correctly that Françoise kills Xavière to save her own interpretation of the truth: "the *right to interpret* is finally what is at stake" (*IW,* 122). We might note that when de Beauvoir wrote *L'invitée,* she established herself as a writer: I exist here, in these words, in my own right. Moi lays out the imagery of Xavière very effectively: "an imagery of sexual menace, suffocation, claustrophobia, and death, and a morbid insistence on the idea of being swallowed, engulfed, poisoned, held down, choked, or strangulated" (*IW,* 115–116). I part with Moi, however, when she argues that Xavière represents de Beauvoir's mother: "the very image of the omnipotent and malevolent archaic mother threatening to devour her daughter" (*IW,* 118). Instead, Françoise and Xavière are two poles of one and the same woman, two diverse philosophical points of view, that de Beauvoir is trying to reconcile.

I object particularly to Moi's identification of de Beauvoir with Françoise and her claim that "for Françoise, to kill Xavière is symbolically to murder her own unconscious, to expel the bad mother from her psyche and to claim total control over body and mind. . . . To kill Xavière is to deny that the repressed ever

103

returns" (*IW*, 124). De Beauvoir's position is far more subtle. In the end, both Françoise and Xavière have completely changed their positions and gone over to the other side. Xavière is angry at Françoise because the older woman has lied to Xavière and has been disloyal to her in regard to Gerbert. But this is Françoise's Kantian value system: to tell the truth, to keep faith with an old friend out of duty or loyalty to the past. Why is Xavière now a sudden convert to Françoise's value system? Likewise, Françoise clearly enters Xavière's world. She acts on her Desire to kill Xavière, but she is horrified at what she has become as she sadly says goodbye to the innocent love she shared with Gerbert. The obvious conclusion is that neither a Kantian idealist nor a Hegelian position of Desire is adequate, although I would not deny completely that this novel has an element of de Beauvoir's revenge against younger women friends. I can imagine a Kojèvian de Beauvoir cackling to herself as she wrote this book: "You may be young and beautiful, and you have made me suffer, but I am a writer. Posterity will remember you as the infantile bitch that Sartre and I once made use of for personal pleasure and career enhancement."

Gabriel Marcel emphasized what is philosophically original in de Beauvoir's novel: her clear expression of the real experience of an Other. Here is the scene: Pierre, Françoise, and Xavière are in a Spanish nightclub watching flamenco dancers. Xavière is first caught up in looking at a particularly good dancer. Then, because she feels slighted that Pierre and Françoise have a closer relationship with each other than with her, Xavière burns her own hand with a cigarette. Françoise finally confronts the otherness of Xavière:

> The atmosphere was stifling, and her thoughts burned like fire. . . . Day after day, minute after minute, Françoise had fled the danger; but the worst had happened, and she had at last come face to face with this insurmountable obstacle, which she had sensed, under vague forms, since her earliest childhood. Running through Xavière's manic pleasure, through her hatred and jealousy, the horror exploded, as monstrous and definite as death. In Françoise's face, yet separate from her, existed something like a condemnation with no appeal: free, absolute, irreducible, another consciousness was rising. It was like death, a total negation, an eternal absence and yet, by a staggering contradiction, this abyss of nothingness could make itself present to itself and make itself fully exist for itself. The entire universe was engulfed in it, and Françoise, forever excluded from the world, was herself dissolved in this void. (*SCTS*, 291, I trans. modified, Fr., 363–64)

104

Here is a truly terrifying description of consciousness as Hegel's *Begierde*: a negating, driving desire that destroys its flesh, burns a hole in its own hand, its being as body, thereby expressing itself as real. As Jacques Deguy has emphasized, *"Il y a Xavière."*[18] Nowhere in *Being and Nothingness* is there any equivalent description that so clearly shows how consciousness as nothingness exists in its body.

De Beauvoir's scene of Xavière's burning her hand should be compared to the similar one involving Mathieu and Ivich in *The Age of Reason*.[19] Here they are, arguably, in that same nightclub. Mathieu is contemplating his future life as a "respectable" man. "My chosen life . . . forever Marcelle's former lover, now her husband, the professor, forever a man ignorant of English, a man who has not joined the Communist Party . . . forever" (*AR,* 244). Ivich, in the scene, represents youthful freedom. " 'Beloved Ivich, beloved freedom.' And suddenly, above his besmirched body, and above his life, there hovered a pure consciousness, a consciousness without ego [*une conscience sans moi*] no more than a mere puff of warm air; there it hovered, in the semblance of a look [*c'était un regard*]" (*AR,* 245). In these passages, Sartre views the for-itself as pure freedom disgusted with the material body as in-itself. Later in the same scene Ivich cuts her hand in an attempt to scandalize a bourgeois couple seated at the next table. Mathieu cuts his hand in imitation. Cutting one's hand is a futile attempt on the part of a gratuitous freedom to deny its own body in an act of bad faith. Mathieu denies his body to avoid taking responsibility for his own acts; he is, indeed, abandoning the woman whom he has impregnated. While Françoise faces the shattering of her empty Kantian life of illusion by the recognition of the Desire of Xavière, Mathieu tries to obliterate bodily existence with cold steel; Françoise opens the Other's oven and a blast of heat scorches her face.

At the end of *L'invitée,* de Beauvoir has posited two characters: an idealistic Kantian and a Kojèvian Hegelian, each of whom gives up her position and accepts the position of the other. Françoise has tried to incarnate her Kantian values with Gerbert, but she cannot sustain this against Xavière's burning desire. Xavière has nothing to show for herself but an aching hole in her hand. When Françoise tries to kill Xavière, Françoise herself ends up with nothing. Here, clearly, is de Beauvoir's conclusion: Neither Kantian idealism nor Kojèvian desire is adequate. These two positions are irreconcilable, and they are both wrong.

By the time she wrote *The Ethics of Ambiguity,* de Beauvoir was able to give an explanation for the negative expression of

Xavière's *moi*.[20] Children believe in absolute values because they do not understand yet that others have established all the order and meaning in the world. The first experience of free choice occurs in adolescence as one negates the values of her parents, her culture, her teachers. Xavière is obviously an example of this negative freedom. She amuses herself because she is less of a child than either Pierre or Françoise, who seriously posit the absolute values of loyalty, fidelity, art, and beauty. In her *Ethics,* de Beauvoir showed how adolescent negativity can grow into a joyful adult experience of concrete freedom. She writes of this *joie d'exister* in a Marxist context:

> In order for the idea of liberation to have a concrete meaning, the joy of existence must be asserted in each one, at every instant; the movement toward freedom assumes its real, flesh and blood figure in the world by thickening into pleasure, into happiness. If the satisfaction of an old man drinking a glass of wine counts for nothing, then production and wealth are only hollow myths; they have meaning only if they are capable of being retrieved in individual and living joy. The saving of time and the conquest of leisure have no meaning if we are not moved by a child at play. (*EA,* 14)

An old man embodies his pleasure as he drinks wine; a child embodies joy in playing with a balloon. The goal of all societies should be to promote these embodiments of joyful freedom in the world. De Beauvoir's position is a combination of the thought of Nietzsche and Marx. An individual incarnates the joy of existence in eating, drinking, playing; labor realizes existence in another way. Without a just distribution of the fruits of labor, old men will not sit and drink wine. But the final purpose of a just distribution of wealth is the expression of the joy of existence. This is the *moi* often expressed by de Beauvoir in her letters: I dance, I ski, I eat lunch, I sleep like an angel, I write, and my writing expresses this life that I am living.

Françoise *prit son élan* toward Gerbert and thus allowed an "original springing forth," *un jaillissement original,* of freedom. This freedom is revealed by existentialist conversion, which de Beauvoir compared to Husserlian *époché.* Just as Husserl brackets all existence claims, "suspending all affirmation concerning the mode of reality of the external world," existentialist conversion puts the will to be in parentheses (*EA,* 15). Once I see that all my values are contingent, limited—in short, *mine*—the creative freedom of my authentic being gushes into the world. "To will oneself free is to effect the transition from nature to morality by establishing a genuine freedom on the original upsurge of our existence" (*EA*, 25). *Il y a liberté!* Sexuality can be one kind of experience of this positive freedom.

De Beauvoir discussed sexuality in this sense in her essay on the young Brigitte Bardot, written in the 1950s. De Beauvoir saw Bardot as a danger to bourgeois values, pointing out the wedding scene in the film *And God Created Woman* where Juliette, a young bride who has long retired to bed with her new husband, comes back to the banquet table in a robe and calmly takes away food and wine, completely oblivious of the somewhat startled guests. De Beauvoir wrote,

> "She cares not a rap for other people's opinions. She follows her inclinations. She eats when she is hungry and makes love with the same unceremonious simplicity. Desire and pleasure seem to her more convincing than precepts and conventions. She does not criticize others. She does as she pleases, and that is what is disturbing."[21]

De Beauvoir claimed that decent French women were infuriated by Bardot and French men did not like her because she refused the artifices that give women mystery. Bardot was always moving: "She walks, she dances. . . . To spurn jewels and cosmetics and high heels and girdles is to . . . assert that one is man's fellow and equal, to recognize that between the woman and him there is mutual desire and pleasure. . . . But the male feels uncomfortable if, instead of a doll . . . he holds in his arms a conscious being who is sizing him up" (*BB*, 20–21). This is de Beauvoir's view of the sexually active woman. She does as she pleases. She walks, she dances, she eats. It sometimes pleases her to give and to take pleasure with others. De Beauvoir's admiration for beautiful, spontaneous, and active women such as Olga Kosakievicz and Nathalie Sorokine originated in her appreciation that they could express a freedom that she, who had been raised by a repressed mother, could not embody.

This account of de Beauvoir's view of sexuality must be reconciled with many other descriptions, especially in *The Second Sex,* that show woman as the Other, the passive recipient of male desire. There are at least two accounts of sexuality in de Beauvoir's works. The first, described in the terms of *Being and Nothingness,* is an example of the bad faith of Sartre. Men avoid acknowledging their contingency and embodiment by pretending to be pure consciousness for-itself and projecting all contingency onto the woman, the Other. The second is de Beauvoir's account of sexuality as the joyful carnal freedom of Bardot's persona, a sexuality that could be, but most often is not, real. Bourgeois con-

107

temporary women are still in this stage of contradiction. Most sexual relationships are in bad faith, but we try as far as possible to embody an ideal that is truly free. De Beauvoir's discussion of bourgeois male fear of Bardot is certainly confirmed today as her younger look-alikes stride down fashion runways, all the better to sell designer jeans and high heels.

De Beauvoir's practice of testing philosophical positions in her own lived experience in literature reveals a contrast to contemporary feminist positions that are ultimately based on Hegel. If we look carefully at de Beauvoir's analysis of Hegel in her first novel, we see not an example of Freudian repression, but rather that there is more to our lives than can be dreamed of by male theorists after Hegel. Philosophical theories must be rethought on women's own terms.

PART IV
READING FEMININE DESIRE:
IRIGARAY

Chapter 7

SITUATING IRIGARAY

Simon Patrick Walter

> From a more strictly philosophical viewpoint, one may
> wonder whether taking into account the sexualization
> of discourse does not open up the possibility of a differ-
> ent relation to the transcendental. Neither simply
> objective nor simply subjective, neither univocally
> centered nor decentered, neither unique nor plural, but
> as the place up to now always collapsed in an *ek-stasis*
> of what I would call the Copula. Which requires the
> interpretation of Being as having always already taken
> on (again) the role of the Copula in a discursive econ-
> omy that denies the Copulative operation between the
> sexes in language.
> —Luce Irigaray, *This Sex Which Is Not One*

Luce Irigaray's rereading of the categories of metaphysics trans-
forms the genealogical discourse inherited from and eclipsing both
Hegel and Heidegger.[1] Yet her explicit sexualization of discourse is
not simply a reactive development in metaphysics. Constitutive of
subjectivity itself, her discourse goes beyond strict hermeneutical
evaluation. From Lacanian linguistics comes a crisis point in reflexive philosophy that can only be resolved by the accommodation of
the body divided. Instead of excluding Woman once and for all from
participation in the significant meaning of the phallic structure, the
repression of sexual difference has been made explicit for the first
time. Woman becomes visible in her absence, disrupting and instigating the rereading of the whole discursive history of subjectivity.

I. Specularization and the Speculative Proposition

Irigaray's rereading does not merely scan the texts of metaphysics to highlight blatant examples of phallocentrism. Rather,

her critique is pitched at a "deeper structure" in the discourse of philosophy. For all of its doubts about the methodology of science, the ontological duality that it involves and the presuppositions about subjectivity that arise from this dichotomy, metaphysics refuses to relinquish the crown of objective neutrality it wishes to supersede. Indeed, despite a continuous process of de-centering, the subject in philosophy remains distinguishable as the autonomous individual, the traditional dynamo of the discourses of history and politics. Centering man outside himself has occasioned his *ex-stasis* within the transcendental (Subject). Here Irigaray identifies the fundamental movement of "reflection" in contemporary philosophy. By emphasizing that the Subject remains dependent on the world of objects to constitute his autonomous distancing from the Other, the status of the Object is to "reflect" back onto the Subject. Subjectivity cannot formulate its own grounding principles spontaneously and refuses to be defeated as the singular objective of metaphysics: The constant in the epistemological equation—the Other—becomes paradoxically the locus of masculinity, in the sense that Being is constructed through exclusion. Man's *ex-stasis* is the "copulative operation of language" in which the Subject projects onto the object in a movement of appropriation. Conceptually, *ex-stasis* is derived from medieval idealism. It is the mystical state in which two lovers achieve a union of their souls by discarding corporeal desire. In Lacanian terms, this idealism disguises the "proper" function of the Copula in the Subject/Object relation, which is the linguistic equivalent of the masculine erection in sexual intercourse. Here *ex-stasis* connotes "blood." For Irigaray the primal trope for the representation of a feminine fluidity becomes solidified in a masculine imaginary in order to become congruent with the necessarily intransigent relation between Subject and Object. It becomes sublated in the Transcendental, and if not always in Absolute Reason then at least in plain male Subjectivity. "Speculation" is the archetypical phallotropic discourse. Not only does it refuse the possibility of alterity—thus engendering an endless circularity of the same concepts—but it also tries to disavow the process of its own production. Although the archaic roots of the concepts of philosophy are no guide—in a Heideggerian manner—to their authentic usage, an etymological glance at a figure's discursive origins reveals the way in which logic is engaged in a continuous process of refining and reifing language's metaphorical base.

The etymology of the word "reflection" is rooted in the Latin verb *reflectere*. In both Greek and Latin philosophy the term has optic connotations.[3] It is the process engendered by mirrored surfaces casting light back, the activity of a mirror representing and duplicating objects in a pictorial sense. This optic metaphoricity is analogous to perception, but not strictly. For a curious plurality of movements occurs before it can become an adequate principle for the foundation of subjectivity. Thus reflection is the structure and the process of an operation that, in addition to designating the action of a mirror reproducing an object, also implies that the mirror mirrors itself, reproducing itself in itself. Subjective consciousness is that figurative mirror that reflects the phenomenological manifold while retaining the capacity of inversion in which it is able to reproduce itself. This movement is the first principle of Descartes's methodology. Through a suspension of the *Cogito*'s relation to the immediate manifold of phenomena, consciousness establishes the apodictic certainty of itself as a result of the clear and distinct perception it has of itself. Conceptual thought becomes a heterogenous duality that knows no certitude save a subject formulated from the self-reflexivity of its own cognition. Differentiated from the world, the *Cogito* becomes emancipated, individuated, before an infinite idealized horizon. But the perceptual process involved in this movement is difficult to realize if the analogy of the mirror that is cognizant of itself is thought through rigorously enough.

To cast the question in Kantian terms: What is the relationship between the objects of sensible intuition and the capacity of comparative understanding of these representations from which the idea of the reflexive self is constructed? Kant's solution was to raise self-consciousness from the categories of the Understanding to a principle of the a priori condition for cognition, and to posit a pure synthetic unity of the Subject and the Subject's representations. Yet a question still remained: What is the relationship between the transcendental ego and the world, in the sense that these two moments of cognition could be differentiated and rendered hierarchical? In the move to Kant the sophistication of the argument almost obscures reflection's metaphorical and analogous foundation in Cartesian philosophy. When Kant proposes that synthetic a priori judgments are possible, he assumes an opacity of communication, an identity between sign and referent, and a simple transitive relation between thought and articulation to which language, determined and determining, is necessarily inadequate. This failure of language itself is made explicit in Irigaray's *Speculum,* in her rearticulation of the Heideggerian conception of linguistics. For Heidegger the origins of language are inexplicable not because of

* a sign b/t the signified /signifier

113

any deficiency in the knowledge of history. Rather, because this anthropomorphic approach is not only situated by and in the language of origins it tries to describe, it also presupposes a Subject prior to the process of subjective construction that language brings about. Linguistics in Heideggerian terms is "neither half nor whole natural science, but, if it is anything at all, mythology."[4] For Irigaray this mythology is the equivalent of a Masculine Imaginary, in which successive generations of philosophers have reified the metaphoricity of the concepts of metaphysics, stripping them of the density and ambiguity of plurality in an attempt to construct one authentic Being as the ground of epistemology. This denial of syntactical multiplicity is analogous to the repression of the possibility of a reciprocal relation between more than one subjective position. When Heidegger attempts to clarify his statement by asking, "How could man ever have invented the power which pervades him, which alone enables him to *be* a man?" (*IM,* 156), he unwittingly confirms that monolithic subjectivity is only an effect of language, while simultaneously clarifying the principle that language does evade the conscious manipulation that Descartes and Kant sought in their affirmation of the transcendental unity of the ego.

In the movement from the metaphoricity of the mirror that reflects objects in the world—and has the faculty of self-reflexivity arising from these representations—to the a priori categories of the understanding that presuppose a transcendental self, an originary separation has evolved that cannot be united by merely claiming an absolute identity of the heterogeneous subject and object. For Kant, philosophical reflection belonged to the understanding that could conceive of the originary synthesis as a union only in the form of an antinomy of absolute dualistic terms. It was a unity that could only be determined in the categories of the understanding by an act of negation, the positing of an opposite to that which was given in intuition. If Being and everything that pertained to it was limited and monolithic, then it must have had in some sense a ground of indeterminacy from which it was differentiated and made intelligible. Yet from the perspective of the Kantian understanding, this indeterminacy was inconceivable. For this "nothingness," from which Being must be distinguished to be perceptible, would necessarily have to be of the same construction as Being: a violation of the logical law of noncontradiction, which is nonsensical in Kantian terms. In the very act of the understanding's positing and determining, there lies a nonpositing and indeterminacy; hence the task of determination was a process that continually evaded closure. At this point Reflection

114

dissolves and passes over into its Other because the oppositions of reflexivity are only oppositions of language.

In the "Preface" to the *Phenomenology of Spirit,* Hegel conceived of the speculative proposition as a resolution of the aporias of the Kantian project. The idea of specularization is the significant move in the phallotropic discourse of masculine subjectivity. While in previous incarnations, the philosophy of reflection had been content merely to negate the otherness of Being—marginalizing an unarticulable "beyond" of representation—with Hegel's absolute reflection. All that is not idealized as One becomes imprisoned within the circulation of masculine meaning as his alienated other.

This process of appropriation becomes evident in the etymology of the trope "Speculation." It is a compound of the Latin *speculatio* and *contemplatio,* both deriving from the Greek *theoria,* meaning "the pursuit of knowledge for its own sake" (*TM,* 142). The root of *speculatio* in Latin is *specio*: "to look" or "to behold." Knowledge in the philosophy of Reflection thus becomes equated with perception in what Irigaray identifies as discursive scopophilia. By broadening *specio* to encompass *speculum*— which, among other things, is a convex surgical instrument for inspecting the cavities of the human body and a mirrored surface of polished metal—the connection is made between the look, the body, and the mirror (the three significant moments in the determination of sexual difference). This happens covertly in the language of philosophy, overtly in psychoanalytic discourse. In "The Blind Spot of an old Dream of Symmetry," Irigaray's critique of Freud's "On Femininity," she identifies Freud's criteria for the differentiation of the sexes as woman's "visible" deviation from the masculine norm (*S,* 11–127). In simple morphological terms, she is Other because she lacks the penis. When this differentiation is translated into the structure of signification in Lacanian linguistics, Woman finds herself deprived of meaningful articulation. Her relationship to representation becomes passive, and she must content herself with a mimetic designation as mere mirror, reflecting the activity of male subjectivity. Yet, as Hegel identified, although he does not acknowledge a plurality of subjective positions, the construction of the homogeneous unity of language necessarily implies an identity and a differentiation as constitutive moments in the teleological sublation of its description of the totality of phenomena. Irigaray emphasizes this paradox: "Sexual difference is a derivation of the problematics of sameness, it is, now and forever, determined within the project, the projection, the sphere of representation, of the same. The differentiation into

115

two sexes derives from the a priori assumption of the same" (*S. 27*).

Hegel's solution to the aporias of the synthetic unity of Kantian transcendentalism was to posit a third moment in the reflective statement in which the object reflected by the mirroring subject was recognized not merely as an arbitrary manifestation of the manifold but as the Subject's symmetrical Other, a representation of its alienated self. In a totalizing embrace, Being and non-Being, the two previously incompatible moments of reflection, are united, yet formally differentiated, in the sublating activity of the dialectic of Absolute Conception.

Reason as thinking expressed in language—whose relation to each other was non-problematic for Hegel—is reflected back onto itself as the reason that animates and surpasses the category of understanding in the subject. As such, the predicate is articulated as a species of Being that exhausts the process of propriation in the subject. This is not a simple reversal of the roles of the judgmental statement but rather a formal identity that radicalizes the status of the Copula. Both passive and transitive, the Copula becomes the subject of the speculative proposition as it brings to realization the absolute totality of the Concept. Thus speculative discourse is only possible insofar as language possesses the reflective capacity to place itself at a distance and to consider itself as such in its entirety as related to the totality of phenomena. In other words, "speculation" is a discourse about language. It addresses its discernable and multiple functions, raising its metalinguistic capacity to thematic proportions while still claiming to represent its extralinguistic referent. This totality of phenomena as articulated in language is equated with conscious thought alone, idealized as Absolute Reason, and the necessarily corporeal designation of subjectivity is excluded. The body lies beyond Hegel's totality. The formal reciprocity between Being and non-Being is merely the articulation of another manifestation of exclusion.

For Irigaray, corporeality is the excess that cannot be embraced by Absolute Reason, merely "idealized" as Otherness. As the perceptible flat reflective surface—the space of projection—its difference is merely the manifestation of the Same. The real alterity—the body—is disavowed in a reinstatement of a hegemony in which subjectivity is an a priori designation, presupposed "always already" before the dialectic begins. Hegelian speculation is merely the return of the heterogeneous dualism of Descartes's mind/body split, translated into the economy of Being and non-Being, thus erasing the materiality of its discursive origins.

[The Copula ensures a dynamic relation between the two moments of speculation, but only an imaginary one—an effect of the rationalist belief that language could be stripped of its ambiguity and placed on an equivalence with mathematics. If the appropriating movement of logic is equivalent with the "idea" as Being, its propriety can only be established if all other manifestations of phenomena are excluded from authentic representation.] In the dark unconscious of Otherness, deprived of the particularity that the light of reason bestows, all that is deposited there becomes unrepresentable; therefore, there will always be an overflow that cannot be conceptually contained by the paradigms of logic. Here the demons antithetical to Reason's originary purpose—that of asserting self-determination for the Subject against the malign forces of the object world—become mythologized in an anti-logic that associates nature with the passions and the body with the feminine. The singularity of speculative reason demands a base of indeterminacy from which it may proceed towards the opacity of absolute self-reflexivity. Yet this indecidability is ultimately its downfall. For while Hegel conceives of non-Being as the flat mimetic surface, Irigaray's critique of this language of exclusion demonstrates that this mirror is necessarily convex; the speculum displays a distorted reflection of reality—a distortion of excess that women must exploit if they are to find a voice. Within this economy:

> the "enigma of Women" would serve as a sign of his progression towards knowledge. For his past, he would have to let into the forces of consciousness this non-knowledge that she seemingly perpetrates, this "unconsciousness" that has been allocated to her without her knowing it. . . . Women would be the basis, the inscriptional space, for the representativeness of the masculine unconscious. For the "Unconscious" of the historical development (of sexuality). For Her, that economy could rate only as "pre-history." And if one day her sexuality was recognized, if it did enter into "History" then his-story would no longer simply take place or have a place to take. (*S*, 111–12)

II. Being and Non-Being

In this attempt to situate the thought of Irigaray within the discursive history of the philosophy of reflection, the Hegelian investment in the formal structure of the speculative proposition is not a sufficient vehicle for an adequate description of subjectivity. Not only does it disavow the role of the body in the constitution of consciousness, it also simultaneously raises masculine self-reflexivity to a state of transcendental omnipotence. Nevertheless, in metaphysics, any attempt to account for sexual difference in speculative representation would not be a simple case of reversing the criteria of Being. Because Hegel identified Being as pure "idea" and hence excluded the possibility of sexual determination from his account of consciousness, it does not necessarily follow that if Being is re-grounded in the perceptible, rather than the strictly intelligible, a more coherent presentation of the pre-scription of the body will be any more forthcoming.

Although Marx turned the Hegelian dialectic "on its head" to form the general principles of historical materialism, in a schematic and maybe oversimplified sense, the discursive economy of philosophy as a whole since the Enlightenment has been a reaction, an enforced confrontation, with the formal perfection of the speculative proposition. But the move away from idealism must also be situated within the increased prominence of the body as the space in which the discourses of knowledge have exerted their power. One only has to consider Lacan's "mirror stage"—in which the analogous "reflection" of Descartes becomes actualized in the child's existential confrontation with itself as the preliminary move in its initiation into the symbolic—as an example of this shift from idealism to materialism. The origins of this shift are not immediately discernable. Indeed, in a move of infinite complexity, like the beginnings of language itself, this origin evades simple archeological recovery. In terms of metaphysics, the relinquishing of the guarantee of scholastic theology and the grounding of certainty in the *Cogito*—although Descartes retained the theoretical Christian dualism—was the first step in the eventual establishment of the corporeal, the body, the Heideggerian "House of Being."[5]

Rather than pure thought being given methodological precedence in Heidegger's "destruction" of metaphysics, consciousness becomes an effect of the faculty of language itself, both simultaneously responsible for the disclosure and concealment of Being as *physis*. This move from Being as *ideos,* the "Idea" in Hegel, to Being as *physis*, the power that manifests itself in the presence of what-is, marks not only the shift from culmination to destruction but also from mind to body or the manifold of phenomena. Structurally the change is slight; the primordial form of the speculative proposition remains intact and the emphasis of the Copula as mediator would seem integral. Now, however, sublation as an abstraction would not take place, and the *telos* of history should not be the revelation of self-consciousness to itself but the bringing to disclosure and maintenance of the Being of beings as a counter-action to the nihilism of scientific appropriation through empiricism. But this is not necessarily the case.

For Irigaray, the paradox of the Heideggerian "body" is: that the perceptible may turn out in the end to be written with a capital letter still marks its subordination to the intelligible order" (*TSO*, 101). The shift of emphasis to the tangible is merely "a detour into strategy, tactics and practice" whose purpose is to found a more substantial—yet in essence congruent, not different—form of Subjectivity. Heidegger is undermined by the idealism implicit in his methodology. He cannot distance himself from Hegel's absolute reflexivity because his discourse is inscribed within the same theological tradition. This tradition considered the corporeal the site of the appetites (in Platonic terms, the *epithemia*) to be the base urges that limit the pursuit of Truth and which must therefore be overcome. For Irigaray, "matter becomes that upon which he [the male subject] will ever and again return to plant his foot in order to spring farther, leap higher, although he is dealing here with a nature that is already self-referential" (*S*, 134). To extrapolate the inference of this statement, a detailed account of the correspondence of the intelligible and of the perceptible in *Dasein's* constitution is necessary. Irigaray's work in this sense is an attempt to reveal the specific site of the body that Heidegger's Being points toward but nevertheless do not discuss.

For Heidegger, metaphysics was accomplished in Hegel, but from "the point of view of sound common sense," his philosophy is the "world stood on its head." The question of metaphysics "has to be put as a whole and has always to be based on the essential situation of existence" (*WM*, 355–36). He differentiates his thought from Hegel's with the distinction between "comprehending the totality of what-is and finding ourselves in the midst of what-is-in-totality. The former is absolutely impossible. The latter goes on in existence all the time" (*WM*, 363). Thus *Dasein* (Being-there-in-the-world) is constituted by a disclosure not of objects but of what is ready-to-hand within-the-world, not as a reflecting subject but as a being always already characterized as Being-in-the-world. This disclosure takes place through states-of-mind, primordial experiences that are presupposed by all immanent reflection: "The affective state in which we find ourselves not only discloses according to the mood we are in, what-is-in totality, but this disclosure is at the same time, far from being a mere chance occurrence, the ground phenomenon of our *Dasein*" (*WM*, 362) Before the subject/object relation, *Dasein* is situated within Being-in-the-world as a totality, irrespective of inner perception and regardless of all faculties of reflection. Reflection in the sense of a turning back becomes only a mode of self-apprehension but not the primary means of self-disclosure. This amounts to a return to the *a priori* subject of Cartesian dualism, reconstituted by Kant as transcendental, but without that self-disclosure that is differentiated from the manifold through the negation of non-Being in logical procedure. This heterogeneous relation to what-is seems to undermine the primordiality of the whole, in which Dasein is supposed to be situated prior to its reflection on its relation to the manifold. To retain a constituted Totality, Heidegger must follow Hegel's proposition that "*Pure Being* and *Pure Nothingness* are, therefore, the same."[6] But how is this speculative statement to be translated into the a priori disclosure of existence if Hegel is dependent on the totalizing effect of language for this assertion? Although according to Heidegger, only through "listening" to language can authentic Being manifest itself, he must resist the sublating movement of self-consciousness in the absolute if Being is to be accepted as *physis* rather than pure *ideos*. For non-Being can be conceptualized in the speculative proposition in the sense that "we can, at a pinch, think of the whole of what-is as an 'idea' and then negate what we have thus imagined in our thoughts and 'think' it negated. [But] in this way we arrive at the formal concept of an imaginary Nothing, but never Nothing itself" (*WM*, 363). By this reasoning, Heidegger sets up an antinomy between the authentic and intuitive grasp of the "feeling" of Nothingness and the logical deduction of Nothingness through conceptual thought. As such this distinction merely restates Plato's heterogeneous antagonism between *nous* (Reason) and *thymos* (the spirit or passions), in the tripartite division of the Soul.[7] But how could mental states be distinguished from reason itself if the reasoning faculty must necessarily be homogeneous in structure to mark its absolute distinction from the body? Heidegger's Being as *physis* can escape the problems of Platonic idealism, but only by explicitly grounding consciousness as an effect of Being-there-in-the-world. Yet Heidegger never talks explicitly about the body—unlike, say, the Nietzschean corporeal, which forms the foundation of the active and reactive forces which constitute subjectivity—merely about instances in which "one feels something uncanny" or when he discusses the "Nothingness" revealed when *Dasein* "loses its bearings" (*WM*, 366). Thus in Heideggerian discourse, the body is simultaneously denied and affirmed. In its guise as Being-there-in-the-world it becomes the site for what is in effect just a more primordial conception of Kantian reflection—*Dasein*'s prereflex-ive self-understanding.

In this sense the body cannot have the ontological status of an effective actuality because, first, the designation of an a priori self-disclosure is in itself a postreflexive concept, and second, because Being animates but is not identical to the corporeal—between apprehension and Being "there is a reciprocal bond" (*IM*, 145)—the states-of-mind of originary self-understanding are not dependent on the body as effects of its being-there, but are rather disclosed in the manner "that we find ourselves placed in the midst of what-is and that this is somehow revealed in totality" (*WM*, 363).

Heidegger's disavowal of the ontological designation of the body, and hence the representation of morphology divided (sexual difference), implicates his revelation of consciousness, circumscribing it within the traditional masculine imaginary, the economy of the Same. When elaborating on the "reality" of "Nothingness," he reproduces the cultural inscription of subjectivity found in the discourse of psychoanalysis. Here, having established that prereflexive states-of-mind are the ground phenomena of *Dasein*, Heidegger asks for a clarification of the relation among the totality, Being and non-Being, and *Dasein*'s emotive sensibility. The revelation of beings is simply asserted in the "joy we feel in the essence of Being" (*WM*, 364). But the more problematic question remains: "Does there ever occur in human existence a mood of this kind through which we are brought face to face with Nothing itself?" (*WM*, 365). The answer in the affirmative occurs when *Dasein* intuitively encounters the finitude of Being. This mood is the dread of non-existence in which the ontological reality of Nothingness is primarily made manifest. For Irigaray, woman's lack of representation in an economy that refuses to acknowledge the crucial role of the body in the constitution of subjectivity marks the feminine ulterior, inscribing her as the "Guardian of the Negative." In this "proliferating desire of the same, death will be the only representative of an outside, of a heterogeneity, of an Other" (*S*, 27). As such, in Heideggerian dread the two predominant concerns of the masculine imaginary come together: otherness and death. The *horror feminae* of the non-symmetrical relation of the sexes becomes equivalent to the realization of the finitude of Being. In a discursive homology in which meaning is equated with the manifest presence of Being, the "beyond"

121

inspires fear and loathing in a manner significantly in harmony with the differentiation of sexuality in Freud's "On Femininity." [Defined from the perspective of a masculine norm, the penis is superficially constituted as the guarantor of authentic being, and within such a scopophilic economy, woman's "lack" must be taken as a deviation, as the locus of the fear of deprivation of the master signifier. Crudely translated into Lacanian linguistics, Being is to beings what the phallus is to male sexuality.]

The body, along with Woman's implicit designation in the Heideggerian imaginary as the representation of non-Being, is further compounded in the process in which *Dasein* constitutes and determines itself:

> Projecting into Nothing, *Dasein* is already beyond what-is-in-totality. This "being-beyond" what-is we call Transcendence. Were *Dasein* not, in its essential basis, transcendent, that is to say, were it not projected from the start into Nothing, it could never relate to what-is, hence could have no self-relationship. (*WM*, 370)

In this manner Dasein formulates "his" own ground. Prior to reflection and to the disclosure of dread, the subject is constituted as an a priori transcendental designation, and as such, the antinomies of the Kantian synthesis between the heterogeneous moments of the manifold of phenomena become, once again, problematic. Nevertheless, Heidegger affirms the crudest form of prereflexive subjectivity, circumventing entirely the structural procedure of speculative philosophy. Non-Being becomes the blank space for the a priori prescription of the phallic circulation of meaning. *Dasein* "projects" into Nothingness, for "he" must appropriate the totality of beings. But unlike Hegelian speculation, where non-Being mirrors and throws back in a semireciprocal sublation toward self-consciousness through the mediation of the Copula as a vital synthesizing effect, Heidegger's reflection is a movement of overpowering. This is *ex-stasis* made manifest. The essence of Being considered as a whole is the motion of power irrupting in the subjugation of non-Being. *Dasein* remains exposed within the "overpowering power," but he is also the "violent one" (*IM*, 151), for in prereflexive states-of-mind, he gathers together this power and brings it to manifestation. Thus the relation between Being and non-Being is necessarily heterogeneous and unaccountable except in that *Dasein* raises himself to the position of domination in a pseudodialectical movement in which otherness is not sublated but appropriated into an economy of the Same. Or, as Irigaray would have it, "Rising to a perspective that would dominate the totality, to the vantage point of greatest power, he thus cuts himself off from the bedrock, from his empirical relationship with the matrix he claims to survey" (*S*, 134).

The nonsymmetrical relationship between Being and non-Being removes any coherent reflexive ground for the foundation of the subject, and as such *Dasein*'s primordial, prereflexive self-understanding is shown to be an incongruous effect of a discourse that claims not to equate thought as authentic being with pure *ideos*, but also suppresses any notion of an outside, of the body's determinations, or of the possibility of a plurality of subjective positions.

By shifting the criteria of authenticity, Heideggerian Being disqualified the transitive and logically reciprocal interaction of the Copula between the two moments of reflexivity in Hegel's speculative proposition. As such, it became a supplementary assertion of the manifest presence of Being. Being simply "is." Heidegger's reconstitution of reflection is merely an affirmation of the verb "to be" as a logically necessary precondition for the existence of language rather than an effect of that language. Heidegger states that without the infinitive of being "there would be no language at all" (*IM*, 82). This confederacy with the Lacanian school of linguists characterizes language as an inadequate relation to the extralinguistic referent. Being or the signified—as the underlying arbiter, constitutive signification—is at once revealed and concealed by the signifier while language can function in its own right as an enclosed totality of differences. In Hegel, Being was *ideos*, and in Heidegger, it is *physis*; but viewed again under the rubric of psychoanalytic linguistics, these terms became no more than euphemisms for the exclusive organization of cultural representation—to the repression of otherness—in a masculine imaginary symbolized by the phallus. Irigaray's textual analysis refrains from taking this form of hermeneutics and from strictly applying it transhistorically to the philosophical canon. Rather, it takes Lacanianism as the genealogical culmination of the metaphysics of reflection—a process of discursive circulation whose center of gravity, authentic male subjectivity, is continuously shifting. From ephemeral idealism to the determinant of masculine morphology, Being—through Lacanianism—has descended from the heavens and rid itself of its ambiguity to become once and for all an explicitly male domain. But, as Lacan admits, due to its imaginary nature, Being can be substantial only if it remains hidden: "That is why the demon [of shame] arises at the very moment when, in the ancient mysteries, the phallus is unveiled."[8]

123

Thus exposed, Being becomes a discursive anomaly, a textual fissure that allows Irigaray to demonstrate the superficiality of its homologous demarcation. It is an opening of resistance against the monosexual incarceration of subjectivity in language. Severely limited in her representations, woman inevitably has a mimetic relation to the protagonist in this economy—a relational distance that it has been the task of the philosophers of reflection to bridge. Irigaray's primary interest is in the articulation of this difference. As such, her "interpretation of being as having always already taken on (again) the role of Copula in a discursive economy that denies the copulative operation between the sexes in language" is not a return to Hegelian speculation devoid of an *Aufhebung* in the realm of absolute consciousness. Nor is it simply an assertion of the manifest presence of the sexualized body. Rather than an ontological reality in the traditional sense, it is a description of being as the figurative trope of difference in the constitution of subjectivity. Being here would be considered an expression of the relational terms of the speculative proposition rather than a substantial revelation of consciousness. If metaphysics has always been an etymological attempt to recover—in the nonidentical equivalence of representation and reference—an imaginary masculine moment of originary fullness, then being has always been a projection of relational difference and not a thing-in-itself. The appropriation of Being is nothing but the manifestation of desire as discursive power in the hierarchical cluster of the structural interdependence of language. Being thus deprived of the status of a significant ontological substance becomes an open space for the inscription of an alternative hermeneutics—the demythologizing of the texts of reflexive philosophy in the movement toward a discourse that acknowledges a plural parity of articulation and requires a reevaluation of the epistemological antinomies of sexuality.

124

Chapter 8

IRIGARAY'S DISCOURSE ON FEMININE DESIRE: LITERALIST AND STRATEGIC READINGS

Dorothy Leland

> Woman's autoeroticism is very different from man's. In order to touch himself, man needs an instrument: his hand, a woman's body, language. . . . And this self-caressing requires at least a minimum of activity. As for woman, she touches herself in and of herself without any need for mediation, and before there is any way to distinguish activity from passivity. Woman "touches herself" all the time, for her genitals are formed of two lips in continuous contact.
> —Luce Irigaray, *This Sex Which Is Not One*

What are we to make of this fragment from one of Luce Irigaray's more famous discourses on feminine desire?[1] At first glance, to my literalist eye, this fragment seems outrageous. It seems to say that my female body, because of its genital morphology, is continuously autoerotic. Lucky me! Unlike a man, I need only the continuous contact of the "two lips" of my vulva to turn me on. My pleasure is all the time.

According to the same discourse, my pleasure is also "all over" because "woman has sex organs more or less everywhere" (*TS*, 28). Everywhere? What could this mean, except perhaps a radically different, nontraditional understanding of "sex organs"? But when I survey Irigaray's discourse, I discover that this is not so. The "sex organs" invoked by Irigaray in her inventory of "specifically female pleasures" are quite traditional—breasts, vulva, clitoris, vagina, uterus—and quite traditionally *not* located "all over" a woman's body.

Although I have only begun to describe what in Irigaray's discourse offends my literalist eye, my concern here is not to chronicle these offenses. In part, I have reservations about the

125

assumptions and yes, even desires, that guide my literalist reading. Perhaps the most important assumption is that Irigaray's discourse is primarily assertive: It makes claims about the nature of
feminine desire. Given this assumption, this discourse offends
because so much of what it claims is false—even ludicrously so.
It offends my desire for truth, and not just my desire for truth in
general. Specifically, it offends my desire for truth which, when
its disaffection is flaunted, screams: "How dare you, a woman, a
philosopher: sloppy, excessive, out of control!"

What tempers my annoyance with Irigaray is a recognition
that her discourse on feminine desire is not exclusively, perhaps
not even primarily, assertive. Rather, her discourse is *strategic*.[2]
The military metaphor is intentional. Her discourse is a trick
played on an enemy, an elaborate artifice or subterfuge designed
to make the enemy look silly. In Irigaray's case, the enemy is
another, more famous, more influential discourse on feminine
desire—the psychoanalytic discourse of Freud and Lacan. Viewed
strategically, Irigaray's texts are playful inversions of psychoanalytic discourse, texts that deliberately "mimic" or flaunt this discourse's more ludicrous aspects.

I want to consider this strategic reading in a bit more detail,
leaving for a moment the literalist, offended me behind. Having
"bracketed" her literalist reading (an old phenomenologist's
trick), I confess: Irigaray's discourse on feminine desire is a
delight. It is witty, ingenious, fun fun fun. Women have sex
organs all over? This is silly, and Irigaray knows it. But the psychoanalytic notion ("penis envy") that only the penis is invested
with symbolic value in the psychosexual development of children—male and female—is equally silly. Irigaray is playing an
"I can do anything you can do better" game, trumping one
extravagant claim with another.

In Irigaray's texts, the literalist me is put off by the persistent
linking of female pleasure and desire to anatomy. My strategic
eye delights in the intricate burlesque of this linkage. If Freud
could get away with his extravagant tale about women's anatomy
and her desire, why not Irigaray? Her discourse on feminine desire
spins an equally extravagant yarn, with one decisive difference.
Irigaray is putting us on.

Specifically, Irigaray is putting us on when she says that a
woman's autoeroticism is very different from a man's because her
genitals are formed by two lips in continuous contact. She should
not be construed as claiming that a woman's autoeroticism is
rooted in the "two lips" of her vulva. Nor should she be criticized

for its lack of empirical warrants or fanciful causal reasoning. To the contrary, this lack of empirical warrants and fanciful causal reasoning is part of Irigaray's point. What Irigaray's discourse provides is a woman-centered fantasy of anatomical superiority in which the "two lips" of a woman's vulva displace the envied penis of the classical psychoanalytic tale.

A decisive moment in this tale is the little girl's misunder- *Sexual* standing of her clitoris as a stunted penis. This misunderstanding *Misunderstandin* is the basis of her conclusion that she does not have (much of) one—the one, the only "sex organ." In addition, the little girl "reasons": The bigger the better, bigger penises get more pleasure. And thus she experiences her own stunted organ as a loss. Even worse, the little girl generalizes her inferior biological equipment to her whole self. She, not just her "sex organ," is inferior. The end result of her "castration" is a lifelong longing for a penis, a desire that, among other things, causes her to change her erogenous zone from the clitoris to the vagina, now valued as a "place of shelter for the penis" (*TS,* 41).

With her "two lips" conceit, Irigaray deftly alters this psychoanalytic tale, beginning with the assumption, attributed to the little girl, that there is only one sex organ. What if, Irigaray in effect asks, the little girl is indifferent to the external look of the male sex organ? What if organ size is irrelevant to her as a measure of sexual pleasure? What if the little girl experiences her own pleasure through touch rather than counting the sites of her pleasure, she might say: "I have at least two of them. Together they caress, hold, and protect my pleasure." Indeed, the little girl might even say: "I have erogenous zones all over my body. My touches here, my touches there, all give me pleasure." Such a little girl would lack the libidinal motivation which for Freud gives rise to penis envy. What the little boy has only "down there," the little girl has (more or less) everywhere. Her pleasure is thus much more—not less, as the classical psychoanalytic tale assumes—than the limited penile men.

Although it might be tempting to object that Irigaray has misrepresented male sexual pleasure, such an objection is barred by my strategic reading. After all, Irigaray's quarrel with psychoanalysis centers on its misrepresentation of female sexuality. Why should she, given her strategic intentions, produce a discourse on sexuality that does justice to men? What Irigaray's discourse does is mimic the focus of psychoanalytic theory on phallic or genital sexuality, which is centered on one organ (the penis) and one aim (orgasmic release of tension). But she reverses the value attached to it. Measured against the multiple sites and multiple aims of female sexuality, male sexual pleasure emerges as limited and deficient. This reversal of value also occurs at the level of anatomical (mis)description. The vulva, not the penis, is the "magic organ," complete within itself, requiring neither the hand nor the "sex organ" of another for its pleasure. Irigaray effects this reversal of value by displacing what she calls "the predominance of the visual" in psychoanalytic accounts of female sexuality with a different sensory modality—that of touch, self-touching in particular. Consider, as an example of her concern, the following fragment from the psychoanalytic discourse of Lacan:

> The feminine genitals have a character of absence, of emptiness, or of a hole which causes them to be found less desirable than the masculine genitals in the latter's provocative [engorged, erect] aspect, and causes an essential asymmetry to appear.[3]

In this incredibly bad piece of reasoning, Lacan argues that certain characteristics of female genitals cause them to be perceived as less desirable than male genitals. But the characteristics he invokes are derived from an implicit comparison that measures the outward appearance of female genitalia against the look of the erect penis. When compared with the erect penis, female genitals present (in Lacan's words) "nothing to see." Moreover, female genitals are found to be less desirable *for this reason.* The missing premise in Lacan's argument is the unexamined assumption that having something to see is more desirable than having nothing to see. Thus rather than explaining the difference in value attributed to male and female genitalia, Lacan's discourse presupposes it. It presupposes that the visible form of the penis, particularly when erect, is desirable. In addition, it presupposes that the desirability of female genitalia is appropriately measured by this penile standard.

Irigaray mocks the "highly anxious . . . attention paid to erection" by Freud and Lacan when they index this concern to male rivalry centered on a boy's narcissistic investment in his penis—for instance, "the 'strongest' being the one who has the best 'hard on,' the longest, the biggest, the stiffest penis, or even the one who 'pees the farthest' (as in little boy's contests)" (*TS*, 25). This comical picture of a peeing contest deflates the high seriousness with which Lacan offers his explanation of why male genitals are more desirable than those of a female. But Irigaray's discourse on feminine desire does more: It displaces "looking" with "touching" as the sensory modality appropriate for describing male and female genitalia, initiating a delicious play on the meaning and consequences of not having "one"—for psychoanalysis, not having the "one" and only sex organ; for Irigaray, not having just "one" sex organ but two and even more.

> When one starts from the "two lips" of the female sex, the dominant discourse finds itself baffled: There can no longer be a unity in the subject, for instance. There will always therefore be a plurality in feminine language. And it will not even be a Freudian "pun," i.e., a superimposed hierarchy of meaning, but the fact that at each moment there is always for women at least two meanings, without one being able to decide which meaning prevails, which is "on top" or "underneath."[4]

My strategic reading provides me with at least a partial rejoinder to the literalist objection that Irigaray often fails to get things right.[5] Saying a woman has sex organs (more or less) everywhere is not quite right. But being quite right, I have suggested, is not Irigaray's point. Indeed, Irigaray delights in being "improper," and her texts invite us to share in outrageous, irreverent pleasures.

Still, the literalist me is not totally pacified. For Irigaray does sometimes "tell things straight," and one of the problems encountered in reading her texts is figuring out just when this is occurring. Sometimes this is obvious, as when Irigaray, without hint of playfulness, punning, or other strategic artifices, presents her views on the French women's liberation movement or on separatism. But in other cases, things are not so clear. For instance, in texts such as "This Sex Which Is Not One," Irigaray's emphasis on touch as the sensory modality appropriate for depicting female sexual pleasure can be seen as a strategic pivot, as a way of "showing up" Lacan's seemingly arbitrary emphasis on the visual form of the penis in his account of the gendering of desire. But this reading seems forced when we encounter the same emphasis in interviews and other formats that invite literalist construals.

This "ambivalence," as I will call it, is expressed in the secondary literature on Irigaray. Irigaray's most vehement critics read her discourse about female sexuality and language literally. This is the case for those critics who attribute to Irigaray an untenable biological essentialism linking woman's "nature" to her genital morphology.[6] On this view, Irigaray makes Freud's mistake, aptly described by Judith Butler as the "conflation of desire with the real—that is, the belief that it is parts of the body, the 'literal' penis, the 'literal' vagina, which cause pleasure and desire."[7] In contrast, strategic readers of Irigaray tend to see something quite different in the persistent links she makes between female labia and female nature. Jane Gallop, for example, treats this as an effort to (re)construct the female body and to (re)metaphorize it in ways that undercut psychoanalytic constructions.[8] Margaret Whitford, to cite another example, argues that the female body as depicted by Irigaray is not an "empirical category"; rather, what Irigaray provides is an "ideal morphology," which helps us to reconceptualize feminine desire along lines less inimical to women.[9] Both Whitford and Gallop thus dispute the underlying premise of those literalists who criticize Irigaray's biological essentialism.

Well, is she an essentialist? Perhaps we are not supposed to know. Perhaps Irigaray constructs texts that are meant to be undecidable, texts that invite multiple, sometimes incompatible interpretations. At times Irigaray says things that (when literally construed) lend credence to this position. If feminine language, like feminine sexuality, is plural, then just as women have multiple "sex organs," so the meanings they express in their speech or writing are multiple. There are always at least two of them, and no one of these meanings prevails over the other(s) as *the* correct meaning. Such polysemantic or ambiguous discourse is said to "baffle" the dominant (masculine) discourse, which values unity over plurality—the "one" sex organ over two or more, the univocal meaning over semantic multiplicity. Rather than resolving the literal/strategic split, this construal of Irigaray's discourse as intentionally ambiguous simply sets it into motion once again. Construed literally, the rationale for Irigaray's textual strategy consists of a set of claims about *"parler femme,"* claims that are rooted in a more general view about the relation between language and desire. Let's listen for a moment to the literalist Irigaray:

> I do not think that language is universal or neutral with regard to the differences between the sexes. In the face of language, constructed and maintained by men only, I raise the question of the specificity of a feminine language: of a language which would be adequate for the body, sex and the imagination (imaginary) of the woman. (*WE*, 62)

Here language is not gender-neutral and, as a consequence, the linguistic resources "constructed and maintained by men" are not adequate for expressing or representing important aspects of women's experiences. More specifically, existing linguistic resources are not adequate for expressing or representing the body, sexuality, and the imaginary of women. This inadequacy, Irigaray further suggests, gives rise to the speculative question that she addresses. What linguistic resources would enable a woman to

130

[margin handwritten note: There is no correct meaning in female language yet there are multiple meanings.]

articulate the "specificity" of her female sexuality (e.g., autoeroticism) and the fantasy life (the imaginary) rooted in her specifically female sexual pleasures?

Irigaray first addressed the issue of how sexual differences correlate with differences in language use, structure, and lexical make up in *Le langage des déments,* which examined the different "dynamics of statements" and different linguistic disturbances characteristic of men and women suffering from schizophrenia.[10] Based on the recording and analysis of samples of the speech of schizophrenic men and women, Irigaray found that women, unlike men, do not articulate their psychosis in language. Rather, women tend to suffer their psychosis directly in the body—for instance, through feelings of corporeal pain associated with beliefs about the physical deformation and transformation of bodily organs. But other texts by Irigaray on the expression of sex differences in language do not follow this empirical, interpretive method. In her early depictions of *parler femme,* she posits an elaborate "isomorphism" between male genitals and language to explain why existing languages cannot express or represent the body, sexuality, and the imaginary of women. So, for example, we are told that nouns, syntax, and other elements of existing languages are artifacts of a man's preoccupation with solid and stable forms, stemming from his narcissistic investment in the erect and visible form of his penis. In contrast, *parler femme* is envisaged by Irigaray as rooted in female autoeroticism. Thus, just as a woman finds sexual pleasure almost everywhere, so too does her language "set off in all directions leaving 'him' unable to discern the coherence of any meaning." The relevant isomorphism here is between the multiple sites of female sexual pleasure and the polysemantic character of female speech.

"Huh? Are you kidding?"

"Yes," says the strategic me, gently forestalling my literalist objections. "Yes, it is a joke. See here, where Irigaray refers to the polysemantic character of feminine language, where she talks about not being able to determine which meaning is 'on top' or 'underneath'? She is making fun of the 'normal' sexual position for intercourse, which is essentially for the sexual pleasure of the man, to bring him to orgasm. Men have the 'dominant' position; they are 'on top.' Irigaray is mocking this hierarchical sexual positioning and the discourse of the 'authorities' that have posited it as the norm for male and female sexual pleasure. She treats this discourse as a product of masculine self-affection, grounded,

131

so to speak, in the man's obsession with the erect form of his own penis. Her specific target is Lacan, who replaces Freud's biological determinism with an appeal to universal structures of language."

I ask the literalist: *"Do you understand? Shall I go on?"*

But the literalist yawns, weary of my convoluted explanation of the joke, wearier still of my constant need to appeal to psychoanalytic discourse to explain Irigaray's strategic intent and artifices.

"What's the point?" the literalist complains. *"Why all the fuss about psychoanalysis and Lacan?"*

The literalist's question has two obvious answers. First, through the agency of Lacan, psychoanalysis has exerted a major influence on French intellectuals unparalleled in North American circles. The second—and probably more important—is Irigaray's own professional relation to Lacan. In 1974, Irigaray was ousted from her position as lecturer at the University of Paris VIII at Vincennes, home of Lacanian psychoanalysis. As viewed by Irigaray, this was directly precipitated by her challenge to Lacan's authority, that is, to Lacan as the authoritative voice on feminine desire. In 1974, Irigaray published *Speculum of the Other Woman,* which criticized the male bias in both philosophy and psychoanalytic theory. Although Irigaray mentions Lacan only in a footnote, her work presents a sustained attack on his treatment of the "mirror stage" for privileging sameness (the *one* sex) and visibility (the erect form of the penis). But the official reason for her ouster was not *Speculum* but a course proposal submitted to the department of psychoanalysis announcing "a rereading of psychoanalytic discourse on female sexuality, and especially on the differences between the sexes and its articulation in language" (*TS,* 168). A three-person commission appointed by Lacan deemed the course proposal "unacceptable," thereby effectively suspending Irigaray from teaching duties.

This political context informs both the content and style of Irigaray's texts. One of Irigaray's persistent targets is the "maleness" of psychoanalytic discourse. With only a few exceptions, the producers of psychoanalytic theory have been men. Moreover, these men have claimed to be authorities not only on male sexual desire but on female sexuality as well.[11] This problem was compounded by Lacan, who blatantly asserted that when women speak of their own pleasure, they "don't know what they are saying." In "Cosi Fan Tutti," Irigaray quotes Lacan's "justification" of this view:

> What makes my suggestion somewhat plausible is that since we
> have been begging them [women analysts], begging them on our
> knees . . . to try to tell us [about female sexual pleasure], well,
> mum's the word. We've never managed to get anything out of
> them. . . . It's quite remarkable. They haven't made the slightest
> progress on the question of female sexuality. There must be an inter-
> nal reason for this, connected with the pleasure mechanism. (*TS*, 90)

Irigaray indicates her displeasure by referring to Lacan's remarks
on women as the "production of ejaculations of all sorts, often pre-
maturely emitted" (*TS*, 91). For Irigaray, these remarks provide a
pivot for her strategic reversals of Lacanian views. In effect, she
says, "Yes, there is a reason for this, and yes, it is connected with
the pleasure mechanism. But the pleasure mechanism in question
is not the phallic pleasure privileged in psychoanalytic discourse.
It is a pleasure specific to a woman, to her 'two lips.' Moreover, it
is a pleasure that cannot be articulated or heard in your psychoanalytic discourse, which recognizes only one sex and which constrains female sexuality to male models and laws."

Many of Irigaray's texts turn on barbs, twists, reversals, displacements, and other strategic artifices that mock the authority
and content of Lacanian views. Thus, getting the point—seeing
the strategy and its effects—often requires a detailed understanding of Lacan. It also requires placing Irigaray's texts in the
proper institutional and political context, reading them as texts
written by a twentieth-century Parisian woman intellectual as
part of her struggle against a very powerful male-dominated psychoanalytic establishment. The clever, often witty, and sarcastic
"play" that Irigaray introduces into her discourse on feminine
desire is a way of getting back at the "Master" (Lacan) by bur-
lesquing his pretension to mastery, by "showing up" the more
ludicrous and offensive features of his texts on feminine desire.
At its best (at least for my strategic tastes), Irigaray's discourse
reduces Lacan to a comical figure—a narcissist obsessed with
whatever mirrors his own self, whose texts are a form of autoaf-
fection, masturbatory instruments in which women appear as the
obliging props of his own penis-centered fantasy life.

Irigaray also produces texts that have a certain lyrical beauty,
for instance, "When Our Lips Speak Together." In this prose poem,
Irigaray extends her "two lips" trope to lesbian love and presents
the compelling vision of a fluid, nonhierarchical interplay of desire
struggling to free itself from the "lips" (the words, the interpretations) and watchful eyes of men. In this work, the psychoanalytic
subtext includes its treatment of female homosexuality, which is

regarded as an imitation of male behavior. A woman "chooses" homosexuality by virtue of a "masculinity complex," that is, by changing herself psychologically into a man, which involves changing her love object from her father to her (phallic) mother. But Irigaray's "two lips" gently differ: "I love you who are neither mother (forgive me, mother, I prefer a woman) nor sister" (*TS,* 209). For while mothers and sisters belong to the "lineage of our fathers," Irigaray's two lips articulate a psychic place where pleasure among and between women flows free of masculine parameters.[12]

So one answer to the literalist's complaint ("What's the point? Why all the fuss about psychoanalysis and Lacan?") is that much of Irigaray's discourse is parasitic on the discourse of psychoanalysis, particularly the psychoanalysis of Lacan. But this answer only partially addresses the literalist's concern. For what provoked her complaint was a requirement of my strategic reading, the constant need to occupy intratextual spaces, to move from Irigaray's texts to other texts and back again to unravel thickets of allusions and intrigues. The literalist is quite willing (now that I have convinced her) to grant that this hermeneutic activity is sometimes, perhaps often, required to "get Irigaray right," even though the matter of just when her texts should be construed strategically rather than literally is far from clear. But she questions why we (for despite our differences, she and I are one) should pursue Irigaray's intratextual spins and whirls, save for the moments of delight and laughter this textual play can bring.

"What does this have to do with women, real ones, not just the props of male fantasy life?" she asks.

"A lot," I answer. "Of course, 'real women,' as you put it, are not just the props of male fantasy life. This is precisely the problem. We women experience our own sexuality through male eyes. We've been taught, for example, to deny ourselves clitoral pleasure. Our real pleasure, we've been told, lies in producing children. Psychoanalysis 'normalizes' such views by making female sexual pleasure a function of a law that completely represses our desires."

"You mean that stuff about changing our erogenous zone from the clitoris to the vagina?"

"That is part of it."

"But hasn't this been known for some time now?"

"Sure. But many people—women and those who 'treat' female sexual dysfunction—haven't yet heard. 'Frigidity,' for example, is still considered by many physicians and analysts to be a specifically female sexual dysfunction. It is defined as a woman's failure or inability to achieve sexual satisfaction in intercourse. But most women don't achieve orgasm during sexual intercourse, and this is not caused by a failure or dysfunction. It is caused by the fact that in most cases the clitoris is not properly stimulated during intercourse. Irigaray talks about this. She says that a woman who believes herself to be frigid has been 'molded into male sexual techniques, which do not correspond to her sexuality' (WE, 66). She contrasts the 'teleology of the male organism' to female sexuality."

The literalist, impatient again, interrupts. "But when you say 'Irigaray says this, and she argues that' you are construing her literally. That's fine. We agreed that Irigaray sometimes 'tells things straight.' That's not what I worry about. I worry about the texts, or parts of texts, that lure us into intratextual play. I worry about the interpretive labor—chasing allusions, tracing reversals, that sort of thing—that sends you deeper and deeper into psychoanalytic texts, all for the purpose of sparing Irigaray from my literalist outrage. Don't we get lost there, don't we lose sight of women and the oppressions they suffer?"

Puzzled, I ask her to continue.

"Consider what Irigaray calls her 'travail du langage.' It seems to me that this 'language work' has very little to do with women. Irigaray describes it as destroying 'the discursive mechanism.' What's that? Well, as far as I can tell, the discursive mechanism is the language system described by Lacan, which supposedly has an invariant universal structure, which operates as an independent force, and which functions to split or castrate every speaking subject. Irigaray talks about this in 'Così Fan Tutti.' She refers to Lacan's claim that the psychoanalytic 'truth' about female sexuality is displayed much more rigorously when discourse rather than biology becomes the primary object of investigations. Here, anatomy is no longer available to serve . . . as proof-alibi for the real difference between the sexes. The sexes are now defined only as they are determined in and through language' (TS, 87)."

"So, working to subvert, jam, smash this discursive mechanism is important to women, real ones, if we want to undo the definitions forced on us by men. . . ."

Suddenly, unexpectedly, the literalist laughs.

"Ha!" she says. "Now look at who is being literal! In order to take Irigaray's 'travail du langage' as an effort to 'jam' the discursive mechanisms that oppress us, we must construe what she says about this discursive mechanism literally. For example, we must believe that Irigaray is 'telling it straight' when she says that the syntactical structure of all existing (Western) languages is the product of male auto-affection and as such is intrinsically alien to female sexual desire and pleasure. Similarly, we must believe that Irigaray is 'telling it straight' when she talks about the need for a *'parler femme'* capable of expressing and representing the specificity of female desire and pleasure.

"Yes," I say, tentatively. "And?"

"A joke. *'Parler femme'* supposedly jams the discursive mechanism, and *'parler femme'* is supposedly rooted in female auto-eroticism. Remember? The isomorphism that Irigaray posits between male genitals and sexual pleasure and the languages that have been produced and perpetuated by men? Just when I was on the verge of throwing a literalist fit, you pacified me by saying that all this was a joke. Irigaray, you told me, is not making an empirical claim when she roots certain characteristics of existing languages in the supposed narcissistic investment that men (all of them, everywhere, in every cultural and historical locus) have in the erect and visible form of their penises. You said, shush, now, shush, Irigaray knows better, she is just getting back at Lacan. Over and over again, she undercuts the empirical worth of psychoanalytic construals of feminine sexuality and desire by reducing these construals to the fantasies of penis-obsessed men. But she really doesn't mean it. She really doesn't think that existing languages are all products of male auto-affection, masturbatory instruments, and therefore incapable of expressing and representing female sexuality and desire. And if she doesn't (literally) mean it, then what she has to say about the features of existing language that oppress us or about the features of another language capable of expressing and representing female sexuality and desire doesn't really have much to do with women. All this has a lot to do with Lacan, with exposing Lacan. . . ."

"A pun?"

"Yes, a pun. Exposing Lacan, stripping him of his pretension and authority. It lets us laugh. Even you and I—together sometimes—when we lightly jump into Irigaray's texts, to join for a little while one of her skirmishes."

"But isn't laughter the first form of liberation from secular oppression (*TS*, 163)?"

"Ah," she says, turning to leave, "that is another question."

To the question of the meaning of the text, only one reply can be given: read, perceive, feel. (*SP*, 192)

Not saying I implies leaving speech, voice, to that which is supposed to be more worthy of articulating our truth. What is the status

If you can laugh @ it then you are free from it.

of this something that could speak better than us? In a *universal* and *neutral* manner?[13]

The conflict between literalist and strategic construals that I have exhibited here is not an all-or-nothing affair in which one side wins and the other loses. Like my small sampling of texts, Irigaray's work usually present us with "mixed discourses" in which truth claims, puns, poetry, burlesque, and so on are freely commingled. Doing justice to her texts thus requires a willingness to experiment with alternative interpretive strategies. It also requires a willingness to allow these strategies to question and contest each other. In this essay I have illustrated just one of the ways in which this contestatory process might proceed. Against the literalist tendency to dismiss Irigaray because much of what she says seems obviously false, preposterous, or ideologically objectionable, I have argued for the importance of looking for traces of deconstructionist artifice that lend themselves to strategic construal. This hermeneutic has its drawbacks, since what seems obviously false, preposterous, or ideologically objectionable to me may not seem so to Irigaray. Hence it is not an infallible principle for "getting Irigaray right." Rather, its value consists in its potential for opening up richer and more rewarding texts, populated less with objectionable truth claims than with intricate and often witty deconstructionist play.

In crafting this essay, I have also taken seriously Irigaray's own hermeneutic advice: read, perceive, feel, and don't suppress the "I" who does these things in favor of a more "universal" and "neutral" discursive style. I have allowed expressions of anger, delight, and frustration to enter my text, not as the tail end of argument or analysis, but as starting points for identifying matters of concern. In addition, I have allowed some of these concerns to be expressed in the form of fictional, first-person dialogue. The result, as one critic has claimed, may be that I have simply replaced (interesting) talk about Irigaray with (not-so-interesting) talk about myself. But, as Margaret Whitford suggests in her introduction to *The Irigaray Reader*, the "interlocutor/reader is often forced to put him/herself into play in order to read [Irigaray's] enigmatic texts, and the response often has as much to do with the reader as with Irigaray" (*IR*, 14). What I have done is to foreground the experience of hermeneutic consternation which Irigaray's texts provoke ("put into play") in readers who have literalist inclinations.

My focus on the strategic character of Irigaray's texts is also an attempt to balance past criticisms of Irigaray based on aggressively literalist construals. I have argued, for example, that Irigaray provides an inadequate account of the gendering of desire, and that part of the reason lies in her Lacanian tendency to ignore the social institutions and practices that contribute to this process.[14] In marshaling this criticism, I ignored the strategic components of Irigaray's discourse, opting instead to focus on just those aspects of Irigaray's texts that seemed *too* Lacanian, too abstract, and too disconnected from historically and culturally specific social relations.

But strategic construals of Irigaray are purchased at a price. Specifically, the price is political. Where should we academic feminists concentrate our energies? What political goods can we purchase with our interpretive labor? Reading Irigaray strategically is a demanding enterprise. We must attune our ears to wordplay, veiled allusions, ironic barbs, and clever reversals, and this often requires knowledge of psychoanalytic and deconstructionist texts. My own strategic construal of Irigaray's trope of "two lips" only grazes the surface of the psychoanalytic subtexts required for a detailed explication. For example, Irigaray's play with the numbers one and two invokes, among other things, Lacan's theory of unconscious counting—which only committed Lacan buffs care to know about, let alone unravel. Similarly, the link Irigaray makes between the "metonymic" (fluid) nature of female sexual desire and the "metaphoric" (solid) nature of male desire plays off texts by both Lacan and Derrida.

But don't we get lost there? Between or among the texts of Irigaray, Freud, Lacan, and others?

This literalist worry has some merit. As Ann Rosalind Jones once asked, "What is the meaning of 'two lips' to . . . African or Middle Eastern women who, as a result of pharaonic clitoridectomies, have neither lips nor clitoris through which to *jouir?*"[15] This question may seem impertinent since it invokes a literalist construal of Irigaray's "two lips" trope. But it nonetheless raises an important issue. Strategic labor can be a profoundly conservative enterprise *if* absorption in the intricacies of textual play is not balanced with an effort to connect this labor to the empirically complex realities (poverty, violence, sex discrimination, racism, etc.) deeply and differently affecting women's lives.

Yet Irigaray's strategic texts do seem to bear a relation to such matters. They foreground some very important issues, not the least of which is the objectification of women as sexual beings—as beings that exist for men, the objects of *their* needs and desires. But the way in which such issues get addressed is often limited by the requirements of Irigaray's strategic maneuvers. For example, Irigaray does not challenge the truth of Lacan's claim that "the problem of [a woman's] position is fundamentally that of accepting herself as an object of desire for men."[16] Rather, she wrests this claim from its (pseudo) scientific context and reinscribes it in the psychological domain as a product of male fantasy and power. In so doing, certain features of Lacan's original analysis of "the problem of a woman's position" are left intact, including his supposition that this problem is a structural effect of language, now strategically construed by Irigaray as a male masturbatory instrument.

But language isn't a male masturbatory instrument, and the sexual objectification of women is not (or not just) a structural effect of the "binary logic" of language. Thus one effect of Irigaray's strategic maneuver is the reproduction of views that mask and mystify the specific oppressions that women bear. For example, to render the sexual objectification of women as a structural effect of language obscures the multiple social and institutional factors (e.g., gender roles, the fashion industry) that actually contribute to this facet of a woman's oppression. Similarly, to treat language as a male masturbatory instrument, intrinsically alien to female sexual desire, occludes actual linguistic practices that can concretely affect a woman's life.

In an important sense, then, my original, literalist-based complaint about Irigaray's discourse on feminine desire transfers to its strategic construal. If Irigaray is not giving an account of the gendering of desire, then she should not be criticized for failing to link this process to historically and culturally specific social relations. But her texts do convey, repeatedly and dramatically, a way of conceptualizing this process closely bound to the psychoanalytic tales she deconstructs. The effect, at least at the level of image and symbol, is to leave women where Freud and Lacan have consigned them, relegated to the realm of the ahistorical, transcultural Other, endowed with a "supplementary *jouissance*" that lies beyond the symbolic, linguistically constituted, phallically oriented world of men.

And where is that?

PART V
WRITING DESIRE: BARTHES AND DERRIDA

Chapter 9

A LOVER'S REPLY (TO ROLAND BARTHES'S *A LOVER'S DISCOURSE*)

Robert C. Solomon

> Gradually it has become clear to me what every great philosophy so far has been: namely, the personal confession of its author and a kind of involuntary and unconscious memoir.
>
> —Nietzsche, *Beyond Good and Evil*

Writers on love undoubtedly and often betray themselves. Much of the best philosophical writing on love, accordingly, is quasi-confessional—Stendhal's romantic travelogue memoirs (*On Love*), Rousseau's *Reveries* and various romantic pleas (*Emile, New Heloise*), Shakespeare's *Sonnets* and several dramatic speeches, the letters between Heloise and Abelard, and Sappho's poetic fragments. Typically, too, the philosophy of love gets semi-fictionalized, for example, in D. H. Lawrence's several analytic novels (notably *Women in Love*), more problematically in Chodoros Laclos's *Dangerous Liaisons*, and in many recent "feminist" novels, such as Marilyn French's *The Women's Room*. Some texts present themselves as fun: Ovid's *Art of Love* and *Loves* and, more recently, Henry Miller's various *Tropics*. Some are both serious and self-undermining, such as Andreas Capellanus's courtly revival of Ovidic seduction lessons in a Christian context that plainly forbade them. There are texts that are obviously polemical, such as de Rougemont's *Love in the Western World* and C. S. Lewis's *Four Loves*, which use love as a ramrod to break through the impious pretensions of the current century in pursuit of a larger agenda.

And then, of course, there is the Philosophy of Love. But as philosophy, the very personal nature of love uneasily clashes with the "objective" stance that philosophy likes to presume, and appropriate treatment of the subject becomes more problematic. How does one theorize about love without losing hold of the fragmentary, very personal nature of an emotion that may mean (as it is usually overstated) something quite different to virtually everyone? Indeed, such an emotion seems to mean something very different to the same person at different times—or even at one and the same time. Which of the several very different speakers in Plato's *Symposium* represents the truth about love— or the views of the author? Is it Socrates? There are good arguments to think perhaps not. All of the symposiasts? None of them? And what about Kierkegaard? How are we to take his "pseudonymous" writings (such as "Diary of a Seducer," in *Either/Or*), which so obviously betray forbidden desires and a halfhearted misogyny and do not conceal the (real) author's loneliness or romantic resentment?

In someone such as Spinoza, on the other hand, the personal and the pathetic ooze out at us through the hard geometrical struts that frame his philosophy. Similarly contemporary "analytic" treatments of love betray what seems to be a basic incomprehension or perhaps an unadmitted fear of love, readily visible through the barbed-wire prose of "suppose that S loves P" and endless dickering about the nature of intentionality and the proper "object" of love (e.g., "Do we love the qualities of a person, or the person as such?"—is this a real question, or a basic misunderstanding of the problem?). Of course, such authors begin by flatly denying that their analysis betrays anything of themselves, confusing the confession of mere details with the revelation of a whole personality. One strategy for so denying the subjective and the personally revealing nature of love is to focus solely on the language of love (an obsession no longer exclusive to philosophy) and to ignore the emotion. And yet love will out, or rather, love outs; love expresses itself in philosophy as philosophy expresses itself in love—even when (especially when) it pretends not to be a personal confession.

In the rich and varied context of this long-evolving literature of love, I want to reread Roland Barthes's *A Lover's Discourse*.[1] Some Barthes fans would object to this reading on the grounds that he is rejecting this entire tradition and is utterly *sui generis*. I doubt the intelligibility as well as the intelligence of this insistence, however, and at the very least I want to see Barthes as confronting this long tradition even as (or if) he deviates from it. But the similarities, I want to argue and then to show, are as striking as the differences—not to mention, whatever current sophistries might indicate to the contrary, the ultimate sameness of a certain basic biology of human affections. The genesis and presentation of

Barthes's book will strike many a familiar chord to readers of *Publisher's Weekly*. Like many of the texts mentioned above, it was written primarily as a popular book (and immediately achieved best-seller status). Like the best of the books above, it was written in an irreducibly personal mode, almost by way of confession despite its dictionary/encyclopedia format. Like so many modern works on love, it begins by denying its personal status and focuses its attention not on love, that is, the feeling of love, but rather on the language of love, the "discourse" of love, the way we describe ourselves and express ourselves when we are, as we say, "in love"—and alone. But love is not only language. However, it does give considerable credibility to La Rochefoucauld's wisdom-filled wisecrack on love: "There are many who would never have been in love, had they never heard love spoken of." And the discourse is not devoid of a "phenomenon" the discourse describes, and the emphasis on "discourse" in the *A Lover's Discourse* need not be mistaken for any excessive claims about ontologically unbridgeable distances between lovers or the utter hopelessness of the love experience. By examining discourse and not the feelings of love, Barthes quite ironically proclaims his work to be impersonal ("there is no question here of a history"). He insists that his dictionary/encyclopedia format yields "no order," only a wholly "arbitrary" list of love words and phrases. But any editor has ample choice—which words are to be included, which synonymic variation is to be represented, whether the verb "to suffer" (*souffrir*) belongs along with or rather instead of "despair" (*désespoir*), whether "pleasure" (*plaisir*) belongs with "joy" (*jouissance*) or vice versa, or whether all should be excluded as derivative or secondary matters.

Indeed, such seemingly lexical decisions are far from arbitrary; they embody for instance, an entire philosophy. Andreas Capellanus and Arthur Schopenhauer, have said that love *is* suffering and that there is no love without suffering. Spinoza, by contrast, has said that love is joy, that joy does not result from—so much as it defines—love. None of these terms appears in Barthes's lexicon as such, although the topic of suffering permeates the text. *Affirmation* is expressed in the language of "suffering," "duty," "doom," and "suicide"(22). Barthes's telltale text is Goethe's *Sorrows of Young Werther*. A choice between two lexical synonyms, (one beginning with "a" the other with "s") may make an enormous difference in terms of the shape and (one uses this term cautiously) narrative of the book. The structure of *A Lover's Discourse* is not arbitrary, and its initial editing as well as its seductive and brilliant writing is revealing. Barthes joins many other authors and insists that "there is no question here of a history" and, more eccentrically, that there is "no author or subject, just discourse produced." We should take this proclamation as part of the writerly lover's discourse, one of those that has become for Barthes de rigueur, like his effort to "discourage the temptation to meaning," his insistence on arbitrary order, and his claim that his text is not "a philosophy of love" but only "fragments."

How does one deal with such a text and such an author? Does one "deconstruct" the text or "analyze" the author? Either seems most inappropriate. Does one give full scholarly treatment to a book that is so self-consciously unscholarly (despite the neat little references to other authors, though rarely the sources, in the margins)? That would miss the spirit (if not also the point) of the book. One could just write one's own discourse on love, but that would miss the book altogether. One could evade the topic altogether and launch into a general discourse on Barthes's rather spectacular intellectual odyssey, his various theories of the "sign," and the now-tedious Saussurean duality of signifier-signified. Predictably, Barthes declares that love is "nothing but signs" (68). He rather insensitively insists that even the most tender caress "touch[es] nothing but a sign" (73). But this fetishism of the sign (or "the sign") is not sufficient for an understanding of love, and Barthes, to his credit, abandons it. One could also treat love as a Barthesian myth: "Love is objectively good, and at the same time, the goodness of love is a myth" and "to believe in love is a coercive collective act."[2] But to dismiss love merely as myth would again be contrary to Barthes's own intentions.

Alternatively, one could violate the author's warnings and his privacy by delving behind the text to dig up those inevitable "dirty little secrets" that no doubt get betrayed on page after page of Barthes's *Lover's Discourse* (not just *"A" Lover's Discourse*), but it is far better that we should bypass the biography and respect the writer and his ironies along with his insistence on distance and disguise (one of the most imaginative chapters of the book is appropriately titled "Dark Glasses"—the paradox of public hiding [*cacher*]). Why should we suspect that the author's own love life, like his discourse, was fragmented? Why should we think that he might have been the sort of lover who kept a list—alphabetized—of lovers? Why should we worry about whether he in fact suffered as much as his book suggests, or enjoyed love only rarely?

146

Would any of this make any difference to our own understanding of love, or for that matter our understanding of Barthes's text—or would it, too, be just another distraction? "No author or subject, just discourse produced," Barthes tells us, but the author has made himself the beloved ("love me for myself, not my writing" [100]), brought an "inexpressible" subject back into public (even "objective") discourse, and through his own discourse made it so obviously the case that love is not just discourse but rather the raw emotion that the discourse expresses. The important La Rochfoucauldian insight, that love is defined and possibly even created through language, does not yield the unsentimental conclusion that love itself is language, nothing but discourse, nothing but signs.

And so I offer a brief reply, in the spirit though not the letter nor the language of Barthes's very personal text. I offer it in alphabetical format (in English) not by way of parody so much as in appreciation, but also to make the point that no such order is arbitrary and what is included (excluded) already circumscribes a "philosophy." A focus on language must be by its very nature a perspective on much else besides, and it dictates if not an order then an emphasis. From an "arbitrary" list of items emerges a portrait, a perspective, a confession. True, what charms and fascinates the reader of Barthes's *Discourse* is its richness of irrelevancies—clouds, ribbons, gossip, dark glasses, mementos, suicide, an orange, a slice of cake, a quote from the *Tao Te Ching,* an observation by Goethe or Blanchot. (It is a book largely written in parentheses, italics and margins.) Nevertheless it provides us with a portrait of love, and it is not altogether a satisfying one. In what follows, I do want to emphasize one problematic point (what some might call a "critique," but I intend it rather as a "complement") regarding Barthes's *Discourse*: It is not a discourse on *love.* What I mean by this will emerge in the following pages, but the core of the "argument" is that love—even love unrequited—is essentially a relationship, a participation, and not just a longing. It is the "affirmative" act of identifying and entangling oneself in the life of another, or, rather, defining one's own life according to the terms of the person whom Barthes misleadingly insists on calling "the other." This emphasis on shared identity is not in any sense a denial of the differences that keep us apart, just as in Aristophanes's allegory (in Plato's *Symposium*) the suggestion of an original unity is not a denial but rather a tragic reminder of the differences that now separate us.

147

Barthes is keenly aware of the projective/introjective aspect of love (his very first entry is "*s'abîmer*" "to be engulfed"), but throughout his *Discourse* he dwells instead on the languor, the waiting, the distance, the suffering of love. I have no desire to replay the "myth" of "the goodness of love" and insist (as has been so often insisted from Plato to the Beatles) that love is always good (and "All you need is . . ."). But neither do I buy the morbid insistence—the favorite theme of cynics and pessimists—that love is suffering, that the joy of love is fraud, that despair is the norm if not the definition of love, that "love and death" go hand in hand. What Barthes captures so brilliantly is the experience (not just the discourse) of despair, but he fails to represent the experience of love, which is a bonding and a rapture, a long dialectical process but not just a "waiting," an ongoing fascination but also an engagement and not "hypnosis." Perhaps because the discourse of despair is so rich and expressive while the discourse of love is so vacuous, Barthes is attracted to the former and negligent of the latter. This would seem to be like the moth flitting to the shadow instead of to the flame. True, "I love you" is one of the least imaginative (but most significant) phrases in our language, except perhaps for the requisite reply. True, "adorable" may be insufficient to describe our fascination with the beloved, but it is not thereby "a failure of language." Such pathetic phrases are emblematic of love's experience— sometimes so dazzling and so visceral that not even the most brilliant verbal expression could do it justice. (But why should language be able to "capture" an experience, or even express it?)

Barthes himself is brilliant on the vicissitudes of lovers' frustrations, for example, on what he calls "the tip of the nose" (the familiar flip-flop—Shakespeare's "alteration"—of love to despair, even contempt), and in his diagnosis of the unimaginative publicity of love ("show me whom to desire" [136]). As anyone who has briefly explored the semantics or the thesaurus of emotion has discovered, our vocabulary for the "positive" emotions is embarrassingly underpopulated, but it does not follow that love is as impoverished as its language. Indeed, Barthes admits that laments are more readily expressed than fulfillments ("Fulfillments: They are not spoken—so that, erroneously, the amorous relation seems reduced to a long complaint" [55]). He nevertheless too readily identifies *Mitleid* with *Mitsein* (57) and dependency and mutuality with humiliation (82). Like his more prosaic but not much more pessimistic predecessor Schopenhauer, he fails to get at the emotion he seeks in his *Discourse*.

What Barthes gives us so artfully is a portrait of the *pathos* of love, not *eros*. Such a portrait is essential to the new image of love and relationships demanded by the fragmented philosophies that constitute postmodernism. But this is not an argument against Barthes, who gets trivialized in such bland *au courant* categories. What follows is an effort to see his discourse through to a happier conclusion. Imitation may be a sincere form of flattery, but a playful impersonation may be more conducive to real appreciation. With real reverence for Barthes's feelings as well as his efforts, I offer my own version of a lover's discourse, not in isolation or at a distance, not even as a "reply" so much as in conversation with Barthes . . . as if in his very presence. (Who in the world ever suggested that "presence" means mastery and control?) In this conversation, also in lexicological form, I want to confront Barthes with some of his own admissions (and omissions), as a way of understanding him.

absence (13) "An episode of language." Obsessive theme in *A Lover's Discourse* evocative of many passions, but none of the "makes the heart grow fonder" variety. Absence rather appears as the essence of love, a mode of despair, a distance essentially present to love, *as* love. Love is waiting (37, 41, 101, 106, 155, 210, 216). Desire in love becomes longing (see **languor**). So, not surprisingly, love engages the ultimate absence; we are "in love with death" (13). Barthes here joins a long line of theorists, most notably and recently de Rougemont, who conflate tragedy (even if only a domesticated, private tragedy) with the essence of love. But though tragedy makes for good theater and absence provides personal pathos, it is not as such love, only a symptom of love, perhaps an *impression* of love, as a face leaves an impression in the pillow when one's lover has paraded happily off to the office. The emphasis on absence mistakes the bond with its (temporary) breach, the relationship with its disruption, and confuses this for love. (Some recent theories of language encourage this, of course, with the word always severed from its supposed "object.") But absence presupposes presence, at the very least in desire. The traditional ideal of togetherness prompts the pained awareness of absence. The metaphysical alternative? "Emotions which are aroused or spring from reason, if we take account of time, are stronger than those which are attributable to particular objects that we regard as absent" (Spinoza, *Ethics*, V, vii).

affect (emotion) Love is emotion, not discourse. There can be love without words, without thoughts, without laments or negotiations: the love of (and for) an animal; the love for (perhaps of) an infant; the

love for and of a lover, which is not created by discourse but encapsu-
lated, encrusted by language (Bertolucci's *Last Tango:* "no words").
But emotions (like discourse) have structures of their own. In love,
that structure (successful or not) is called (banally) a relationship.

affection   "No one is interested in the problems of sentimentality" (as
opposed to sexuality) (178). Is affection in the lover's "discourse" a
mere implication, a presupposition, an absence? Where is the shared
"sweetness" that so embarrasses intellectuals but remains the hall-
mark of greeting cards and alone warrants love (if only in fleeting
instants between abuse)? Where is the consolation (this is already giving into *pathos*) that justifies and prolongs the desperation? Cf. "tenderness" (224): "bliss, but also a disturbing evaluation of the loved
object's tender gestures." (A very short chapter!) In the torrent of
longing and resentment, needing, touching and hoping, where is simple affection? Could one have a true lover's discourse—or a lover's
true discourse—without it? (See **engulfed**.)

anxiety   (29) "If there is such a figure as 'Anxiety,' it is because the subject sometimes exclaims (without any concern for the clinical sense of
the word): '*Je suis angoissé.*' " Anxiety too is a discourse. Cf. William
James: "imagine two steel knife-blades with their keen edges crossing
each other at right angles, and moving to and fro." That is the experience of anxiety. "Discourse" only follows, and to no avail. (Cf. Jean-
Paul Sartre, who rightly points out that anxiety is, first of all, my own
relation to myself [12].)

beauty   Curiously subdued, buried in various references to Plato (the
Symposium) and odd figures of fascination, hypnosis, enchantment.
But the philosophy of beauty (as in Plato) pours through the text: the
emphasis on "attraction" (fixation), the idea that love is a reaching
out, a longing for ("intentionality"), not participation (even Platonic).
But love is to beauty not fascination but engagement, a way of seeing
not something found or longed for. It is not recognized but created in
love. (Cf. *Mythologies,* "plastic": "more than a substance, plastic is the
very idea of its infinite transformation" [97].) Where in Barthes (cf.
Socrates) is beauty enjoyed? See Paul Valery: "The definition of
beauty? That's easy. Beauty is that which makes us despair."

being with   (*Mitsein*) The essence of love, as opposed to absence, as
opposed to "the other." (One is not merely "*with* the other.") Even
in frustrated, unrequited love, one is (if only in one's thoughts and
desires) together with one's lover, a twosome—one out of two (the
Aristophanic element of the *Symposium,* that Barthes brushes so
quickly past). Barthes takes being-with to be an illusion, in any case
a disappointment; every instance of being-with converts into a shattering being-without. For example, consider "com/passion": "At the

same time that I 'sincerely' identify myself with the other's misery, what I read in this misery is that it occurs *without me* . . . the other abandons me" (57).

blind (229) "Love is blind: The proverb is false. Love opens his eyes . . . produces clear sightedness." But what does one *see?* Vision is from a distance, the being-with already broken. What does one see when one looks face-to-face with one's lover? Not his/her eyes, but *into* the eyes. And what does one see there? One does not "see" at all.

body (see **skin**)

castration (230) "The lover botches his castration? Out of failure, he persists in making a *value.*"

choice (62) "What is to be done?" The question is not how love is to be expressed. It is, rather, the "futile problems of behavior" (62) (in Barthes, see "embarrassment" (*gêne*), ("monstrous"). Barthes resists the temptation to consider the possibility that we *choose* to love, choose whom to love and how to love. He notes rather that "I choose not to choose," a familiar phrase indeed; it already suggests—if not entails—"bad faith." Jean-Paul Sartre permeates *A Lover's Discourse,* only sometimes by name. (He remained thoroughly nameless in Barthes's notorious first book about him.[3] Is this an elevation or a demotion—just another "author"?)

commitment Barthes occasionally employs commercial images (e.g., 84), but rarely such quasi-legal metaphors. It is refreshing, therefore, to read an entire lover's discourse that does not hammer (like any good red-blooded American magazine) on the joys and importance of "commitment," a contractual notion more appropriate to institutions (e.g., marriage) than to "affairs of the heart." The dangers of "discourse" include the temptation to commitment, of *meaning* if not of contract. Barthes of course resists this "temptation." Happily, much of this language doesn't *mean* anything at all (however fraught with meanings the signs to which it responds may be). Cf. *Mythologies* (on wrestling); it "abolishes all motives and all consequences" (15).

death (see **absence**)

desire Oddly second-rate. (Competing French thinkers obtained an earlier copyright.) Desire is desperation and design, not pleasure. "Fulfillment" (predictably one of the shortest chapters) mentions it only by way of a put-down ("Delight exceeds the possibilities envisioned by desire"). Desire counts in love only insofar as it is transformed into something else: "Desire is everywhere, but in the amorous state it becomes something very special—languor" (155). Alternative: "The Satyr says: I want my desire to be satisfied *immediately.*" Subtlety versus vulgarity. Descartes: "An agitation of the soul caused by spirits which dispose it to wish for the future of things which represents itself as agreeable" (*Les passions de l'âme,* art. LXXXVI). Emphasis on "agitation."

embrace (104) A "motionless cradling" but "within this infantile embrace, the genital unfailing appears."

engulfed (10, also 24) (as *s'abîmer,* Barthes's first entry) Helplessness in the face (mouth?) of love. Not a decision. Not willingly. "I fall, I flow, I melt. . . . This is exactly what *gentleness* is" (10). "The gentleness of the abyss . . . I have no responsibility here" (11). "In love with death? An exaggeration" (11).

falsification "Passionate love (the lover's discourse) keeps succumbing to falsification" (118) (see also **blind**). Does Barthes (like so many other writers) confuse *illusion* with *idealization?* Illusion indeed falsifies; idealization glorifies. If I find Barthes's prose (or your nose) "exactly right," I need not falsify my standards for noses or proses. I recast those standards, first to include, then to highlight the prose, your nose, as a perfect example of itself. One's lover becomes one's ideal, if only *as* a lover. Of course, in love (as in all emotions) there is ample room (even an invitation) to self-deception, but deception is no more essential to love than it is to admiration. Not rationalization (Freud's sense, not Hegel's) but sentimentality. See also **weeping** (kitsch).

friendship Not included by Barthes, but alphabetically it would appear near the beginning. What a different shadow that would cast on the rest of the *Discourse!* In Plato and Aristotle's Greece, there was very little distance between *eros* and *philia* (a merely phallic distance, one scholar has suggested—off the record). Friendship involves (and requires) intimacy (another key word missing from Barthes's lexicon), closeness (oneness) and not distance. There is little room for absence in friendship; distance does not make the heart grow stronger. Why should we think it so in love?

idealization (see **falsification**)

I love you (147) "I love you has no usages: Like a child's word, it enters into no social constraint; it can be a sublime, solemn, trivial word, it can be erotic, pornographic word. It is a socially irresponsible word" (quoted in Solomon, *Love: Emotion, Myth and Metaphor*).[4] Or rather, I love you is an action, not a word. It looks like a report, a psychologically descriptive sentence, but it is a performance, an act of aggression. It is only rarely a confession, and then double-edged (like the "confessions" of Jean-Baptiste Clamence in Camus's *La chute,* evoking guilt in the reader rather than relieving it in Clamence). If I love you is not understood, it cannot be explained. If it is unheard, it has not been uttered. If blurted out, it no longer matters that you didn't really mean to say it. Once done, it cannot be undone. I love you does not *express* one's love. Indeed, love may not yet be there. Sometimes *I love you* creates love; it comes into being with the utterance, like the name of a ship or a baby at a christening. *I love you* puts the other on the spot. "I'm flattered" is inappropriate; "That's interesting" is offensive. "Why?" is humiliating. There is only one response, and that is I-love-you-too, also a performance but always under duress (no matter how relieved or overjoyed). *I love you* may become a ritual, a meaningful-meaningless repetition, and never say a thing. I-love-you can also be a cry (as Barthes suggests), a lament, a warning ("Don't push your luck"), an evasion ("Don't even ask me"). It is often an apology, an excuse, a reminder (but not of love), a trap, a blessing (*"Te absolvo"*), a disguise. I-love-you: "What a terrible thing to say to someone." "Tell me you love me." (The performance has just been undermined.) I-love-you is language that destroys language, Barthes would say. Once said, it can never be said again. (But once said, it must be repeated.) Barthes: It is "released"— shot out like an arrow. A weapon and not mere discourse at all. "*I love you* is in my head, but I imprison it behind my lips. . . . *I keep myself from loving you*" (234).

jealousy   (144) A debatable consequence of love, too readily raised to the status of a sitcom criterion. If one loves, then one will (logically) be jealous. Economic premise: "There is only so much love to go around," a "zero-sum" quantity. Barthes begins with (Werther's) Charlotte, who as a cake, is divided up; each has his slice. (Jealousy as a species of greed.) "'When I love, I am very exclusive,' Freud says (whom we shall take here for the paragon of normality). To be jealous is to conform." To conform, of course, is almost as odious as being "reasonable," and so jealousy does not fare well in Barthes's *Discourse*. "As a jealous man, I suffer four times over: because I am jealous, because I blame myself for being so, because I fear that my jealousy will wound the other, because I allow myself to be subject to a banality—I suffer from being excluded, from being aggressive, from being crazy, and from being common" (146). But is there an escape? "Inverted conformism: one is no longer jealous, one condemns exclusivity, etc." (145).

joy   (fulfillment) (54) As "excess" ("for me, *enough* means *not enough*"), "the utopia of a subject free from repression" (55). "The fulfilled lover has no need to write, to transmit, to reproduce" (56) (cf. Spinoza: "True love is bliss"—*Ethics*). But also, the joy of love as "eternal success" (54). "Joy wants itself, wants eternity, the repetition of the same" (56). "Eternal"? "Success"? See Barthes, *Mythologies* (on wrestling), "a spectacle of success" (15). Love as wrestling? "The thrill of victory" (even prescripted)? See also Descartes: "Joy is an agreeable motion of the soul in which consists the enjoyment that the soul possesses in the good." Joy as "possession"? As "excess" and

153

"overflowing." See Sartre: joy as a (chosen) mode of irresponsibility (*The Emotions: Outline of a Theory*).[5] (See **pleasure**.)

language "The ego discourses only when it's been hurt" (54). "To escape disreality, I . . . link myself to the world by bad temper. I *discourse* against something" (88). "Love has of course a complicity with my language" (98). "To try to write love is to confront the *muck* of language, that region of hysteria where language is both *too much* and *too little*, excessive and impoverished" (99). "Language is a skin: I rub my language against the other" (73). But this contact with the other is limited, remote: "The lover's discourse stifles the other" (165). ("I am odious [*monstreux*]"). It is not discourse with or to: "Love is not always told to but told by." "Speaking within himself, *amorously*, confronting the other (the loved object) who does not speak" (3). Discourse to, however, is manipulative, strategic: "It is by language that the other is altered" (26). It is through discourse that the other becomes anonymous (as in Socrates?): "The love story, subjugated to the great narrative Other" (7). "The lover's discourse is today of an extreme solitude . . . spoken, perhaps, by thousands of subjects (who knows), but warranted by no one; it is completely forsaken by the surrounding languages: ignored, disparaged, derided" (1). As in Proust, it is "a whole scene through the keyhole of language" (27) (cf. 4).

languor (155) Desire as hemorrhage, waiting, absence. "Love seeks not its fulfillment but its prolongation." Serious ambiguity: languor as *prolongation* and as *longing*, the first as a romantic style (cultivated rather than merely "delayed" gratification), the latter as self-imposed abstinence and frustration. Languor can be the continuous delight of exquisite desire—the "infinite yearning" that Aristophanes describes in the *Symposium*—or it can be taken to be the wrongheaded fantasy of the troubadours, celibate but still singing. Would it change our conception of the history of love to learn just how often and how much courtly lovers enjoyed their consummations, and kept on loving? (Cf. Andreas Capellanus, on consummation with discretion.) What misunderstanding of sexual fulfillment has led to its equation with disillusion and death? (See **terminal**.)

love at first sight (188) Scholarly name: "enamoration." (See also, in Barthes, "magic.") "Love at first sight is a hypnosis" (189). Or is it rather déjà vu—the recognition of fantasies long cultivated? "Is love at first sight possible?" Why not? But it is so only in retrospect, looking back amorously (or regretfully) on a first meeting from the viewpoint of love developed and matured. *Love takes time*. It is a process, not a state. The lover's discourse is not a description, nor a lament; it is a structuring of time together.

loving love (31) "Explosion of language during which the subject manages to annul the loved object under the volume of love itself: By a specifically amorous perversion, it is love the subject loves, not the object. "How is it possible to "love love"? Does one love the sense of excitement (hardly unique to love), the novelty (hardly love), the burst of emotion, the languor? But even love loved requires an "object," some putative (if only convenient) beloved. (Scholarly name: "intentionality.") And if one does not love that "other," then it cannot be love that one loves.

object Amorous fetishism (cf. Werther's knot of ribbon). An odious term, inherited from Freud (Brentano and the Scholastics), which Barthes uses throughout the *Discourse* to refer to the "Other," the "object of love"—for example, "confronting the other (the loved object)" (3). But to say "object" is to designate a *target,* to suppose a distance and a distinction: "subject" (who discourses) and "object"— always "about." It is to cut out of discourse the "we" (a rare pronoun in the *Discourse*) and deny the we-ness of love. Why such fear of "we"? "Love object," like "sex object"—something to be *played with.* "Aside from these fetishes, there is no other object in the amorous world" (174).

obscene (175) Not sex or perversion but love's sentimentality and seriousness. ("The obscenity would cease if we were to say, mockingly, 'luv.'") Love is embarrassing, humiliating, disgusting. See *Mythologies* (on striptease): "The end of the striptease is then no longer to drag into the light a hidden depth, but to signify, through the shedding of an incongruous and artificial clothing, nakedness as a *natural* vesture of woman, which amounts in the end to regaining a perfectly chaste state of the flesh." Striptease is a "sport" (*Mythologies* 85–86). Love lacks the art of the striptease. It is no longer natural, nor chaste, nor flesh. Love that denies rather than celebrates the body; an intellectual in love: "extreme stupidity" (176).

other Like "object," an obscene way of systematically referring to the beloved. The "other" is the one talked about, not necessarily present. "Imagine oneself talking about the loved being with a rival person— the strange pleasure of complicity" ("connivance" [65]). In such discourse (with a third party) "the loved being is . . . virtually de trop." In the lover's discourse, we find ourselves "confronting the other, who does not speak" (3). So not surprisingly, "The other is impenetrable, intractable" (134, also 22).

philosophy of love "What do I think of love—as a matter of fact, I think nothing at all of love. I'd be glad to know what it is, but being inside, I see it in existence, not in essence. What I want to know (love) is the very substance I employ in order to speak (the lover's discourse)" (59). But can one speak of love "from the outside"? (Cf. Kierkegaard on third-party descriptions of love.) Why can't one know "from the inside"? (Whatever happened to phenomenology?) "I begin *classifying* what happens to me." In love, one tends to philosophize: "From *you* I shift to *he* or *she*. And then from *he* or *she,* I shift to *one*: I elaborate an abstract discourse about love, a philosophy of the thing, which would then in fact be nothing but a generalized suasion" (74). But the "thing" in question is an emotion and the philosophy a conceptual endorsement: How could it not be a "suasion"? "Every discussion of love (however detached its tonality) inevitably involves a secret allocution" (74). If for Socrates the philosopher was the ultimate lover, Barthes takes philosophy to be the mark of failure: "I am . . . doomed to my own philosophy" (23).

pleasure "*Gaudium* is the pleasure the soul experiences when it considers the possession of a present and future good as assured. *Laetitia* is a lively pleasure" (Cicero, Leibniz). But unable to obtain the former, I dream of falling back on the latter—"a lunatic project" (51) (Cf. Spinoza: "Love is pleasure"—*Ethics*). But is pleasure the point of love, even of desire? (Cf. Sartre, on pleasure as a distraction in love.) A pleasureless joy (*jouissance*) that ends in melancholy. Better, instead, "the pleasure of the text."

port(s) of call (102) "A compulsion to speak which leads me to say 'I love you' in one port of call after another . . . my wandering, my errantry continues . . . all the meanderings of my amorous history" (105).

power Love as impotence ("engulfed," ravishment," "will-to-possess") (see **resentment**). "I experience reality as a system of power" (89). "The lover's solitude is not a solitude of person (love confides, speaks, tells itself), it is a solitude of system: I am alone in making a system out of it" (212). Alexander Nehamas tells us that Nietzsche made such a system of *himself* (*Ecce Homo*). Is Nietzsche (as Socrates) the ultimate lover? (Barthes's book ends on a "Nietzschean accent": "Not to pray any longer—to bless" [234].)

reason(s) Warranted, caused, legitimated ("affirmation"). "The wealth of 'good reasons' for loving differently, loving better, loving without being in love, etc." (22). See Spinoza again: "Emotions which are aroused or spring from reason, if we take account of time, are stronger than those which are attributable to particular objects that we regard as absent." Love has its reasons; it is not, therefore, "unconditional." But what if those reasons were stubbornness, obstinacy, the dubious joys of a cultivated unhappiness? (Cf. Capellanus: "Love is suffering.")

reasonable A term of abuse (e.g., 147).

relationship (see **being with**)

resentment (200) The "fundamental mode of amorous subjectivity: a word, an image reverberates painfully in the subject's affective consciousness." An antithesis of love, the beloved as *other,* a source of irritation. Love (as resentment) as a lack of power. Love (as *ressentiment*) as an exquisite, debilitating sensitivity. Resignation (but not *amor fati*). "Not the man of resentment, but of fatality" (70, 214, and passim). "The lover lives in a universe of signs" (Culler on Barthes, *Barthes,* 110).[6] Looking for signs everywhere, creating signs. A fetishism of the sign? But the relation between signs and between sign and signified is not intratextual but contextual, and in love this primarily involves a confrontation with another human being. How much of this is "projection" and how much "the real person"? And how much of what cynics call "projection" is nothing but ordinary intentionality and the confusion of the lover with an "other"? The semiotic problem (in love): "The amorous subject has no system of sure signs at his disposal" (214).

skin (71) The body proper; also a language. "I rub my language against the other" (73) (see **language**). A medical question: What, then, is *in* the body? An improper question: what does one sexually "penetrate"? Not skin. The language of the body (discourse?): "Every contact, for the lover, raises the question of an answer: The skin is asked to reply" (67). ("A squeeze of the hand—enormous documentation") (67). The dermatologist's dilemma: To see the skin is to ignore the body, and miss the person. (Cf. eyes [**blind**].)

solitude "The lover's discourse is . . . an extreme solitude" (1). See Rilke: lovers as guardians of each other's solitude. But isn't love the end of solitude? (A naive question.)

strategy "The lover's discourse is not lacking in calculations: I rationalize, I reason, sometimes I count" (85).

terminus ("fade-out") (112) Love ends. Why?

union (fusion, merging) (226) "I spent an afternoon drawing what Aristophanes's hermaphrodite would look like. . . . I persist, but get nowhere" (226–27). "I might as well return to the pursuit of the multiple" (228). "Dreams of total union: Everyone says this dream is impossible, and yet it persists. I do not abandon it" (228). But perhaps Aristophanes is right: "I am no longer myself without you" (F. Wahl, quoted). "I am Heathcliff!" (Cathy, in *Wuthering Heights*). "The identity theory of love" (Solomon, *Love: Emotion, Myth and Metaphor*).

vulnerability "Flayed" (95). (See **resentment**.)

weeping (180) Suffering, but also joy overflowing ("I am not wounded"). But is it the lover or the romantic who weeps? (180) The sentimentality of love ("an obscenity" [178]). Cf. Milan Kundera on kitsch: "Kitsch causes two tears to flow in quick succession. The first tear says: How nice. . . . The second tear says: How nice to be moved. . . . It is the second tear that makes kitsch kitsch" (*Unbearable Lightness of Being,* 251). But see Barthes: "I remain dry, watertight. My identification is imperfect" (57).

writing "Two powerful myths have persuaded us that love could, *should* be sublimated in aesthetic creation: the Socratic myth and the romantic myth. Yet . . ." (97). "You do not love me for my writing (and I suffer from it)" (79). And again, "Fulfillments: They are not spoken—so that, erroneously, the amorous relation seems reduced to a long complaint" (55). "Love . . . cannot be *lodged* in my writing" (98). *"I cannot write myself"* (98).

Perhaps I have yielded too easily to both the Socratic and the romantic myths myself, enamored by writing (but not *my* writing) and, quite frankly, turned off by the long complaints that are so often confused for love. Indeed, perhaps it is the thought of being loved *as a writer,* or worse, writing oneself as a lover, that explains so much of the sour passion that now replaces the traditional saccharine and naive (if not hypocritical) musings on "merging" and "fusion" and happy togetherness. But writers are only sometimes (perhaps rarely) successful lovers, and the distance created by writing may indeed be part of the problem. Love, I suggest, is not discourse, much less discourse at a distance, and as we complete our lexicon the silent conclusion is a palpable longing for "the other." With some luck (for it is not an ontological impossibility), he or she will be there.

For Kathy, who is and always will be

Chapter 10

IN THIS TEXT WHERE I NEVER AM: DISCOURSES OF DESIRE IN DERRIDA

Nancy J. Holland

Three texts at three different times across the thirty years of his career reveal at least two different discourses of desire in the work of Jacques Derrida. One could easily be coded "male"—discursive, abstract, centered on the master texts of the philosophical tradition. It *talks* about desire, but in so doing makes explicit the phallogocentrism of the economy of desire in that tradition. Here I will focus on three versions of this master text of mastery, all published in 1967 in *Writing and Difference*.[1] The second discourse of desire could as easily be coded "female." Allusive, indirect, literary/artistic, it *embodies* desire, appearing to best advantage in "Restitutions," a "'polylogue' (for n + 1 *voix—féminine*)," published in *The Truth in Painting* in 1978.[2] I have already discussed that happier text in some detail elsewhere.[3] Here I will trace instead my disillusion with Derrida's fictive polylogues of female desire in two later texts: *Cinders* (1980),[4] and *Memoirs of the Blind* (1990).[5] The paradox of this alternation/alteration from a male voice that seems to provide a framework for what could be a feminist understanding of philosophical desire to a fictive female voice that ultimately seems to preclude such an understanding tells us less, I believe, about Derrida than about desire itself, about the maleness of any desire that would call itself philosophical.[6]

I. "Delirious"

The first discussion I had as a "professional" philosopher came at closing time in a Boston hotel bar, when a dean who was, as it turned out, unable to give me a job instead gave me permission to think seriously about the fact that the great philosophers were overwhelmingly not only men but unmarried men.[7] ("Impotence, here, is a property not of the critic but of criticism. The two are sometimes confused" [*WD*, 302 n].) Neither of us wished to say that homosexuality or celibacy per se were determinate factors in the history of philosophy (as a male graduate-school colleague jokingly claimed), but the fact under consideration did seem to suggest that neither gender nor sexuality were entirely irrelevant to the philosophical enterprise. ("Bataille's writing thus relates all semantemes, that is, all philosophemes, to the sovereign operation, to the consummation, without return, of meaning" [*WD*, 270].) The effects of that conversation on my subsequent career have been immeasurable, but have centered on the role of gender in philosophy rather than on the role of sexual desire. At the same time, however, the maleness of philosophy is deeply intertwined with what is, in our culture at least, a very male-centered view of sexuality and desire. ("Sovereignty dissolves the values of meaning, truth, and a *grasp-of-the-thing-itself*" [*WD*, 270].) And the texts from *Writing and Difference* made the role of this masculine desire in the philosophical tradition clear to me.

What is female desire in the restricted hom(m)oerotic sexual economy of philosophy, of language in general? How can we speak its name, tell its story? We all know what a story is: boy meets girl, boy loses girl, boy gets girl, and gets her again. Subject, verb, object. How to tell the story of the subjectivity of the object of desire, and especially, how to tell it at the moment when that subjectivity itself desires, desires to become object, desires, it might easily seem, only to play its masochistic role in the eternal narrative of male desire? Is there female desire, or simply an abyss, the thrill of falling in a dream only to awaken, terrified, in the Father's bed once again?

In "From Restricted to General Economy," Derrida comes at Hegel through the work of Georges Bataille, while in "La Parole Soufflée" and "The Theater of Cruelty" he presents Antonin Artaud, in his madness and his homosexuality, as the type of the anti-Hegelian. Whereas Hegel offers a restricted economy of desire (and one ultimately so restricted to the family *oikonomos* that the ideal love is that between Antigone and her brother, or Hegel and his "mad" sister, as Derrida points out in *Glas*), Artaud seeks a theater of the moment, never to be repeated or represented, that is, an economy of pure loss, of spending without reserve or return, of risk and death desired and embraced.[8] Antigone's death as a virgin suicide, however, suggests that all the roles in both versions of this play of the economics of desire are necessarily male. What Derrida does in these texts is to provide a

160

path through the cave in which Antigone is imprisoned, a path not to freedom, but to what might be an understanding of why female desire, like Antigone, can only die there.

Derrida comes at Artaud through his madness, through the relationship between critical and clinical evaluations of his work, or rather, through their common ground in a dualistic metaphysics that Artaud seeks to destroy in "a pure creation of life" (*WD*, 175). Artaud's search is for a speech that will do what Bataille suggests laughter does: exceed the system without being able to be reincorporated into it as negation. "Not the absence but the radical irresponsibility of speech, irresponsibility as the power and the origin of speech" (*WD*, 176). Because such original speech is impossible, Artaud's project is necessarily a futile one: "As soon as I speak, the words I have found (as soon as they are words) no longer belong to me, are originally *repeated*" (*WD*, 177). He is haunted not only by having one's words, breath (*souffle*), stolen by this "always already" of language but also by the parallel theft of the body, stolen by God at birth. The only defense against this necessary theft is to maintain the original, integral word in theatrical speech, to maintain the original, integral body:

> A true man has no sex, for he must be his sex. As soon as the sex becomes an organ, it becomes foreign to me, abandons me, acquiring thereby the arrogant autonomy of a swollen object full of itself. The swelling of the sex become a separate object is a kind of castration. (*WD*, 186)

Madness, indeed, but a madness that in its confusion of body and word, desire and loss, is of a piece with metaphysics itself.

In *La Parole Soufflée*, Derrida suggests that in economizing in this way, in seeking to limit loss, Artaud only repeats the gesture of reincorporation into the system: "The transgression of metaphysics through the 'thought' which, Artaud tells us, has not yet begun, always risks returning to metaphysics" (*WD*, 194). Later, in "The Theater of Cruelty," Derrida returns to Artaud, but with a perhaps greater understanding of the difference between mimetic necessity and "representational *mimesis*" in the usual sense. He begins by noting that, to the extent that today "all theatrical audacity declares its fidelity to Artaud," a "theater of cruelty" must in some sense be possible.[9] It becomes so by ending the dominance of the spoken word and its author/God. Theater will no longer be defined by the desire to represent what is not present; speech will be replaced by, will become, gesture. On this borderline between speech and nonspeech will be sacrificed "the difference between the soul and the body, the master and the slave, God and man, the author and the actor" (*WD,* 240). From this deicidal sacrifice will arise a sacred theater of the divine, a carnival of pure spending: "Nonrepetition, expenditure that is resolute and without return in the unique time consuming the present, must put an end to fearful discursiveness, to unskirtable ontology, to dialectics" (*WD,* 246). Artaud thus becomes, for Derrida, the non(anti)thesis of the Hegelian system: "In this sense the theater of cruelty would be the art of difference and of expenditure without economy, without reserve, without return, without history" (*WD,* 247).

The abolition of the mastery of the text in the theater, and of the slavery of the actor, leads down yet another corridor from Artaud to Hegel, one that might seem closer to the pathway of desire. But both master and slave remain resolutely male in Hegel. The difference that might be thought to generate desire is erased in the need that the roles be interchangeable, that the slave be the master of the master, as language is the master of the subjectivity that would control it. The consequence of this gender neutral discourse in Hegel is, as always, the disappearance of women in the reciprocal self-desire of the Same.[10] As already noted, Bataille makes the Other of this self-identical discourse not a festival of cruelty, but laughter: "The burst of laughter is the almost-nothing into which meaning sinks, absolutely" (*WD,* 256).[11] Laughter is the excess of meaning, which the system cannot recapture. By the same account, however, it also cannot be captured in language, is excessive to it. Thus Bataille's critique of Hegel is, like Artaud's theater, an impossible one. "Necessary and impossible, this excess had to fold discourse into strange shapes," not least because, Derrida goes on to say, "all of Bataille's concepts here are Hegelian" (*WD,* 253).

The Hegelian master, Bataille tells us, is willing to risk, to put his life at stake in the achievement of meaning. However, since he cannot bring that meaning to consciousness once dead, the risk can never truly be run if the system is to work. Death is another form of pure loss, like the woman who represents it, whom it represents—"the little death of the bed." Hegelian risk is always part of an "economy of life [that] restricts itself to conservation, to circulation and self-reproduction and the reproduction of meaning"(*WD,* 255–56). As opposed to this limited loss, laughter, like the theater of cruelty, is the desire for true risk, the risk of desire: "This gaiety is not part of the economy of life, does not correspond to 'the desire to deny the existence of death,' although it is as close to this desire as possible" (*WD*, 258). What Bataille finds here, Derrida says, is the affirmation of a life that is not just the negation of death: an *other* side of positivity, a non(anti)thesis that cannot be reassimilated into the economy of the Same. This other side is a blind spot in Hegel, marked by death, but also by laughter and play. Like Artaud, Bataille risks imitation, repetition, but offers instead a nonrepetition in which:

> a barely perceptible displacement disjoints all the articulations and penetrates all the points welded together by the imitated discourse. A trembling spreads out which then makes the entire old shell crack. (*WD*, 260)

This is not "representational mimesis," but the necessary irony of a mimetic nonrepresentation unable to escape what it would destroy.

Again, what exceeds the system is sacred, but Bataille does not limit that excess to a particular scene of language: "The poetic or the ecstatic is that *in every discourse* which can open itself up to the absolute loss of its sense, to the (non-)base of the scared, of nonmeaning" (*WD*, 261). The desire for meaning, by contrast, runs no risk, so that in Hegelian terms it is a servile desire. A non-servile language would not be silence, but a non-language that always risks making sense, risks becoming Hegel. But it does so furtively (another semanteme from Artaud), always remembering that "the transgression of meaning is not an access to the immediate and indeterminate *identity* of a nonmeaning, nor is it an access to the possibility of *maintaining* nonmeaning. Rather, we would have to speak of an *epoché* of the epoch of meaning" (*WD*, 268).[12] Such a language of sovereignty (as opposed to a mastery tied to the slave and the grasp of things) would conform to what Bataille calls "general economy." It generates a writing that would be neither true nor false, but "fictive," not a loss of meaning, but a "relation to the loss of meaning" (*WD*, 270). Hegel, by contrast, gives us only "a restricted economy: restricted to commercial values, one might say, picking up on the terms of the definition, a 'science dealing with the utilization of wealth,' limited to the meaning and the established value of objects, and to their *circulation*" (*WD*, 271). And woman, the object of circulation par excellence, appears again, if only to neutralize this dialogue among men.

Such a neutralization—irremediable, irreconcilable non-negation—is affirmed, in both Bataille and Derrida, as transgression. The closed economy of desire that Hegel seeks to create and control is always already open, as desire, to what is outside it, to the inassimilable Other. This transgression of the Hegelian dialectic and its restricted economy is paradigmatic of, resonates with, all the displacements of Bataille's nonrepetition of it. And Derrida's conclusion resonates with all I have said about Artaud, and will have to say about Derrida:

> From one to the other, totally other, a certain text. Which in silence traces the structure of the eye, sketches the opening, ventures to contrive "absolute rending," absolutely rends its own tissue once more become "solid" and servile in once more having been read. (*WD*, 277)

In these texts, this transgression never progresses beyond an Other that would be only another form of the Same. Still, the necessity of this unlawful congress among men, in which women appear only by indirection, is clearly drawn here. The traditional economy of desire is a restricted one, an economy in which desire is figured as risk, loss, and death, rather than as plentitude, passion, or pleasure. In the history of European philosophy that Hegel both summarizes and consummates, the restricted economy of desire is, as Derrida makes clear, a male one.

II. *Descendre*

When I was a child, it was my job to light the incinerator at the back of the yard to burn our trash. This was rather an ordeal for me, since I was afraid of lighting the match, afraid I would burn myself when it exploded into flame. ("I do not like this verb, 'to incinerate'; I find in it no affinity with the vulnerable tenderness, with the patience of a cinder. The verb is active, acute, incisive" [*C*, 35].) Eventually, by doing the chore several times a week, I overcame my fear and got used to the explosion, which might be one reason my mother persisted in making me do something I found so frightening. What my mother probably did not intend, although she may have known about it, was that I then became obsessed with fire and went through a period of preadolescent pyromania, playing with matches, votive candles, and a long red stick of sealing wax. ("She plays with words as one plays with fire, I would denounce her as a pyromaniac" [*C*, 61].) A metaphor is building up here: The parallel between fire and sexuality that, in my case at least, followed a similar path of fear, familiarization, and fascination. ("But the urn of language is so fragile. . . . And if you entrust it to paper, it is all the better to inflame you with, my dear, you will eat yourself up immediately" [*C*, 53].) Is this a story that happens only to women, a uniquely feminine relationship to fire/desire? I have no way of knowing, but I would never pretend that I did. In *Cinders*, however, Derrida engages in exactly such a pretense.

I loved philosophy platonically once, but when I both read and felt the pleasure of the text, small streams of desire began to flow around the source of what and how I thought. These streams sank quickly into the dry sand of what the tradition said I should know and care about, or, better yet, know and not care about at all. On friendlier soil, the streams became rivers in which I could not step twice (which is hera-clitean and therefore wrong, the old Aristotelian said); the rivers became an ocean that covered the undifferentiated earth. What are the criteria of interpretation when we are all adrift? And who asks? Who seeks to control my drift, my desire? My desire for philosophy was not philosophy's desire—my desire was outside its discourse. Yet how could I not desire the French postcard? There is a place where male desire wants to rub up against female desire, tries to find its voice in our voices, its beauty in our beauty. There is a place where difference is almost erased, but always as already reinscribed in a discourse that can see only an abyss where that which would be neither the phallus nor desire for the phallus might exist. There is a male voice there, but in falsetto, able to sing both parts only because of technology, which always ultimately means control.

In talking about *Cinders* and *Memoirs of the Blind,* my topic will be doubly dual: about women and the blind, on the one hand (and what the hand means is part of these texts of Derrida), and about death and religion on the other. Religion here is doubly figured, as sacrifice and transcendence, or—not in any way analogously, but in an entirely different register—as Jewish and Christian, or, again with the same proviso, as Biblical and Greek. But this dual topic is also a divided one, divided between the Others of the philosophy mastered by the Hegelian text, because the oneness of the Other is an illusion that mirrors the illusion of the Same. If philosophy both fears and desires the Other, it must fear the desire of the Other insofar as the Other cannot be the Same. But the secret here is that the Other can always, in some respects, be the Same. The only question, then, would be the economy of respect.

Cinders thus attempts to give a voice to female desire, to gain diversity within unity, by presenting itself as a polylogue between an unknown number of individuals of indeterminate genders, a polylogue that is presented in chiasmic intertext with related quotations from other works by Derrida. However, the diversity is patently illusory and its relationship to the content of the text seems contrived rather than either natural or artful. This governing conceit, in both senses of the term, which seemed so liberatory some twenty years ago when I first read "Restitutions," has come to seem less the discourse of a fractured, polymorphous Subject and more a way in which Derrida, like Plato, can engage in a dialogue with himself.[13]

The fictive polylogue in *Cinders* chains together themes that reach back to both *Writing and Difference* and *Dissemination,* the original source of the reference to cinders. The themes are familiar from Hegel: woman, death, the tomb/crypt, writing, proper names, property, capitalism, the Father, family, and race/blood. The key text is still *Antigone.* However, this carefully constructed chain of concepts has a few weak links, such as the dichotomy Derrida tries to create between cinders and smoke:

> What a difference between cinder and smoke: the latter apparently gets lost, and better still, without perceptible remainder, for it rises, it takes to the air, it is spirited away, sublimated. The cinder—falls, tires, lets go, more material since it fritters away its word; it is very divisible. (*C,* 73)

But, of course, smoke *is* cinders—small, light ashes that float away. The dichotomy fails because it rests on a figuring of cinders as only one thing, as purely feminine, so that smoke can have no part of it.

In a continuation of the gesture toward an undifferentiated, "pure" feminine, the she/it/you within the "polylogue" also becomes not only, of course, Cinderella (*C,* 55), but also Little Red Riding Hood (*C,* 53, quoted above) and, by implication, a widow practicing suttee (in quotations from *The Post Card,* at *C,* 74, 76).[14] Even the printed English text of *Cinders* is figured as "feminine," split and even doubly split: The left-hand pages quote Derrida's other works, the right-hand ones give us the text of *Cinders,* but each page is also printed in two columns, the left lower and in French, the right higher and in English, each of the four columns printed in a different typeface. Would this be a case of protesting too much?

Someone might point out here that the false dichotomy between cinders and smoke comes from a voice in the polylogue that is not necessarily Derrida's (just as the layout of the English text is not his doing). My only answer is to ask again, "Whose voice is it (i.e., Who author-ized the text)" We have seen that Derrida is one of the most consistent voices naming the restricted hom(m)oerotic economy of philosophy (and I would add that "Plato's Pharmacy" also echoes loudly here), so the introduction of an ambiguously female voice into this text may be an affirmative neutralization of that tradition:[15]

> Above the sacred place, incense again, but no monument, no Phoenix, no erection that stands—or falls—the cinder without ascension, the cinders love me, they change sex, they re-cinder themselves, they androgynocide themselves. (C, 61)

Still, so long as language is an instrument of power and power is figured as male, philosophy will remain hom(m)oerotic, an economy of the Same, and the pretense of a female voice will remain an illusion, even in Derrida's text (and my own). To figure the feminine as any one thing, even such a thing as cinders, is only to make it the Same again and hence to fall back into philosophy.

> The mortal throw of the die that is the exhalation of a vocable, at once delivers the gift and the debt, dissemination and grace, the necessity and the impossibility of return; thus cinders fall to ash, "dé:cendre." (C, 79 n)

In *Cinders* at least, women constitute something of a blind spot for Derrida, even as he thematizes the female voice, just as the possibility of pure loss is a "blind spot" for Hegel, even as he thematizes negation and risk. Not an accidental blind spot, but one the necessary structure of which is perhaps made clearer in comparison with *Memoirs/Memories of the Blind*. This text is also presented as a patently false dialogue. The interlocutor, whose gender is never indicated, appears only rarely to raise such questions as "You seem to fear the monocular vision of things. Why not a single point of view? Why two hypotheses?" (*MB*, 1). Obviously this person is not a regular reader of Derrida's work. He/she/it does, however, tend to want to return to bits of Derrida's autobiography that are relevant to why he chose the subject of blindness for the exhibition at the Louvre for which this book was the catalogue: "This really is looking like an exhibition of yourself. You are inscribing in your memoirs, in short, the chronicle of an exhibition" (*MB*, 32). If this solicitude to personalize the narrative is an attempt to figure the interlocutor as female, however, one could say that Derrida has done women no great favor. He does so, moreover, in a context in which this slightly inane Other, *if* female, is more or less clearly indicated to be a variation of himself in drag—"What then is to be made here of sexual difference? And of the Tiresias within us?" (*MB*, 128).

This level of discourse is not the norm for *Memoirs of the Blind,* which is in many ways the kind of intelligent, insightful work we expect of Derrida. The passages we might not have expected of him, however, generally seem to be tied to the feigned dialogue, if not to an attempt to introduce a fictive female voice into the text. One might think that this effort, as well as unfortunate in its outcome, would also be an unnecessary move toward diversity in a book that would seem to speak of another oppressed group within our culture. Wisely, however, and in contrast to what he does with regard to women in *Cinders,* Derrida makes it quite explicit that it is not the blind of whom he wishes to speak here, but of the meaning of *blindness* as it is represented in Western culture, especially European painting (and especially European paintings available to the Louvre). Thus, he says, "Here is the *second hypo-thesis* then . . . a drawing of the *blind* is a drawing *of* the blind. Double genitive" (*MB*, 2). That is, the artist or draftsman (always male here) is blind precisely at the moment that he draws, because he must either look at the model and not see what he is drawing (on the paper) or look at the paper and not see what he is drawing (the model) (*MB*, 43). "The blind" as such are not the issue here, except perhaps insofar as Derrida's own temporary blindness in one eye is the precipitating event of the whole enterprise, that is, insofar as this *Memoir* would be, as the interlocutor insists, autobiography.

Of course, blindness represents many things in the discourse or iconography of the West. The usual Hegelian list of preoccupations can be developed here—debt, money, capital, the Father, inheritance, death, burial—but to these are added concepts tied to the Biblical use of these themes, linking this chain both to blindness and to religion: knowing as seeing, truth, conversion, circumcision, skepticism, belief. The key narratives here would be the story of Jacob and Esau, or that of Saul on the road to Damascus. These preoccupations have a heavily masculine coding, centering as they do on blindness as castration, the Medusa, and sacrifice as an access to transcendence, that is, as a way to evade the death that is always already coded as female. Derrida himself acknowledges this more than once, for instance in a context somewhere between the Biblical and Greek narratives of sacrifice:

> Why does sacrifice, in its own moment, make one go blind, regardless of what is at stake? And this, whether it be a matter of the act of

choosing or of the beings who are chosen—chosen quite often in order to be sacrificed: the only son, the unique son, one son for the other—or the daughter, more invisible than ever. (*MB*, 100)

Early in the book, he notes (literally) that these narratives, and the paintings based on them, speak of blind *men* because these are stories of the filiation between fathers and sons, Father and Son. Blind women are not heroes, but saints (*MB*, 5–6 n).

Two other texts, then, one about women and death, one about sacrifice and resurrection, but two texts that do not seem to see each other, or not clearly. Does Derrida merely note a tradition in which women and the death they represent cannot be incorporated into narratives of redemptive sacrifice, or do these texts participate in that tradition in spite of themselves? When his fictive dialogues are done well, as in "Restitutions," the gesture seems clearly mimetic in the almost literal sense of an act of ironic imitation. In these two texts, where it is less successful as a literary device, the repetition of the exclusion of women from the realm of transcendence (or their merely fictive inclusion in it) also edges closer to "representational mimesis" of the Same. Would it be a case, as with the draftsman or in Diderot's letter to his mistress, of drawing or writing "without seeing" (the letter is cited twice: *MB*, 1 and 102)? Or can death and sacrifice find a common ground in smoke—or tears?

> —In drawing those who weep, and especially women (for if there are many great blind men, why so many weeping women?), one is perhaps seeking to unveil the eyes. To say them without showing them seeing. To recall. To pronounce that which, in the eyes, and thus in the drawing of men, in no way regards sight, has nothing to do with it. Nothing to do with the light of clairvoyance. One can see with a single eye, at a single glance, whether one has one eye or two. . . .
> —Isn't that in fact what happened to you, as you explained earlier? (*MB*, 127)

Where does the voice of female desire stand to name itself? Since I must stand somewhere, the impurity of that stance is the first excuse the phallogocentric tradition provides me for not wishing to speak of female desire at all. My desire may simply be the product of a mind narrowed by its European, Protestant, heterosexual, middle-aged, middle-class, married, mothering world to a singular point that is no longer a place to stand or a voice to speak. If I describe female desire as polymorphous, undifferentiated pleasure without object, as definitive of a self and a world, as the Other of the restricted hom(m)oerotic sexual economy of philosophy, even if I am wrong, at least I have not let the fear of these questions (which are themselves formed largely within the discourse of a tradition I am trying in many ways to step beyond) silence me once again. The questions from outside are much harder: Where does female desire stand in the face of the other Others, those who suffer from and challenge the white man's power without the easy option of giving up and going to bed with it, without the option of desiring it for the pleasure it can give, for the privilege of writing this text and having you read it?

PART VI
PRODUCTIVE DESIRE:
DELEUZE AND GUATTARI

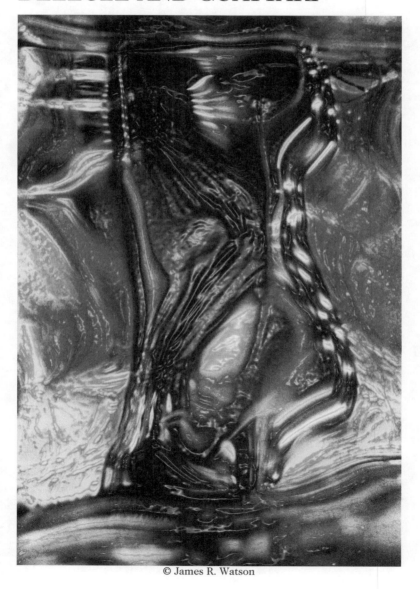

Chapter 11

SPINOZA, NIETZSCHE, DELEUZE: AN OTHER DISCOURSE OF DESIRE

Alan D. Schrift

And now, said Socrates, bearing in mind what Love is the love of, tell me this. Does he long for what he is in love with, or not?

Of course he longs for it.

And does he long for whatever it is he longs for, and is he in love with it, when he's got it, or when he hasn't?

When he hasn't got it, probably.

Then isn't it probable, said Socrates, or rather isn't it certain that everything longs for what it lacks, and nothing longs for what it doesn't lack? I can't help thinking, Agathon, that that's about as certain as anything could be. Don't you think so?

Yes, I suppose it is. . . .

Well, then, continued Socrates, desiring to secure something to oneself forever may be described as loving something which is not yet to hand.

Certainly.

And therefore, whoever feels a want is wanting something which is not yet to hand, and the object of his love and of his desire is whatever he isn't, or whatever he hasn't got—that is to say, whatever he is lacking in.

Absolutely.

—Plato, *Symposium*

Socrates's remarks here seem perfectly intuitive: of course one can only desire what one does not already have. The conceptual link between desire and absence or lack seems natural, and we should not be surprised to find this conceptual link running throughout the history of Western philosophical discourse. In Hobbes, for example, we find the absence of the desired object as the defining characteristic that allows us to distinguish desire from love:

173

> That which men desire, they are also said to LOVE: and to HATE
> those things for which they have aversion. So that desire and love
> are the same thing; save that by desire, we always signify the
> absence of the object; by love, most commonly the presence of
> the same. So also by aversion, we signify the absence, and by hate,
> the presence of the object.[1]

Descartes makes a similar point when he defines desire in *The Passions of the Soul* in terms of its temporal modality: Desire is futural, and inasmuch as the future is not yet present, desire is always a longing for what is absent.

> For not only when we desire to acquire a good which we do not yet
> have, or avoid an evil which we judge may occur; but also when we
> only anticipate the conservation of a good or absence of an evil,
> which is as far as this passion may extend, it is evident that it ever
> regards the future.[2]
>
> *The definition of Desire.* The passion of desire is an agitation of the
> soul caused by the spirits which dispose it to wish for the future the
> things which it represents to itself as agreeable. Thus we do not only
> desire the presence of the absent good, but also the conservation of
> the present, and further, the absence of evil, both of that which we
> already have, and of that which we believe we might experience in
> time to come. (*PS*, art. 86)

We find this same link between desire and absence, to cite one final example, in Locke's *Essay*:

> The uneasiness a man finds in himself upon the absence of anything
> whose present enjoyment carries the idea of delight with it, is that
> we call desire.[3]

Whether rationalist or empiricist, whether ancient or modern, the history of philosophy displays a remarkable consensus among the views of those philosophers who discuss desire. While acknowledging the relative infrequency of these discussions, we must note that when desire does become the object of philosophical reflection, almost without exception it is conceived as the consequence of the lack of the object desired.

When we look to the twentieth century, we again find the link made between desire and lack, but this time this link is brought to philosophical center stage. Here we could cite numerous examples, but two stand out as exemplary: Lacan and Sartre.[4] Both draw on Hegel, and both make desire-as-lack a defining characteristic of human being. Lacan designates the function of desire "as *manque-à-être,* a 'want-to-be,' " and he defines psychoanalysis itself as being "engaged in the central lack in which the subject experiences himself [sic] as desire."[5] Following Hegel's account of desire in the *Phenomenology of Spirit,* Lacan offers the formula "man's desire is the desire of the Other."[6] Whether as objective genitive (the Other as the object desired) or subjective genitive (desiring the Other's desire or what the Other desires), Lacan tells us that the desideratum is lacking:

> One lack is superimposed upon the other. The dialectic of the objects of desire, in so far as it creates the link between the desire of the subject and the desire of the Other—I have been telling you this for a long time now that it is one and the same—this dialectic now passes through the fact that the desire is not replied to directly. It is a lack engendered from the previous time that serves to reply to the lack raised by the following time. (*FC*, 215)

"The Other, the locus of speech, is also the locus of this want, or lack" (*E,* 263), that is desire, and this lack of the Other as object of desire allows Lacan to posit the phallus as signifier of the Other/desire:

> The fact that the phallus is a signifier means that it is in the place of the Other that the subject has access to it. But since this signifier is only veiled, as ratio of the Other's desire, it is this desire of the Other as such that the subject must recognize. (*E*, 288)

In other words, the phallus, ultimate signifier of desire, is ultimately lacking.[7]

Sartre, on the other hand, identifies freedom, consciousness, and being-for-itself with desire as lack:

> The for-itself is defined ontologically as the *lack of being*, and possibility belongs to the for-itself as that which it lacks. . . . The for-itself chooses because it is lack; freedom is really synonymous with lack. Freedom is the concrete mode of being of the lack of being. . . . Fundamentally man is *the desire to be*, and the existence of this desire is not to be established by an empirical induction; it is the result of an a priori description of the being of the for-itself, since desire is a lack and since the for-itself is the being which is to itself its own lack of being.[8]

As future-projecting beings, humans are what they are not yet, and as self-motivated beings, they seek to become the future/project that they currently lack. In the end, Sartre ties this ontological account to the *desire to be God:* as a free for-itself, human being ultimately seeks what it does not have—the ontological status of being-in-itself. But the for-itself does not seek simply to become a thing. Instead, seeking to have its cake and eat it too, the for-itself desires to be a being-in-itself-for-itself, that is, to be a being that would be its own foundation—to be God. Such a project, however, would entail that one both lack *and* at the same time possess what one lacks, which is an ontological impossibility. As a consequence, Sartre concludes, "man is a useless passion."[9]

Several other instances of the view of desire as lack could be provided, but these few examples should suffice to indicate the relative uniformity on this issue in the discourses of psychology, ontology, and philosophy. However, another discourse of desire runs through our tradition and has been brought more clearly to the center in the recent work of Gilles Deleuze. This other discourse supplements the discourse highlighted above by recognizing the productivity of desire. Where the philosophical mainstream has focused on the *desideratum,* the object of desire, as lacking, this other discourse focuses on the motivational force of the *desiderare,* the act of desire, as productive.

Deleuze does not claim to be the originator of this discourse. Rather, he seeks to highlight the history of this discourse in addition to articulating its current importance. The investigation of this history leads to the two philosophers with whom Deleuze feels the greatest affinity: Spinoza and Nietzsche.[10]

Spinoza's relevance to this other discourse of desire emerges at two points. First, desire is marked as the essence of being human. "Desire," Spinoza writes, "is man's very essence, insofar as it is conceived to be determined, from any given affection of it, to do something."[11] The essence of something, according to Spinoza, is "the striving [*conatus*] by which each thing strives to persevere in its being" (*SE* III, prop. 7). He thereby concludes that "the power of each thing, *or* the striving by which it (either alone or with others) does anything or strives to do anything . . . is nothing but the given, *or* actual, essence of the thing itself" (*SE* III, prop. 7). By identifying desire as the power to act (*conatus*), and in particular as the power to act that is conscious of itself (*SE* III, prop. 9), Spinoza's discourse on desire first raises the potential productivity of desire as an issue requiring examination.[12]

The second Spinozist contribution concerns his articulation of the primacy of desire in relation to its object. Contrary to the moral drawn from Plato's *Euthyphro,* we do not desire things because they are good; rather, we constitute things as good because they are the objects of our desire:

It is clear that we neither strive for, nor will, neither want, nor desire anything because we judge it to be good; on the contrary, we judge something to be good because we strive for it, will it, want it, and desire it.[13]

Here we recognize a major point of intersection between the projects of Spinoza and Nietzsche.[14] Like Spinoza, Nietzsche views value as a consequence of desire or will. "Our values," he writes, "are *interpreted into* things [*Unsere Werthe sind in die Dinge hineininterpretiert*]."[15] No intrinsic values in things create in us a desire for them. Only our imposing will bestows upon things their value *as desirable*. Nietzsche's name for this imposing will is, of course, will to power, and although he does not make frequent use of the specific language of "desire" (*Begierde, Wunsch, Sehnsucht*), will to power, as the form- and value-giving force of interpretive imposition, performs the function for Nietzsche that others attribute to desire.

Nietzsche frames the discourse of desire by examining the construction of the "true" or "real" world of the metaphysicians.

It is our needs [*Bedürfnisse*] *that interpret the world*; our drives and their For and Against. Every drive is a kind of lust to rule; each one has its perspective that it would like to compel all the other drives to accept as a norm.(*KSA*, 12:7 [60]/*WP*, 481)

On the basis of these needs, the metaphysicians have judged the world of becoming as a deception and have invented a world beyond it, a *true* world, the world of Being. This true world of Being is "fabricated solely from psychological needs" (*KSA*, 13:11 [99]/*WP*, 12), as we see in the case of Plato. Confronted by a world of becoming that lacks unity, aim, purpose, stability, Plato is unable to cope. He lacks the courage to make his way in such a world and instead creates a fictional, ideal world in which the values he desires will be located: "Plato is a coward in the face of reality—consequently he flees into the ideal."[16] Plato's idealism, like all idealism, is "a figment of the imagination."[17] And like all figments of the imagination, it is a construct of desire. In a passage from the *Nachlass* that appears under the section heading "Toward the Psychology of Metaphysics," Nietzsche succinctly terms such metaphysical constructs "false conclusions":

Suffering inspires these conclusions: fundamentally they are *desires* [*Wünsche*] that such a world should exist; in the same way, to imagine another, more valuable world is an expression of hatred for a world that makes one suffer: the *ressentiment* of metaphysicians against actuality is here creative. (*KSA*, 12:8 [2]/*WP*, 579)

The link between desire and creativity appears frequently in Nietzsche's texts. In section 370 of *The Gay Science,* entitled "What Is Romanticism?" Nietzsche distinguishes Dionysian creativity from Romantic creativity in the following way: "Regarding all aesthetic values I now avail myself of this main distinction: I ask in every instance, 'is it hunger or superabundance [*Uberfluss*] that has here become creative?'"[18] Hunger prompts Romantic art as a reaction to a state of affairs that is currently felt to be intolerable. Superabundance produces Dionysian art—the result of an overflowing of excess creative energy that no longer could be contained and must become its own future. Romantic art is prompted, reactive; Dionysian art is productive, active. The Romantic artist (Wagner, Schopenhauer) suffers "from the *impoverishment of life* and seek[s] rest, stillness, calm seas, redemption from themselves through art and knowledge, or intoxication, convulsions, anaesthesia, and madness." The Dionysian artist (Goethe, Rubens, Hafiz) suffers from the "over-fullness of life" and cannot refrain from the creation of new forms.

This distinction between overfullness and impoverishment of life is the fundamental evaluative distinction operating within Nietzsche's texts. Whether expressed in the language of ascension/decline, health/decadence, enhancement/impoverishment, superabundance/lack, overflowing/hunger, or strength/weakness, Nietzsche bases his conclusions regarding the assessment of value in terms of this fundamental genealogical distinction.[19] Applied to the work of art, this distinction prompts the following question: Does this creative transformation of becoming originate from strength and the desire to make a more beautiful world, from a creative act that imposes form and creates a world? Or does this creation have its origin in a lack, the need to fix, the need for Being, to make the world as it *ought* to be (because the world as it *is* ought *not* to be)?[20]

Applying this genealogical distinction more generally to the domain of knowledge raises the question of the relation of knowledge and interest. In *On the Genealogy of Morals,* Nietzsche suggests something of an instrumental account of knowledge: One gets the sort of knowledge one "needs," and what one "needs" is conditioned by what one "wants," one's *interests*. About "objectivity," Nietzsche writes that it should be understood not:

as "contemplation without interest" (which is a nonsensical absurdity), but as the ability *to control* one's Pro and Con and to dispose of them, so that one knows how to employ a variety of perspectives and affective interpretations in the service of knowledge.[21]

He goes on to caution philosophers to guard against the dangers of a Kantian disinterested subject of knowledge. To eliminate the will (read "desire"), to posit a "pure, will-less, painless, timeless knowing subject," would mean "to *castrate* the intellect" (*GM* III, sec. 12). Moreover, such an elimination is not possible: The notion of a "disinterested subject" is a "conceptual fiction [*Begriffs-Fabelei*]" that allows one to put forward one's *own* interested perspective in the guise of a disinterested, value-neutral objective judgment. Nietzsche rejects the linking of disinterestedness and justice that has animated the epistemological tradition from Plato to Kant. Instead, disinterest is viewed simply as a facade in which some put forward their own pros and cons. To the free spirits seeking to liberate themselves from the illnesses of pessimism to which all idealists are subject, Nietzsche advises them to become masters over themselves and also over their own virtues. They must:

> learn to grasp the sense of perspective in every value judgment—the displacement, distortion and merely apparent teleology of horizons and whatever else pertains to perspectivism; also the quantum of stupidity that resides in antitheses of values and the whole intellectual loss which every For, every Against costs us. You shall learn to grasp the *necessary* injustice in every For and Against, injustice as inseparable from life, life itself as *conditioned* by the sense of perspective and its injustice. You shall above all see with your own eyes where injustice is always at its greatest: where life has developed at its smallest, narrowest, neediest, most incipient and yet cannot avoid taking *itself* as the goal and measure of things and for the sake of its own preservation secretly and meanly and ceaselessly crumbling away and calling into question the higher, greater, richer.[22]

Injustice is at its greatest when one's own perspectives (will/desire) are put forward as the *only* perspectives possible. Nietzsche singles out the incarnations of the ascetic ideal, particularly the Church and its moralists (whether philosophical or theological), as the primary perpetrators of this injustice. Church history is a history of exclusion, and one of the things that this history has sought to exclude is desire. In fact, partly on the grounds of its *desire* to exclude desire, Nietzsche judges Church practice to be hostile to life. Because it was too weak-willed to discipline the passions, the Church sought to control them by the only means it had at its disposal—"castration, extirpation." It sought "to *exterminate* the passions [*Leidenschaften*] and desires [*Begierden*] in order to do away with their folly and its unpleasant consequences. . . . But to attack the passions at their roots means to attack life at its roots." The practice of the Church, Nietzsche concludes, "is *hostile to life.*"[23] Nietzsche's implication here is clear: Had the ascetic priests not understood desire as lack and had they not (perhaps subconsciously) feared the productive potential of desire, they might have recognized the life-negating forces that were at work in their attempt to eliminate the passions. But they were not capable of such a recognition, and it was left to others, with a healthier understanding and respect for the productivity of desire, to explore these passional possibilities.

As Deleuze himself notes, in *Nietzsche and Philosophy,* "it is difficult to deny a Spinozist inspiration" in Nietzsche's view that will to power is manifested both as the capacity to affect and the capacity for being affected.[24] The Nietzschean distinction between active and reactive forces that lies at the heart of Deleuze's reading of Nietzsche is itself prefigured if not inspired by the Spinozist distinction between active affects and passive affects (*SE,* III, prop. 58). Active affects are self-generating in the sense that they arise from our desire to act out of an adequate understanding of self, while passive affects (strictly speaking, the *passions*) are generated by external causes. Indeed, Nietzsche's fundamental genealogical distinction between a weak will to power that seeks only to conserve or preserve itself and a strong will to power that seeks to enhance itself may be modeled on the subtle Spinozist distinction between two characterizations of *conatus,* that which "strives to persevere in its being" and that which strives to "increase or aid the body's power of acting" (*SE* III, prop. 12).

Perhaps this connection, above all, leads Deleuze to share Nietzsche's opinion that, following the pre-Socratics, Nietzsche had no real predecessor other than Spinoza. And Deleuze, in *Nietzsche and Philosophy,* is certainly motivated to focus on the link between desire and will to power, and to draw from his interpretation of will to power in terms of the productivity of both active and reactive forces the conclusion that desire is productive. In *Anti-Oedipus,* however, and the works that followed, Deleuze confronts directly the view of desire as lack, particularly in terms of how this account of desire underpins psychoanalysis, whether Freudian or Lacanian:

> Desire: who, except priests, would want to call it "lack"? Nietzsche
> called it "Will to Power." There are other names for it. For example,
> "grace." Desiring is not at all easy, but this is precisely because it
> gives, instead of lacks, "virtue which gives." Those who link desire
> to lack, the long column of crooners of castration, clearly indicate
> a long resentment, like an interminable bad conscience. . . . Lack
> refers to a positivity of desire, and not the desire to a negativity of
> lack. Even individually, the construction of the plane is a politics,
> it necessarily involves a "collective," collective assemblages, a set
> of social becomings.[25]

In psychoanalysis, the (negative) lack as the absent object
which the subject desires to possess can also be understood as
the (positive) product that desire seeks to create. But this formulation is itself deceptive, for in reality, there is no desire in
any substantive sense. Echoing Foucault's claim, in his discussion of power relations, that Power, *"le" pouvoir,* doesn't exist,[26]
Deleuze and Guattari claim that "there is no desire but assembling, assembled desire."[27] Where Foucault talks about power
existing only as part of a network of relations of force operating
within social and discursive practices and systems, Deleuze and
Guattari talk about desire existing as part of an assemblage
(*agencement*). Assemblages "are compositions of desire. . . . The
rationality, the efficiency, of an assemblage does not exist without the passions the assemblage brings into play, without the
desires that constitute it as much as it constitutes them" (*TP,*
399). Desire, in other words, must be freed from the dialectic of
acquisition and lack in order to be displayed as productive, as
the process of production itself.

The productivity of desire, which Deleuze and Guattari reiterate throughout their works together, appears as a central theme
in their interpretation of Kafka:

> There isn't a desire for power; it is power itself that is desire. Not
> a desire-lack, but desire as a plenitude, exercise, and functioning,
> even in the most subaltern of workers. Being an assemblage, desire
> is precisely one with the gears and the components of the machine,
> one with the power of the machine.[28]

In *Anti-Oedipus,* Deleuze and Guattari introduce the desiring
machine as a machinic, functionalist translation of Nietzschean
will to power. A desiring machine is a functional assemblage of a
desiring will and the object desired. Their goal here is in part to
place desire into a functionalist vocabulary, a machinic index, so
as to avoid the personification/subjectivation of desire in a substantive will, ego, unconscious, or self. In so doing, they can avoid the

paradox Nietzsche sometimes faced when speaking of will to power while refraining from positing a subject doing the willing. To speak of desire as part of an assemblage, to refuse to reify or personify desire (as psychoanalysis does), is to recognize that desire and the object desired arise together. Desire does not arise in response to the perceived lack of the object desired. Desire is not a state produced in the subject by the lack of the object. "Desire does not lack anything; it does not lack its object. It is, rather, the *subject* that is missing in desire, or desire that lacks a fixed subject."[29]

Desire is, as it were, a part of the infrastructure. It is constitutive of the objects desired as well as the social field in which they appear.[30] One could say that the structure of desire is intentional in the hermeneutic-phenomenological sense: There is no object of desire without a desiring consciousness to constitute the object *as desirable*. But contrary to the view of desire-as-lack, the experience of desire is not derivative upon the object; rather, it precedes and "produces" the object desired. Unlike phenomenology, there is no ontological problem concerning the ideal status of the noematic desideratum: whether or not the desired object qua object preexists desire, its production as desirable is immanent to the social space insofar as desire is always already at work within this space. As Deleuze and Guattari put it, *"There is only desire and the social, and nothing else"* (AO, 29).

The desire on the part of Deleuze and Guattari to introduce desire into the social field at all levels motivates their whole critique of psychoanalysis. Freud viewed libidinal social investments as subliminal, and as a result, he interpreted all social relations as desexualized representations of unconscious desire. Furthermore, when sexual relations do appear in the social field, they are interpreted by Freud as symbolic representations of the Oedipal family. Deleuze and Guattari reject this reductive familialism that sees only the family while it obscures all relations of wealth, class, gender, and race, that is, all social relations outside the family. For example, they criticize Freud for failing to acknowledge the sexual dimension of economic dependence, as he does when he consistently reduces women of subordinate social standing ("maids," "peasant girls," etc.) to substitutes for incest with the mother or sister (cf. the "Rat Man" or the "Wolf Man") (AO, 352–54). For Deleuze and Guattari, on the other hand, every investment, libidinal or otherwise, is social (AO, 342). The social field is, they claim, desexualized: Social production is libidinal and libidinal production is social.

> The truth is that sexuality is everywhere: in the way that a bureaucrat fondles his records, a judge administers justice, a businessman causes money to circulate; in the way the bourgeoisie fucks the proletariat; and so on. And there is no need to resort to metaphors, any more than for the libido to go by way of metamorphoses. Hitler got the fascists sexually aroused. Flags, nations, armies, banks get a lot of people aroused. (*AO*, 293; trans. modified)

Revising both Marx and Freud, Deleuze and Guattari conclude that insofar as desire is constitutive of the social field, "social production is desiring-production *under determinate conditions*" (*AO*, 243).

The question of desire is, *pace* Freud, a question not of dramatic familial representation but of material production, which is to say, a political question. As with Nietzsche's critique of Plato, Deleuze and Guattari imply that Freud did not have the courage to confront what his investigations of the unconscious disclosed to him: "It is as if Freud had drawn back from this world of wild production and explosive desire, wanting at all costs to restore a little order there, an order made classical owing to the ancient theater" (*AO*, 54). The productive potency of desire "is reduced to mere fantasy production. . . . The unconscious ceases to be what it is—a factory, a workshop—to become a theater, a scene and its staging. And not even an avant-garde theater, such as existed in Freud's day (*Wedekind*), but the classical theater, the classical order of representation. The psychoanalyst becomes a director for a private theater" in which the dramas of familial romance are staged.[31] This point cannot be emphasized too strongly: the great discovery of psychoanalysis was the discovery of "the production of desire, of the productions of the unconscious." But as soon as psychoanalysis turns to *Oedipus Rex*, Oedipus wrecks; with the introduction of Oedipus, desire was restricted to the production of fantasy, representation was substituted for production, units of expression replaced units of production, "and an unconscious that was capable of nothing but expressing itself—in myth, tragedy, dreams—was substituted for the productive unconscious" (*AO*, 24). To liberate desire from its enslavement within the theater of representation and to overturn this theater "into the order of desiring-production: this is the whole task of Schizoanalysis" (*AO*, 271).

The link between desire and material production is central to Deleuze and Guattari's analysis in *Anti-Oedipus*, which we must recall is the first volume of *Capitalism and Schizophrenia*. Making the association of Oedipus with idealism and showing how psychoanalysis restricts the productivity of the unconscious to fantasy production is crucial to their critique. Equally crucial is their development of the real, material libidinal productivity that is made possible by reversing the relation between desire and lack. Desire is not the effect of lack, but rather the reverse: "Lack is the countereffect of desire. . . . Desire is not bolstered by needs . . . needs are derived from desire: They are counterproducts within the real that desire produces" (*AO*, 27).

Deleuze and Guattari here follow a line of argumentation that is clearly Marxist in its orientation. Lack is a social product; it is "created, planned, and organized" in accordance with the interests of the dominant class. It is never primary; it is a deliberate creation as a function of a market economy that "involves deliberately organizing wants and needs amid an abundance of production; making all of desire teeter and fall victim to the great fear of not having one's needs satisfied" (*AO*, 28).[32] This production of organized lack, which Deleuze and Guattari name "antiproduction," is a defining characteristic of capitalist economies that operates at the heart of capitalist production itself (*AO*, 235). And we can see here why the schizo is such a threat to capitalism: for capitalism to function, it must be able to control (code, decode, recode) desire, to construct and insinuate need and lack at the center of abundance. But the schizo's desire cannot be controlled, as Freud himself was forced to concede. Because the schizo's desire productively exceeds the limits of capitalist and psychoanalytic control alike, the schizo provides a "line of flight" that Deleuze and Guattari pursue through the pages of *Anti-Oedipus*.

Like Nietzsche, Deleuze and Guattari recognize that the productions of desire may be dangerous. For Nietzsche, the value of the will to power animating the ascetic ideal was ambiguous. Although Nietzsche encouraged the maximization of strong, healthy will to power, he acknowledged the necessity, the inevitability of weak, decadent will to power. In *On the Genealogy of Morals,* Nietzsche offered an account of the will to nothingness as preferable to not willing and bad conscience choosing to make itself suffer rather than relinquish the pleasure in making itself suffer. Nietzsche saw this ascetic desire to will nothingness and make itself suffer as perverse but fundamentally *active* and ultimately *positive,* for through this perverse desire, "*the will itself was saved*" (*GM* III, sec. 28). Analyzing this phenomenon of desire seeking its own repression is one of the goals of Deleuze and Guattari's schizoanalysis, and we should notice the structural similarity between desire desiring its own repression and Nietzsche's discovery in the *Genealogy* that the will would rather will nothingness than not will. Championing the productivity of desire does not prevent Deleuze and Guattari from recognizing that desire is sometimes destructive and at times has to be repressed while at other times it seeks and produces its own repression.

From their observations of Nietzsche and Wilhelm Reich, whose account of the links between psychic repression and social repression allowed him to explain the phenomenon of fascism not in terms of the masses's false consciousness but in terms of the desires of the masses to repress themselves, Deleuze and Guattari draw the following conclusion: desire is productive, it must be productive, and it will be productive.[33] If a social field does not allow for desire to be productive in nonrepressive forms, then it will produce in whatever forms are available to it, even those that it recognizes to be socially or psychically repressive. As did Nietzsche regarding will to power, Deleuze and Guattari claim that desire must be analyzed locally, relative to the social field in which it operates. There can be no global, universal, or totalizing judgment concerning desire. Nor can there be a full recognition of desire's productive potency until its analysis is freed from the constraints imposed by our tradition's continued adherence to what Foucault called the "repressive hypothesis." One of modernity's most privileged myths, the "repressive hypothesis" emerges for Deleuze and Guattari in one of its guises as desire framed by the ideology of lack. Freeing desire in its multiple forms from the constraints imposed by the ideology of lack animates their questioning of political and psychoanalytic practices, as it animated the emancipatory projects of their predecessors in articulating this other discourse of desire.[34]

Chapter 12

DELEUZE AND GUATTARI: FLOWS OF DESIRE AND THE BODY

Dorothea E. Olkowski

The role and function of desire in human activities has been central to Western philosophy since Plato. Dominique Grisoni has traced the philosophical history of this concept in order to show to what extent it has been associated with negativity and lack and what the effect of this has been on thought and action.[1] Grisoni begins with Plato, whose bivalent treatment of desire has set the stage for all subsequent philosophical accommodations of this concept. Plato's manipulations of desire are grounded in his hypothesis that "man [*sic*] is not perfect *because* his Being is incomplete" (*OD*, 170). Desire enters the picture as a sign only, a mark of both "man's" "essential" or "ontic" incompleteness and its source (*OD*, 171). Yet, for Plato, desire also assumes positive characteristics: desire propels "man" toward full, complete Being, which, Grisoni argues, Plato identifies with "reason: culture, civilisation, the city, etc." (*OD*, 171).

Hidden in this trajectory is another story; this story is about power. Desire is aligned with power insofar as in Plato's story (here the *Symposium*) "man" climbs the ladder of Diotima in search of Being, "and so *submits himself to the laws* directing him towards this goal" (*OD*, 172, emphasis added). Grisoni concludes that once Plato established this "circuit of desire," moving from lack to reason and Being, it remained immutable (*OD*, 172). Reasserted and augmented by Freud, the relation of desire to power as good desire (life instincts) and bad desire (death instincts) was linked to the ever-present primal lack (*OD*, 177).

Gilles Deleuze and Félix Guattari take exception to this history and rewrite it. For them, desire is transformed into an activity, a process of production which, by assembling singularities, "manufactures effects" and is the real itself, not a sign of the real; desire orders and organizes bodies (*OD*, 178). Rather than following the paths of power, the law that regulates totalization, desire experiments and tinkers with what is aleatory and momentary (*OD*, 179). In short, desire manages to evade the power of law that is the mark of social power. However, social power cannot tolerate the multiplicity and freedom this conception of desire claims—for if it were truly desire, the power of negation (what Nietzsche calls "slave morality") would disappear as a cause.

Feminist philosophers have taken strong exception to this reading of and by Deleuze and Guattari. Among those who reject Deleuze's reformulation of desire, none has played a larger role than Judith Butler. In *Subjects of Desire: Hegelian Reflections in Twentieth-Century France,* Butler argues that Deleuze makes desire "the privileged locus of human ontology" (*SD*, 206), an ontology that is not historicized.[2] The absence of *specific* social and historical conditions qualifying Deleuze's conception of desire leads Butler to conclude that desire is an "ontological invariant," "a universal ontological truth" that Deleuze has managed to release from an interminable period of suppression. Butler refers to Deleuze's notion of desire as "emancipatory" (*SD*, 213) "a precultural eros" (*SD*, 214), "an originally unrepressed libidinal diversity," and "an ahistorical absolute" (*SD*, 215). "Libidinal diversity" is an odd condemnation, especially coming from Butler, since the willingness to locate desire in purely social and historical terms is principally what leads her to favor the work of Michel Foucault. Foucault, she believes, makes it possible for philosophy to break with the Hegelian system that always already accounts for any rupture with itself. Presumably, this is because Foucault investigates specific historical moments and orders.

Libidinal diversity, however, does not seem to run counter to an historical approach. So the problem must lie in the question of its relation to the ahistorical absolute. Are Deleuze and Guattari committing themselves to an ahistorical conception of desire? Or are they insisting upon a philosophical framework that provides an account, on an ontological level, of the constitution, deconstitution, and constitution again of libidinal diversity? Why do Deleuze and Guattari refuse to simply historicize desire and instead propose a philosophical framework, an ontological level that guarantees the flows of libidinal diversity? Obviously the dehistoricizing aspect of Deleuze's approach is in some sense central to everything Deleuze alone and Deleuze and Guattari together write. They confirm that "we are not, of course, doing history: we are not saying that a people invents this regime of signs, only that at a given moment a people effectuates the assemblage that assures the relative dominance of that regime under certain historical conditions."[3] How is it possible to insist upon an ontology that at least promotes certain modes of comportment while simultaneously insisting upon the real if not actual and material aspects of desire? These questions must be addressed in order to make sense of how and why there is no universal, original desire, no naturalized libido, but that even creative desire can only arise if guaranteed by a certain level of absraction. In order to do this, I will also begin to address Deleuze (and Guattari's) notion of bodies insofar as bodies and desire are inseparable in their thought, both conceptually and pragmatically.[4]

From the very beginning of Deleuze's work, he has played with and upon the notion of desire. Such play almost always turns upon a conception of the body. In *Nietzsche and Philosophy,* Deleuze articulates a multiplicity of connections involving the body, the notion of force, and desire.[5] He writes:

> What is the body? We do not define it by saying that it is a field of forces, a nutrient medium fought over by a plurality of forces. For, in fact, there is no medium, no field of forces or battle. There is no quantity of reality, all reality is a quantity of force. (*NP*, 44/39)

The body is not a medium, and body does not designate substance; but it does express the relationship between forces. Precisely because the relationship between forces is not constituted out of some kind of preexisting medium or preexisting reality, forces are never known, but only available for interpretation. With the term *body,* then, Deleuze is not simply referring to the psychophysiological bodies of human beings, but to "body" in its broadest sense. Bodies may be chemical, biological, social, or political, and the distinction between these modes is not, as Deleuze argues in *Difference and Repetition,* ontological.[6] If anything, it becomes, for Deleuze (with Guattari), semiological, a function of different regimes, different organizations of life.[7]

Ultimately, the "body" is too general a concept for Deleuze and Guattari and so is in need of greater articulation on a pragmatic and conceptual level. Even in the Nietzschean context, the forces that constitute a body are already differentiated by Deleuze as quantitative and qualitative. The difference in quantity between two forces is their "differential" element, but this is not another quantity; it can and must be a qualitative difference existing between two forces of different quantities. For if differences are not qualitative, then they are not real differences; they are not

188

differences in kind but only differences in degree. This is what makes it possible to speak of force as active or reactive in relation to other forces. Furthermore, without quality, in addition to quantity, bodies (chemical, biological, social, or political) would simply be motionless and dead. Hence forces are constituted differentially. A differential element, the relation to other forces, must always be present. No force can be quantitatively determined apart from its relation to other forces, and forces are differentiated qualitatively as different from all other forces. Equality would mean the elimination of any determination of force at all.

A body that actively dominates in one situation may well find itself dominated by other, stronger forces, and this has to be accounted for. When bodies are reactive, they *act* by reacting to other bodies. Thus, for Deleuze, desire is connected to active and reactive force. Citing Plato's *Gorgias,* Deleuze comments on Socrates's discussion with Callicles, and introduces a certain conception of desire. Like Callicles, Deleuze characterizes "law" as whatever separates (active) force from what it can do. The upside-down mirror image of reactive forces and negative will serve this function. For Callicles, as for Nietzsche, Deleuze argues, the weak cannot form a stronger force by banding together; rather, reactive forces can only stop active forces from doing what they do by confronting them with the upside-down image. Like Nietzsche, Callicles maintains that the slave does not cease to be a slave when he is triumphant; "from the point of view of nature, concrete force is that which goes to its ultimate consequences, to the limit of power (*puissance*) or desire" and which consequently has the strongest capacity for being affected (*NP,* 66–67, 59). And with regard to the body, "The more ways a body could be affected, the more force it had" (*NP,* 70, 62). But Socrates can only comprehend desire as pain followed by a pleasurable satisfaction—thus only as a reaction, or as the properties or symptoms of reactive forces—whereas for Deleuze, desire is the limit of a power and not its negation, so that "every body extends its power as far as it is able."[8] Limit ceases to be negation and is understood as "that point from which it [a thing] deploys itself, and deploys all its power" such that "the smallest becomes the equal of the greatest as soon as it is no longer separated from that which it is capable of"(*DR,* 55). As such, desire is what Nietzsche calls "will to power," and desire—here, will to power—is an immanent and qualitative principle; it is what experiments with forces.[9]

This articulation of desire characterizes Nietzsche's conception of force as that which goes to the limit of its power, as opposed to a notion of desire as reactive force, that is, the experience of pain negated by the experience of pleasure. This idea of desire as a reactive force is found in *Anti-Oedipus,* within a system that may be far more complicated than that of *Nietzsche and Philosophy,* but within a system that nonetheless relates desire to bodies.[10]

From a feminist point of view, *Anti-Oedipus* has been viewed suspiciously. Alice Jardine represents this position forcefully. Her criticism of Deleuze and Guattari is that they have abandoned the familial-psychoanalytic and even the academic-textual point of view for a cosmic vision of the world that is more likely to address "[s]ea animals, computers, volcanoes, birds, and planets than the bourgeois family hearth and its books."[11] Initially, Jardine claims that Deleuze and Guattari do away with "*any* concept of the body" (*GYN,* 211, emphasis added).[12] She finally, however, reassesses their work and comes to the none-too-flattering conclusion that their cosmic empiricism produces "denaturalized Bodies of all kinds—and most especially the human one." Such empiricism culminates in the notion of the "body without organs," a body emptied of fantasies so as to make way, not for a new body, but for new processes of production.[13]

The conception of "bodies without organs" is remarkable, original, and revolutionary in Deleuze and Guattari's work. If desire has been conceptualized in psychoanalysis as connected to bodies in such a way that desire is nothing but a reaction to the past that seeks images of the "impossible real," then, as Jacques Donzelot has argued:

> Deleuze and Guattari moved from this . . . [to the] retort that desire is the real itself. Why, they ask, see anything other than a difference in regime between desiring activity and social, technical, artistic, or political activity?[14]

Insofar as desire is never a desire for something, but is itself material production that can be regulated just like the rest of the social field, Deleuze and Guattari's is truly a nonhumanistic point of view. This means, however, that their argument is not about some kind of utopic projection. Rather Deleuze and Guattari argue that "it is correct to retrospectively understand all history in the light of capitalism" (*AO,* 163, 140), but only insofar as the desiring-production of bodies cannot be differentiated from the social production of capital which alone of all social machines "liberates flows of desire" (*AO*, 163,139), opening up the flows that realize the body without organs and desiring production. Desire, bodies, the real, the social—none of these make sense apart from an analysis of capitalism.

In *Anti-Oedipus*, Deleuze and Guattari address multiple issues and carry out many philosophical tasks at once. To name a few: the critique of psychoanalytic fantasy in the form of Oedipus, the extension of Marxist materialism to desire as well as a reconception of desire as positive, the refusal of Lévi-Strauss's conception of society as a structure of exchange, a refutation of Baudrillard's conception of a Lacanian unconscious enslaved to signs, and an examination of the limits of Wilhelm Reich's explanation of fascism, a schizoanalysis of capitalism, a celebration of artistic freedom at the threshold of capitalist economy. *Anti-Oedipus* is also the product of a certain era: the end of the alliance between Freud and Marx, the crumbling of Lacanian orthodoxy and Hegelian dialectics, and a refusal of the structuralism ushered in by Foucault's archeology. While I cannot hope to follow all these diverging movements, I will nonetheless trace out here some of the chief concepts involved in the "revolutionary" reconception of desire and the body.

One of Deleuze and Guattari's introductory images in *Anti-Oedipus* is a quote from Georg Büchner's *Lenz*:

> He [Lenz] thought that it must give one a sense of infinite bliss to be thus touched by the individual life of every form of creation, to have a soul that would communicate with stones, metals, water, and plants, as in a dream to absorb into oneself every being in nature, as flowers absorb air according to the waxing and waning of the moon.[15]

What attracts Lenz is being touched by the individual life of every form of creation, a soul in communication with every form of living thing (stone, metal, water, plant . . .), in short, to exist on a microlevel prior to the categorizations imposed by consciousness-culture. From a certain point of view, this would be, a kind of nothingness, but not the empty nothingness of negation. Lenz, Deleuze and Guattari conclude, has projected himself back to a time before the man-nature dichotomy, and lives nature as nothing but a process of production, so that "the self and the nonself, outside and inside, no longer have any meaning whatsoever" (*AO*, 8, 2). Yet even if we accept the determination that Lenz has "projected himself back" to a predichotomous era, it seems that Lenz has done this in the midst of a society that creates such dichotomies: man-nature, self-nonself, inside-outside. All these

191

and more impose themselves upon Lenz until he is forced to find relief in extreme actions just to "recall himself to consciousness" (*L*, 60). He throws himself into an icy fountain in the middle of the night; he jumps out a window, breaking or dislocating his arm; he attempts to pray, even to preach. These are all efforts to bring himself back to his "senses," to resocialize, to redichotomize, to conform to the social regime (in this case, the despotic semiotic of God and family).

But Lenz's initial insight into the connection between the stars, the sky, the mountains—all teeming with production—and himself is the insight that guides Deleuze and Guattari in their discussion of desire. Neither "man" nor nature, but rather the process of production "produces one within the other" and couples various processes together. The radicalized body, the molecular and micro-body communicating with stone, metal, water, and plant, is what they call "desiring-machines" (*AO*, 8, 2). Deleuze and Guattari articulate the first aspect of "process" in their explanation of "process of production" in precisely these terms. While such processes are unconscious, they are not necessarily "the secret repository of a meaning to be deciphered, but rather the state of coexistence of man and nature" in which there is nothing to express (*AS*, 30, 838). So they must not be characterized simply in human terms, and especially not in humanistic terms. Desiring-machines are everywhere; they are actively synthesizing with respect to all chemical, biological, social, and political bodies, all of which are the expressions of the relations between forces. Although these relations are pure processes, they are not purely arbitrary—elements or particles undergo syntheses and are "selected" by a process that is local, partial, and perceptual in nature. The first articulation, the production of production, in the geological formulation of *A Thousand Plateaus* is presented as "the process of 'sedimentation,' which deposits units of cyclic sediment according to statistical order" (*TP*, 55, 41). The second articulation is the process of recording that "sets up a stable functional structure and effects the passage from sediment to sedimentary rock"(*TP*, 55, 41). In other words, a stable functional structure is constituted, whether as geological formations or social formations. Each process involves coding, though the first is merely the creation of a certain order, while the second is already organized, thus overcoded, centered, unified, integrated, hierarchized, and finalized.

Processes of production, recording, and consumption are modes of ordering and organization called "syntheses." All syntheses are unconscious productions of desiring-machines, requiring the rethinking of all distinctions such as those between man-nature, industry-nature, society-nature, and their correlative spheres of production, distribution, and consumption. These dichotomies have long been taken for granted not only in philosophy but also in social and economic spheres. Likewise, the correlative spheres of production, distribution, and consumption are presumed to be separate. But, as Marx argued, if production, distribution, and consumption are taken to be separate from one another, this is only because capitalist industry believes that it extracts raw materials from nature, that it creates industrial products opposed to natural occurrences, and that the refuse and/or environmental pollutants it dumps back into the earth are simply the price "nature" must pay since all production emanates from the body of capital and presupposes "not only the existence of capital and the division of labor, but also the false consciousness that the capitalist being necessarily acquires, both of itself and of the supposedly fixed elements within an over-all process" (AO, 9, 4).[16]

Hence all distinctions between production, recording, and distribution, as well as all distinctions within these three syntheses of production (Deleuze and Guattari specifically name actions and passions, distributions and their coordinates, and sensual pleasure, as well as anxieties and pains) are part of one and the same process of production. From the point of view of capital, the productive nature of the three syntheses is invisible, and production is mapped, studied, and understood in specialized fields of knowledge organized according to industrial and social utility. Yet recording processes (those processes that set up stable, functional structures) are immediately utilized (thus, consumed), and consummations are immediately reproduced, such that there is nothing but process "incorporating recording and consumption within production itself, thus making them the productions of one and the same process" (AO, 10, 4).

As Lenz wished (and Marx's analysis determined), no differentiation is to be made between humans and nature. This is the second meaning of "process." Humans and nature are not opposite terms; they are not polar terms in relations of causation, ideation, or expression (subject and object) because all such differentiations are merely *idealizations* of the process of production. Instead, humans and nature are caught up in the essential reality of "the producer-product," the process for which desire serves as an immanent principle.

The third aspect of "process" is not a goal or an end in itself, but neither can it be extended indefinitely. Every force extends its power only as far as it is able, so the end of any process is simply its completion. When Deleuze and Guattari point out that productive and reproductive desiring-machines reach their completion, they are simply pointing to the fact that all desiring-machines are binary. Desiring-machines obey laws or sets of rules that govern the associations whereby one machine is coupled with another. "Production of production" has been characterized as a moving series of *conjunctions,* which have the logical form of " 'and . . . ' 'and then . . . ' " (*AO,* 11, 5) and are thus open wholes rather than unities that transcend their parts.[17] A flow is produced by one machine but interrupted or diminished by another machine, for while "desire causes the current to flow," it also "flows in turn, and breaks the flows" (*AO,* 11, 5).

In addition to being far from any kind of "emancipated desire," neither does the unconscious symbolize, imagine, or represent desire.[18] Donzelot expresses this point of view when he argues that Freud had certainly already made it possible to conceive of desire as extended to all "surfaces of contact" (polymorphous perversity), but what is different in Deleuze and Guattari's conception of desire is that "desire is no longer viewed as a desire *for something . . .* [but as] *the simultaneous desubstantialization and demystification of sexuality,* such that desire no longer has a precise substance or a meaning" (*AS,* 30). Indeed, given that the concept "body" must be taken in the broadest sense, and that productive syntheses assemble, in the least, stone, metal, water, plant, and animal, we can no longer make claims about desire as private, or subjective, or irrational, or directed by or toward the Imaginary, that is, by images of social norms.

Desiring-production is wholly social production; nature and society are neither opposites nor separate in any way, but express differences in intensities: increased or decreased heterogeneity and differentiation and different modes of organization, that is, forms of content and forms of expression. Insofar as it is not substantial, desire is simply machinic (not mechanical), that is, it *makes connections.* Lacan would call it the impossible "Real" (the process of production, which for Deleuze and Guattari is precisely not impossible). For Deleuze and Guattari, productive, unconscious desiring-machines are "the domain of free syntheses . . . [of] endless connections, nonexclusive disjunctions, nonspecific conjunctions, partial objects and flows" (*AO,* 63, 54).[19]

Following Deleuzes analysis of series in *Difference and Repetition,* unconscious desiring-production produces connections unless it is captured and "subjected to the requirements of representation." Representation demands that desiring-production yield to its hierarchy and to substance. Thus it must represent something like Oedipus, the despotic signifier, where production is no longer the production of real, unconscious processes but the reproduction of Oedipus as an imaginary thing, the "unconscious expression" (*AO,* 63–64, 54–55). When the Oedipal code converts all the flows of desiring-production into the detached signified "phallus," it provides the nonsignifying signs with a signifier, assigns sexuality to one of the sexes, and recasts the history of partial objects (machinic connections) into that of castration (lack)(*AO,* 87, 73).

The second, or disjunctive, synthesis is that in which desiring-machines attach themselves to the "body without organs" (the earth in primitive society, the despot in barbaric society, and capital in capitalist society), such that all the acts of humans and nature appear to emanate from social formation. Deleuze and Guattari maintain that restrictive Oedipal uses can be opposed but that the risks are high. For this synthesis imposes and demands negation in the form of either/or. When limited by Oedipus, the acts of the second synthesis force a choice, producing parent *or* child, man *or* woman, alive *or* dead—never both at once. As Brian Massumi points out, neither Oedipus nor capital can tolerate multiple identity; no unconscious desiring-production as trans-parentchild, transsexual, trans-alivedead affirmative use of disjunctive syntheses; no spanning between the disjuncts.[20]

The third syntheses, conjunctive syntheses, are those in which the productions of connective and disjunctive syntheses are brought together to constitute "races, cultures, and their gods" (*AO,* 101, 85). They indicate a social field. Once again, conjunctive syntheses are *both* segregative *and* exclusive (where one proclaims oneself part of the superior race or culture) or/and nomadic and polyvocal (where one finds "the outsider" as well as "minor becoming") (*AO,* 125, 105).

In *Anti-Oedipus* and *A Thousand Plateaus,* Deleuze and Guattari discuss what happens when these three syntheses of desiring-machines are subject to their exclusive Oedipal use and translate into the three great strata that bind us through social repression: the organism, significance, and subjectification, that is, lack, law, and signifier. Because desire is never the sign of lack or law but of force or power (*puissance*), what a body is *able* to do, the task of the body without organs is to "disarticulate" these strata, to disassemble them in order to open the body to connections (*TP*, 197, 159–60). Desiring-production confronts both social production and the "repression that the social machine exercises on desiring-machines," that is, the reproduction of psychic repression through social repression. Yet desiring-production does not posit an original free-flowing eros; rather, it assumes the existence of the "unconscious libidinal investment of sociohistorical production" (*AO*, 117, 98). As Eugene Holland argues, "Deleuze and Guattari insist on placing the family [Oedipalized desire] in its sociohistorical context and considering culture and society as a whole."[21] For them, social and cultural regimes always "override" the relatively limited Oedipal complex.[22] There are many forces that "Oedipalize" the unconscious (transgression, guilt, castration), and psychoanalysis merely reinforces the segregative and exclusive use of all the syntheses of the unconscious, stopping up creative flows (*AO*, 133, 112).

In the English preface to *Anti-Oedipus*, Michel Foucault argues that Deleuze and Guattari confront fascism, and not merely Oedipus, as their main adversary. However, their argument is not only against the historical fascism of Germany and Italy; more particularly, what they challenge is "the fascism in us all, in our heads and in our everyday behavior, the fascism that causes us to love power, to desire the very thing that dominates and exploits us" (*AO*, xii). Above all, this is a fascism of the body, the body of desiring production in all its articulations. Thus while Oedipus is clearly the signifier that stratifies and overcodes desiring-production in the capitalist social formation, it nonetheless only operates and can only operate within the context of a social system that needs it, that produces Oedipus as a fascism of the body.

In order for Oedipus to restrict desire, a "displacement" first takes place. What I have been referring to as "law" prohibits some aspect of desire, thereby persuading its subjects that *they* had the intention of trespassing against this law. Why bother? Why go to such lengths to control desire? Because, Deleuze and Guattari answer, desire *is* revolutionary. Their astonishing response is worth repeating at length:

> If desire is repressed, it is because every position of desire, no matter how small, is capable of calling into question the established order of a society: not that desire is asocial, on the contrary. But it is explosive; there is no desiring-machine capable of being assembled without demolishing entire social sectors. (*AO*, 138, 116)

Entire social sectors! An amusing hypothesis, they call this. Desire compromises exploitation, servitude, and hierarchy (exclusive connective, disjunctive, and conjunctive syntheses). Desire threatens the very being of a society when that society is organized in terms of these structures. The conclusion: Society must repress desire in order to continue reproducing itself. The problem is often how to distinguish "real" desiring-production from the social production that represses it and from the family, which is nothing but the agent of psychic repression (*refoulement*) bearing down on desire in the service of the social, displacing it through a process of disfigurment (*AO,* 142, 119). Under these conditions, in place of desiring-production, an Oedipal formation is synthesized: incest, desire for the mother, narcissism, hysteria. The upside-down mirror of Callicles appears again, this time in front of desire.

Even when unimpeded by the signifier, desiring-production is involved in some sort of ordering or organization. *Anti-Oedipus* articulates three types of "machinic" connections in both their nonrestrictive and restrictive uses. The nonrestrictive connective syntheses add together and so couple desiring-machines to produce localized and partial objects as well as the flow of production. They oppose the Oedipal, thus parental and conjugal restrictive syntheses that are subject to use by a despotic signifier that operates by "assigning lack to each position of desire" and, as Grisoni warns, "fusing desire to a law" (*AO,* 131, 110). Thus molar collective formations take precedence over molecular and multiple partial objects. Not Lenz's connection to stone, plant, metal, water, but hierarchical consciousness and consumable landscapes.

Too often, readings of *Anti-Oedipus* reflect only the restrictive and limitative aspects of the three syntheses. Yet nonrestrictive desiring-productions seem to be operating everywhere. Deleuze and Guattari punctuate their text with literary, musical, and visual-arts references to disruptions of social production as if this were the chief arena of action in which creative flows struggle for realization. Such flows and breaks of desiring-production are found in Marcel Proust's *Remembrance of Things Past,* where "the two sexes are both present and separate in the same individual: contiguous but partitioned and not communicating, in the mystery of an initial hermaphroditism."[23] Within the same entity, then, one finds heterosexual series, homosexual series, and transsexual series, which, on the *molar* level, indicate the existence of certain global persons who are fixed subjects and

197

fixed bodies, complete objects with regard to their sex (*AO*, 83, 70); but molecularly, they designate "the coexistence of fragments of both sexes, partial objects which do not communicate. *And it will be with them as with plants*" (*PS*, 120, emphasis added).

Molecularly (on the level Lenz longs for), elementally, we are all transsexual, flowing across all sexualities (*AO*, 82, 70). In every case, desiring-production produces the coupling and breaks the coupling. Such a process is a bricolage, indicating:

> the ability to rearrange fragments continually in new and different patterns or configurations; and as a consequence, an indifference toward the act of producing and toward the product, toward the set of instruments to be used and toward the over-all result to be achieved. (*AO*, 13, 7)

Thus, desiring-production is indifferent to capitalist divisions of process into production, recording, and consumption.

When couplings break and desiring-machines "break down," they are actually working at their best. In such circumstances they are destabilizing, deterritorializing, releasing flows that otherwise would be channeled into a (social) organism. Deleuze and Guattari also draw our attention to artists freely creating desiring machines which break down "within an object of social production." Ravel, for example, ends his compositions with "abrupt breaks, hesitations, tremelos, discordant notes, and unresolved chords, rather than allowing them to slowly wind down to a close or die away into silence," thereby breaking down or exploding the machines of social production (*AO*, 39, 31–32). In so doing, Ravel converts the regime of technical (capitalist) machines or social production into a regime of desiring-machines. Alternatively, one can look at the work of contemporary "sitework" artists such as Robert Smithson and Alan Sonfist, whose declared preference is to work with the "'infernal regions' like slagheaps, strip-mined wastelands, and polluted rivers," the dismal, silent, ugly, broken, and leftover.[24] Their sites and non-sites are likewise instances of the conversion of the regime of technical machines or capital and industrial production into the regime of desiring-machines, thereby breaking down social production. Similarly the artist Barbara Kruger writes: "If we experience life *only* through the filters of rigid categorizations, and binary oppositions, things will definitely be business as usual."[25] In Kruger's visual work, commercial slogans or popular clichés appear over the top of black-and-white images so as to multiply the possible senses of and put into question both those slogans and clichés and the social formation within which they have become banalities. In the process, Kruger deterritorializes rigid categorizations and binary oppositions to make way for sites of force that are otherwise unseen and unheard, unfelt and unknown.

In spite of the makeshift nature of the process of production, in spite of how desiring-machines continually break down, such a desire does not correspond to the negative and reactive desire of Socrates, which merely fills a lack, then disappears. Nor do the component pieces of desiring-machines fall apart and return us to a kind of nothingness, to "a pure fluid in a free state, flowing without interruption, streaming over the surface of a full body." Although pure fluids flowing without interruption are characteristics of the body without organs, nomadic flows of unstable matters are subject to an "important, inevitable phenomenon that is beneficial in many respects, and unfortunate in many others: stratification" (*TP,* 55, 40). "Desiring-machines make us an organism . . . [though] the body suffers from being organized in this way, from not having some other sort of organization, or *no organization* at all" (*AO,* 14, 8, emphasis added).

The body suffers from the organization of desiring-machines in the process of production, but also from no organization at all. This statement problematizes desire in a way not indicated in Deleuze's Nietzsche text. As such, the entire notion of desire comes into question in *Anti-Oedipus.* Clearly, there is no emancipatory, precultural eros, for desiring-machines are precisely what constitute our organization, what give us an order or an organism by means of their constant couplings and uncouplings, and what produce even the body without organs. And the body without organs, the "*field* of forces" (chemical, biological, social, and cultural), the field over which desiring-machines extend themselves, is the "body without an image," which—unless it escapes production by identifying producing and product in the process of production itself, which produces the nonproductive body without organs—suffers from the division of the production of production into production, distribution, and consumption. As Deleuze and Guattari claim, it would be better not to have any objects at all, which is not at all a matter of taking vows of poverty, but of affirming becoming.

In *Anti-Oedipus,* Deleuze and Guattari argue that the body without organs suffers the dichotomous organization of desiring-machines. It resists this organization by setting up a counterflow, reproducing itself, "putting out shoots to the farthest corner of the universe" (*AO,* 16, 10). For example: "In order to resist using words composed of articulated phonetic units, it utters only gasps and cries that are sheer unarticulated blocks of sound . . . 'primary repression' . . . this *repulsion* of desiring-machines by the body without organs" (*AO,* 15, 9). Such is the case in Antonin Artaud's translation of Lewis Carroll's "Jabberwocky." In *The Logic of Sense,* Deleuze compares Carroll's nonsense verse

> Twas brillig, and the slithy toves
> Did gyre and gymble in the wabe
> All mimsy were the borogoves,
> And the mome raths outgrabe[26]

with the schizophrenic Artaud's unarticulated blocks of sound:

> When Artaud says in his "Jabberwocky" "Until rourghe is to rouarghe has rangmbde and rangmbde has rouargnambde," he means to activate, insufflate, palatalize, and set the word aflame so that the word becomes the action of a body without parts, instead of being the passion of a fragmented organism. (*LS,* 110, 89–90)

Artaud's "breath-words" or "howl-words" correspond "to an organism without parts which operates entirely by insufflation, respiration, evaporation, and fluid transmission" (*LS,* 108, 88). This repulsion of desiring-machines is a repulsion by the body without organs; it actively repulses the organization of the body into organs that stratify the body in an act of capture that operates like a "black hole," overcoding and territorializing, even while the body without organs flees from territorialization, seeks to become destratified and deterritorialized, and sends out shoots and rhizomes (*TP,* 54, 40).

As in the case of Lenz, he functions, or tries to function, as an open system of desiring-production. "He" is a constant process of ordering and making connections, but this constant becoming-other takes place in a social framework that continually demands conformity to socially appropriate norms: praying, marrying, common sense. What is at stake is not simply a body trying to remain fluid, but a multiple-becoming resisting the imposition of certain kinds of desiring-machines by the social formation or social machines in the midst of a society that wants to limit this body within restricted parameters. Thus Deleuze and Guattari's analysis of the operations of capitalism conceptualizes the motion of bodies at the limit of their power and bodies dominated by stronger forces. For if the fluid body without organs is "captured" by the black hole of stasis and overcoding (the stable structural formations described above), there is another layer in this process: the social or cultural milieu, an even greater, that is, more powerful force which likewise captures the body so as to produce a surplus of consummation/consumption (*consommation*).

Every process of "social production" begins with a full body (whether that of earth, tyrant, or capital), that is, a *socius*, which, according to Marx, precedes the process of production of the body without organs. In fact, for Marx, there cannot be a production process without an already existent society holding land in some form (*G*, 88); in order for there to be becomings, there must be the body of the earth, the despot, or that of capital.[27] But the *socius* is more than land, for land is just another kind of body. The *socius* includes all types of bodies in processes of becoming, as well as a set of cultural norms with which to form them, to stop them up: law in the guise of the social, as Grisoni called it. So the *socius* often acts as the very apparatus of capture, the black hole, referred to above, which Lenz and Artaud flee in their efforts to become, to remain fluid bodies. Hence, the *socius* manifests an "unengendered nonproductive attitude, an element of antiproduction" (*AO*, 16, 10) or stasis, along with production.

Antiproduction, arresting the desiring-machine, is one of the body-without-organ's modes of resisting capture by social formations and explains why the body without organs is always at the limits of the social formation. This schizophrenic or absolute limit is not descriptive of schizophrenia as a pathology, rather, it is the organized and overcoded *socius* when its codes are scrambled or deterritorialized, that is, destabilized. However, it is not the only limit. The "genius" (I use that term guardedly) of capitalism is that it is the only social formation that makes use of decoded flows by substituting something even more oppressive than a code—a "quantifying axiomatic"—for the codes that would otherwise organize bodies in social formations. Thus capitalism is always the "relative limit" of any social formation (*AO*, 207, 176).

It would be a mistake to overvalorize primitive social formations given that the codes governing savage societies are both cruel and repressive. Alphonso Lingis describes the rituals of the Egret people, who brought their newly born children to the temple of Tlaloc, where the females would be bled from the ear and the males from the genitals, while adults drew blood from their own earlobes, tongues, thighs, upper arms, chests, or genitals.[28] These rituals "existed to drain ever greater multitudes of bloodsacrifices toward the pyramids of the sun the Aztecs erected on the *earth,* that monster whose maw swallows the setting sun, the remains of the dead, and sacrificial victims" (*AB,* 12, emphasis added). These practices, radically determinate as they are, have to do with connecting organs to the earth and marking bodies, prior to the existence of any state. Lingis also discusses the arrival of the Spanish conquerors, whose "imperial-despotic order seeks to extend its administration over subject societies and economies" (*AB,* 12). They demanded filiation, not with the earth, but with the despot, a coding directly opposed to that of primitive territorial alliances (*AO,* 229, 193), even though the primitive code continues to haunt or inhabit certain aspects of the despotic *socius* (*AO,* 230, 194).

Primitive and despotic social formations do whatever they can to ward off the capitalist social formation, the free flows of money and production that would open the door to quantification. To use money to buy something which, in turn, is sold for money is a process of quantification that cannot be coded, although it makes use of what is already coded to carry out these transactions. As a social formation, the body of capital is without a fixed center or an established authority figure, even while "exchange value and the market ruthlessly undermine and eliminate all traditional meanings and preexisting social codes" (*SA,* 407). Even though capital decodes every previous formation, opening desiring-production socially for the first time, free flows of desiring-production are not the outcome of capitalism.

The existence of capitalism is not the inexorable outcome of previous social coding; it has arisen due to the chance conjunction of two of these deterritorialized flows (a chance that required numerous conditions).[29] On one hand, some workers have nothing and are therefore forced to sell their labor in order to survive; and on the other hand, money is available to buy this labor (*AO,* 266, 225). Capitalism succeeds by appropriating for itself *all* the forces of production so that it appears to be the cause of all production coming from all bodies. Here Marx's analysis holds true, for:

> [T]hese productive powers and the social interrelations of labour in the direct labour-process seem transferred from labour to capital. Capital thus becomes a very mystic being since all of labour's social productive forces appear to be to capital, rather than labour as such. (*AO,* 17, 11)

As freely flowing desiring-production, the schizo-flows of Lenz or Artaud are one limit of capital; complete capture by despotic hierarchies is the other. We cannot simply assume that capital's desiring-production actually produces becoming. For, given that capital takes over the entire field of social production, it immediately operates to recapture free flows into "a world axiomatic that always opposes the revolutionary potential of decoded flows with new interior limits" (AO, 292–93, 246). Capital thus operates as a field of immanence, of which the schizo-flows are the exterior, the outside.

Capitalist machines decode and deterritorialize the previous machines, those of primitive or despotic societies, by

> transforming preexisting modes of production and consummation/consumption. Yet, territorial despotic machines reemerge within the capitalist machine (in the form of Oedipus in the family and in the form of reaping profits on previous investments in the social sphere) to code and recode, territorialize and reterritorialize the flows of desire that capitalism decodes. (SA, 408)

The nuclear family is one of the effects of recoding. It is an entity cut off from the social formation so as to be reterritorialized. The desiring-production of those caught in it is fixed on the objects "Mommy, Daddy"; psychoanalysis can attend to the Oedipal desire of the nuclear family with relative success precisely because of its overwhelming isolation from other social formations (SA, 410, 416 n. 13). But today, as the nuclear family continues to break down, "blame" is placed on a lack of paternal authority and maternal care. Deleuze and Guattari would point instead to the social formation itself.

In part, this condition is a function of something like the "integral atheism" Pierre Klossowki discovers in the work of the Marquis de Sade. Klossowski argues that, for de Sade, atheism is already operating within the norm of reason. "This atheism, the supreme act of normative reason has to institute the reign of the total absence of norms."[30] Normative reason presupposes atheism, which in turn guarantees human freedom, such that villainy is an act of freedom within rationality. However, by appealing to reason to justify villainy, de Sade's libertines also deride reason insofar as it claims to guarantee positive human behavior.

A further breakdown of the social structures is due to the force of market relations (SA, 411): "the bourgeoisie . . . has put an end to all feudal, patriarchal, idyllic relations . . . and has left remaining no other nexus between man and man than naked self-interest, than callous 'cash payment.'"[31] As such, Marx concludes, no occupation is honored; lawyer, priest, poet, and scientist are all reduced to wage laborers and to the axiomatic of cash (*SA*, 416 n. 14). These social phenomena account for the decoding of desiring production and the freedom that accompanies that decoding. According to Deleuze and Guattari, "capitalism tends toward a threshold of decoding that will destroy the *socius* in order to make it a body without organs," in order to make it possible to unleash flows of desire on the deterritorialized field (*AO*, 41, 33).

Yet within the capitalist social formation,

> as the nuclear family breaks down and increasingly fails to perform the oedipal reinscription of desire . . . psychoanalysis steps in to finish the job. If need be, the psychoanalyst shoulders the mantle of the despot in the famous "transference." (*SA*, 410)

In contemporary society, however, psychoanalysis performs this role less and less. Today the political state retains or resumes the despotic role. One only has to remember Senator Robert Dole's televised response to the U.S. President's 'State of the Union address' of January 1996. Again and again he urged Americans to go back, to return to the values they had abandoned: "We must . . . put parents back in charge of our schools, untie the hands of our police, restore justice to the courts and put our faith once again in the basic goodnesss, wisdom and self-reliance of our people."[32]

Unlimited parental authority, uninhibited police power, and an unrestricted punitive juridical system are all aspects of the despotic regime where the hierarchical arrangement of power remains the model for family, police, and juridical functions. Situating those claims amidst decreased funding in the United States for environmental protection and for the impoverished is a function of the capitalist social formation itself, a formation that sacrifices all desires to those of the capitalist machine. If there is a profitable way to protect the environment and care for the impoverished (an unlikely scenario), only then might the capitalist machine embrace these values.

One of the tasks of *Anti-Oedipus* is to question the right of the Oedipal or despotic image (referred to above as "law") to determine the organization of production. Deleuze and Guattari comment on the problem of the Oedipal image in *Anti-Oedipus*, noting that the great discovery of psychoanalysis was the production of desire, by which they mean production of the unconscious:

But once Oedipus entered the picture, this discovery was soon buried beneath a new brand of idealism: a classical [Oedipal Greek] theater was substituted for the unconscious as a factory; representation [the image] was substituted for the units of production of the unconscious; and an unconscious that was capable of nothing but expressing itself [as subject]—in myth, tragedy, dreams—was substituted for the productive unconscious. (AO, 31, 24)

Still, it is understandable how on the one hand, a people can come to desire their own repression or how, on the other hand, an individual can (in the midst of segregation and from out of a center of domination) proclaim herself to be revolutionary. If unconscious desiring-production is both segregated and Oedipalized, as well as polyvocal and nomadic, this is because every "social form of production exercises an essential repression of desiring-production" and "every position of desire, no matter how small, is capable of calling into question the established order of a society" and its global bodies; desire is "explosive," and every desiring-machine is completely capable of demolishing entire social sectors (AO, 138, 116). As I have emphasized above, the same set of syntheses produces both desire and its repression. Only the chemical, biological, social, or political body—nomadic and polyvocal or segregative and biunivocal—makes the difference.

The problem is that Western thinkers operate with the Platonic logic of desire. It is only a means to satisfying a need, or as Deleuze and Guattari state it, as part of an acqusition that makes desire into something negative, even nihilistic (AO, 32, 25). They credit Kant with at least conceiving of desire as a cause, even if it is the cause only of hallucinations and fantasies, of psychic realities, a definition tailor-made for psychoanalysis, which conceives of desire's fantasy object as the "double" of the "real" object of social production (AO, 32, 25). Ultimately, such an interpretation of desire only reinforces the Platonic conception of desire as lack of an absolute object, for the substitution of fantasies for "Ideas" is theoretically insignificant. Deleuze and Guattari argue, however, that desiring-production does not produce hallucinations; it is a *material* process of production, and naming desire as the cause of psychic realities only reinforces the conception of desire as "lack of a real object."

The Lacanian solution is unsatisfactory. According to Deleuze and Guattari, for Lacan, need, not desire, is what gets defined in terms of lack. But, desire, even while producing both itself and the fantasy (by detaching from the object), makes the lack absolute, never fulfillable. Thus the relation of need to the object

205

as something absolutely lacking remains the underlying support of the theory of desire, since even though desire produces the fantasy, there is always an object missing from the world, the one object that would fulfill the lack (*AO,* 33, 26).

For Deleuze and Guattari, if desire is to be construed as productive, rather than as negative and nihilistic, needs are simply derived from desire as a "countereffect of desire," an indication of the loss of desire and the loss of passive syntheses: a loss of the ability to produce within the realm of the real, the void that Deleuze and Guattari see ever so clearly as "the loss of the objective being of man" (*AO,* 35, 27). Such lacks are not the result of human nature or essence; rather, they are the *planned* result of social production that "falls back upon" and appropriates productive force. The market economy in the hands of its "dominant class" "deliberately organiz[es] wants and needs in the midst of an abundance of production" (*AO,* 35, 28). Such a power is indeed great insofar as it is able to fell desiring-production, to silence productive syntheses, under the force of the great fear (a created fear) of not having one's needs satisfied. Lack, then, is the effect of the separation of the process of production and the object, placing the real object outside of desiring-production (in the realm of the rational), and confining desiring-production to the production of fantasy.

Desire, however, as productive, must produce real products, not just the psychically real. Thus "desire is the set of *passive syntheses* that engineer partial objects, flows, and bodies, and that function as units of production. . . . Desire does not lack anything; it does not lack its object. It is, rather, the *subject* that is missing in desire" (*AO,* 34, 26). In the "autoproduction of the unconscious" the object is real; there is no place for a "fixed subject." And since there is no distinction between the process of production and the product, there is no distinction between desire and the objects of desire. As such, "desire is a machine, and the object of desire is another machine connected to it" (*AO,* 34, 26), the machine of the first machine. In order for there to be a "product," something gets detached from the process of desiring-production, making a place, a *residuum,* for the "nomadic subject," the subject that is not fixed. This "deterritorialization" of desiring-production is possible because, as Deleuze and Guattari state, "desiring-production is first and foremost social in nature, and tends to free itself only at the end" (even though social production derives from desiring-production under determinate conditions as well) (*AO,* 40, 33). The body without organs is the "ultimate residuum of a deterritorialized *socius*," that is, of a *socius* that ceases to "codify the flows of desire" by ceasing to inscribe and regulate them, thereby destablizing the *socius* (*AO*, 40, 33). This is in contrast to the revolutionary residual subject, in whom desiring-production "cuts across the interest of the dominated exploited classes, and causes flows to move that are capable of breaking apart both the segregations and their Oedipal applications" (*AO*, 125, 105). As the outsider, as deterritorialized, becoming is possible—becoming any dominated or exploited class, anything but the master nation, religion, or race, anything but the global body.

NOTES

CHAPTER 1: *ALETHEIA, POIESIS*, AND *EROS*: TRUTH AND
UNTRUTH IN THE POETIC CONSTRUCTION OF LOVE

1. Plato, *Symposium*, trans. W. R. M. Lamb (London: Heinemann, 1961), p. 111.
2. Michel Foucault, *The Use of Pleasure (The History of Sexuality,* volume 2) trans. Robert Hurley (New York: Pantheon Books, 1985), p. 225.
3. Stendhal, *Love,* trans. Gilbert Sale and Suzanne Sale (Harmondsworth, England: Penguin Books, 1975), pp. 275–78.
4. *The Poems of Sappho,* trans. Suzy Q. Groden (Indianapolis: Bobbs-Merrill, 1966), p. 20.
5. Ovid, *The Metamorphoses,* trans. Horace Gregory (New York: Viking Press, 1958), Book XV, p. 421.
6. Denis de Rougemont, *Love in the Western World,* trans. Montgomery Belgion (New York: Harper and Row, 1974). Henceforth cited as *LW*.
7. "Just as the simple taboo created eroticism in the first place in the organized violence of transgression, Christianity in its turn deepened the degree of sensual disturbance by forbidding organized transgression." Georges Bataille, *Eroticism: Death and Sensuality,* trans. Mary Dalwood (San Francisco: City Lights Books, 1986), p. 127.
8. "In the psychiatrization of perversions, sex was related to biological functions and to an anatomo-physiological machinery that gave it its 'meaning,' that is, its finality [i.e., reproduction], but it was also referred to an instinct which, through its peculiar development and according to the objects to which it could become attached, make it possible for perverse behavior patterns to arise and made their genesis intelligible." Michel Foucault, *The History of Sexuality (volume 1): An Introduction,* trans. Robert Hurley (New York: Random House, 1980), p. 153.
9. "It is evident . . . that every emission of semen, in such a way that generation cannot follow, is contrary to the good for man. And if this be done deliberately, it must be a sin. Now, I am speaking of a

way from which, in itself, generation could not result: such would be any emission of semen apart from the *natural* union of male and female. For which reason, sins of this type are called contrary to nature." Thomas Aquinas, *On the Truth of the Catholic Faith,* III, I, trans. Vernon J. Bourke, quoted in *Sexual Love and Western Morality,* ed. D. P. Verene (New York: Harper and Row, 1972), p. 121, emphasis added.

10. "A law being that which is *laid* down, *law* not too surprisingly comes, through Middle English *lawe,* earlier *laghe,* from Old English *lagu,* law, akin to and probably from Old Norse *lög,* law, originally the plural of *lag,* a layer or stratum, a due place, synonym Old Saxon *lag,* Old Frisian *laga.*" Eric Partridge, *Origins: A Short Etymological Dictionary of Modern English* (New York: Greenwich House, 1966), p. 353. Pokorny (the *American Heritage Electronic Dictionary*) and the *Shorter Oxford English Dictionary* give similar accounts.

11. See M. C. Dillon, "Sex, Love, and Natural Law Morality," in *The Ethics of Postmodernity: Contemporary Continental Perspectives,* ed. G. B. Madison (Evanston: Northwestern University Press, 1998).

12. The lived body provides an ambiguous but nonarbitrary measure for modes of erotic regulation. Castration of preadolescent males preserves the soprano range in their voices. Clitoridectomy may or may not dampen the development of erotic interest among preadolescent females. Circumcision seems to have salubrious effects, but perhaps at the expense of pleasure. The list goes on: Some cultures tattoo the bodies of the youth; others pierce earlobes, nipples, penises, noses, tongues; some bind feet, and others elongate necks or flatten heads. No culture leaves the body intact, unaltered, unadorned, unpainted, unstyled. Call it mutilation or enhancement, we modify the bodies of our youth in order to adapt them to our purposes and usually without soliciting the consent of the individual. I take bodily motility or functionality as a paradigm of freedom, and freedom as a measure of civilization. The point here is tenuous and might be defended better than I have, but it is worthy of consideration: The lived body provides a measure of the deployment of power lurking behind social construction.

13. See M. C. Dillon, *Semiological Reductionism: A Critique of the Deconstructionist Movement in Postmodern Thought* (Albany: SUNY Press, 1995). Chapter 6, in particular, offers a critical exegesis of Derrida's account of desire.

14. André Malraux, *La Monnaie de l'absolu,* p. 125. As quoted by Merleau-Ponty in "Indirect Language and the Voices of Silence," *Signs,* trans. Richard C. McCleary (Evanston: Northwestern University Press, 1964), p. 57.

15. "Of Don Juan we must use the word *seducer* with great caution. . . . This is not because Don Juan is too good, but because he simply does not fall under ethical categories. . . . [Don Juan] does not seduce. He desires, and this desire acts seductively. . . . I suppose he is a deceiver, but yet not so that he plans his deceptions in advance; it is the inherent power of sensuousness which deceives the seduced, and it is rather a kind of Nemesis." Søren Kierkegaard, *Either/Or,* vol. 1, trans. David F. Swenson and Lillian Marvin Swenson (Garden City, NY: Doubleday, 1959), p. 97. Tell that to Donna Anna, Søren, or to her father, the Commandatore, who sends Don Giovanni off to hell in a triumph of moral outrage.
16. "As letting beings be, freedom is intrinsically the resolutely open bearing that does not close up in itself." Martin Heidegger, "On the Essence of Truth," trans. John Sallis, in *Martin Heidegger: Basic Writings,* ed. David Farrell Krell (New York: Harper and Row, 1977), p. 133. Cf. endnote 9. Henceforth cited as *ET.*
17. "The inordinate forgetfulness of humanity persists in securing itself by means of what is readily available and always accessible. This persistence has its unwitting support in that bearing by which Dasein not only ek-sists but also at the same time *in-sists*" (*ET,* 135).

CHAPTER 2: BATAILLE'S EROTICISM, NOW:
FROM TRANSGRESSION TO INSIDIOUS SORCERY

1. Michel Foucault, "A Preface to Transgression," in *Language, Counter-Memory, Practice,* ed. Donald F. Bouchard (Ithaca: Cornell University Press, 1977), p. 43.
2. Georges Bataille, *Visions of Excess: Selected Writings, 1927–1939,* trans. Allan Stoekl (Minneapolis: University of Minnesota Press, 1985), p. xxiii. Henceforth cited as *VE.*
3. Georges Bataille, *Inner Experience,* trans. Leslie Anne Boldt (Albany: State University Press of New York, 1988), pp. 93–97. Henceforth cited as *IE.*
4. In situating this discussion in the discourse of desire, I insinuate Foucault's notion of "discourse" such that we might consider the ways by which it constitutes bodies, subjects/authors, and social relations. Thus I intimate Bataille's position vis-à-vis the development of a postmodern critical social theory, and the questions I raise here are akin to issues raised by Poster in his inquiry about the "mode of information." I do not, though, flesh out a critical theory here, nor am I focusing on electronic media, but I am asking about a certain "mediated eroticism." See Mark Poster, *The Mode of Information: Poststructuralism and Social Context* (Chicago: University of Chicago Press, 1990).

5. This phrase, and the chapter's epigraph, are from Georges Bataille, "The Sorcerer's Apprentice," in *The College of Sociology, 1937–39,* ed. Denis Hollier (Minneapolis: University of Minnesota Press, 1988), p. 21. Henceforth cited as *SA.*

6. Georges Bataille, *Oeuvres complètes,* vol. VI. *La Somme athéologique II. Sur Nietzsche. Memorandum. Annexes,* eds. Henri Ronse and Jean-Michel Rey (Paris: Gallimard, 1973), p. 429.

7. Georges Bataille, *Eroticism: Death and Sensuality,* ed. Robert Kastenbaum (New York: Arno, 1962; reprint, 1977), p. 17. Henceforth cited as *DS.*

8. Michele H. Richman, *Reading Georges Bataille: Beyond the Gift* (Baltimore: Johns Hopkins University Press, 1982), p. 70. Henceforth cited as *R.*

9. Georges Bataille, *My Mother, Madame Edwarda, The Dead Man,* trans. Austryn Wainhouse (London: Marion Boyars, 1989), p. 222.

10. Hélène Cixous, *Souffles* (Paris: Des femmes, 1975), pp. 9–10. Henceforth cited as *S.*

11. Georges Bataille, *The Impossible,* trans. Robert Hurley (San Francisco: City Lights Books, 1991), p. 9. Henceforth cited as *I.*

12. Georges Bataille, *Oeuvres complètes,* vol. III. *Oeuvres littéraires. Madame Edwarda. Le Petit. L'Archangélique. L'Impossible. La Scissiparité. L'Abbé C. L'Être indifférencié n'est rien. Le Bleu du ciel,* ed. Thadée Klossowski (Paris: Gallimard, 1971), p. 536.

13. Georges Bataille, "L'Existentialisme," *Critique.* 41, (October 1950): 83.

14. Georges Bataille, *Oeuvres complètes,* vol. II. *Écrits posthumes, 1922–1940,* ed. Denis Hollier (Paris: Gallimard, 1970), pp. 131–32. Henceforth cited as *VI.*

15. Allan Stoekl, *Politics, Writing, Mutilation: The Cases of Bataille, Blanchot, Roussel, Leiris, and Ponge* (Minneapolis: University of Minnesota Press, 1985), p. 131. Henceforth cited as *PWM.*

16. Georges Bataille, *Oeuvres complètes,* vol. VIII. *L'Histoire de l'erotisme. Le surréalisme au jour le jour. Conférences, 1951–53. La Souveraineté,* ed. Thadée Klossowski (Paris: Gallimard, 1976), p. 135. Henceforth cited as *HE.*

17. Paul Virilio, *Pure War* (New York: Semiotexte, 1983), p. 83; Jean Baudrillard, *Forget Foucault* (New York: Semiotexte, 1987), pp. 128–29.

18. Georges Bataille, *The Tears of Eros,* trans. Peter Connor (San Francisco: City Lights Books, 1989), p. 20.

19. Steven Shaviro, *Passion and Excess: Blanchot, Bataille, and Literary Theory* (Tallahassee: Florida State University Press, 1990), p. 116.

20. Georges Bataille, *Theory of Religion* (New York: Zone Books, 1989), p. 43.

21. Alphonso Lingis, *Libido: The French Existential Theories* (Bloomington: Indiana University Press, 1985), p. 7. See also *IE*, p. 60, for how this possible mockery is not the "ecstasy" and *non-savoir* Bataille took to be so important for human destiny.

CHAPTER 3: THE (NON)LOGIC OF DESIRE AND WAR: HEGEL AND LEVINAS

1. Georg Wilhelm Friedrich Hegel, *Phänomenologie des Geistes* (Hamburg: Felix Meiner, 1952); *Phenomenology of Spirit,* trans. A. V. Miller (Oxford: Oxford University Press, 1977). Henceforth cited as *PhG*. German pagination is cited first, followed by the English page reference.

2. Georg Wilhelm Friedrich Hegel, *Wissenschaft der Logik,* 2 vols. (Hamburg: Felix Meiner, 1951); *Science of Logic,* trans. A. V. Miller (New York: Humanities Press, 1969). Henceforth cited as *WL*. (German, then English pagination).

3. Hyppolite deals with this question at both the beginning and the conclusion of his massive study on Hegel, but acknowledges that "it is a problem which fundamentally will remain insoluble because it will lead us to ask whether Hegel's philosophy is itself a phenomenology or an ontology. It is both, no doubt, but which is the authentic proceeding, which is the source of Hegelianism? Is Hegel's logic independent of all phenomenology?" Jean Hyppolite, *Genesis and Structure of Hegel's Phenomenology of Spirit,* trans. S. Cherniak and J. Heckman (Evanston: Northwestern University Press, 1974), p. 56.

4. This essay develops and coalesces under the thematic of desire ideas presented in my *Altared Ground: Levinas, History, and Violence* (New York: Routledge, 1996). There I focused on the broader themes of the history of philosophy and the constitution of ethical subjectivity and intersubjectivity.

5. In order to distinguish Levinas's conception of Desire *(désir)* from Hegel's *(Begierde),* I will employ a capitalized "D" when referring to Levinas's usage of the term.

6. I will follow the convention in the English translations of Levinas's work by translating *autrui* (the personal other/s) as "Other" with a capitalized "O" and *l'autre* (otherness in general; alterity) as "the other."

7. Plato, *Republic,* 509b.

8. Georg Wilhelm Friedrich Hegel, *Die Wissenschaft der Logik. Erster Teil, Enzyklopädie der philosophischen Wissenschaften* (1830), ed. F. Nicolin and O. Pöggeler (Hamburg: Felix Meiner, 1959); *Logic: Part One of the Encyclopedia of the Philosophical Sciences,* trans. W. Wallace (Oxford: Clarendon Press, 1975), §215.

9. On the logic of Levinas's argument against Hegel, see Jean-François Lyotard, "Levinas's Logic," trans. I. McLeod, in *Face to Face with Levinas,* ed. R. Cohen (Albany: SUNY Press, 1986), pp. 117–30. Lyotard writes that "Levinas struggles to escape the Hegelian persecution" (p. 121) by attacking "Hegelian alterity so as to show that it is only a caprice of identity" (p. 119).

10. Emmanuel Levinas, *Totalité et infini* (La Haye: Martinus Nijhoff, 1961), pp. 5–6; *Totality and Infinity,* trans. A. Lingis (Pittsburgh: Duquesne University Press, 1969), p. 21. Henceforth cited as *TI* (French, then English pagination).

11. Levinas characterizes traditional forms of metaphysics, including Hegel's and Heidegger's, as "ontology." Even though he does not retain the term "metaphysics" in his later work, I will continue to use it in reference to his philosophy. Depending upon the context, I will distinguish it from classical or traditional metaphysics.

12. See Edith Wyschogrod, "Derrida, Levinas, and Violence," in *Derrida and Deconstruction* (Continental Philosophy–II), ed. H. J. Silverman (New York: Routledge, 1989), pp. 183–200, esp. p. 191.

13. According to Adorno, a "preponderance of the object" requires "a total self-relinquishment" of the subject. Theodor W. Adorno, *Negative Dialectics,* trans. E. B. Ashton (New York: Continuum Press, 1973), p. 183 ff.

14. Alexandre Kojève, *Introduction to the Reading of Hegel,* trans. A. Bloom and J. Nichols (New York: Basic Books, 1969), esp. pp. 3–70. Also see Judith Butler, *Subjects of Desire: Hegelian Reflections in Twentieth-Century France* (New York: Columbia University Press, 1987) for an overview of the French reception of Hegel; and Vincent Descombes, *Modern French Philosophy,* trans. L. Scott-Fox and J. M. Harding (Cambridge: Cambridge University Press, 1980) for an analysis of the relation between Kojève's interpretation of Hegel and nihilism.

15. See Robert Bernasconi, "Hegel and Levinas: The Possibility of Reconciliation and Forgiveness," in *Archivio di Filosofia* 54 (1986): 325–46; "Levinas Face to Face—With Hegel," *Journal of the British Society for Phenomenology* 123, no. 3 (1982): 267–76.

16. See Piotr Hoffman, *Violence in Modern Philosophy* (Chicago: University of Chicago Press, 1989), esp. p. 149, on this point.

17. See Drucilla Cornell, *The Philosophy of the Limit* (New York: Routledge, 1992), p. 91 ff.

18. See Emmanuel Levinas, *Autrement qu'être ou au-delà de l'essence* (La Haye: Martinus Nijhoff, 1974), pp. 129–56; *Otherwise Than Being or Beyond Essence,* trans. A. Lingis (The Hague: Martinus Nijhoff, 1978), pp. 81–98; "Phenomenon and Enigma," esp. pp. 64–66, and

"Language and Proximity," pp. 109–26, in *Collected Philosophical Papers*, trans. A. Lingis (Dordrecht and Boston: Kluwer Academic Publishers, 1987).

19. See Emmanuel Levinas, *En découvrant l'existence avec Husserl et Heidegger* (Paris: J. Vrin, 1967, 1988), p. 207 ff.; "Phenomenon and Enigma," in *Collected Philosophical Papers*, p. 64 ff.; revised trans. R. Bernasconi and S. Critchley, "Enigma and Phenomenon," in *Basic Philosophical Writings*, ed. A. Peperzak, S. Critchley, and R. Bernasconi (Bloomington and Indianapolis: Indiana University Press, 1996), p. 69 ff.

20. Jacques Derrida, "Violence and Metaphysics," in *Writing and Difference*, trans. A. Bass (Chicago: University of Chicago Press, 1978), p. 93.

CHAPTER 4: INSCRIBING THE "SITES" OF DESIRE IN LEVINAS

1. See Vincent Descombes, *Le même et l'autre, Quarante-cinq ans de philosophie française (1933–1978)* (Paris: Editions de Minuit, 1979), chapters 2 and 3, pp. 71–130, here p. 119. Henceforth cited as *MA*. English translation by L. Scott-Fox and J. M. Harding, *Modern French Philosophy* (New York: Cambridge University Press, 1980).

2. For his discussion of numerous twentieth century philosophies'— most notably Heidegger's—call to return to "Life" in its sensuous fullness, see Gianni Vattimo, *Introduzione a Heidegger* (Rome: Gius Laterza & Figli, 1971/82). French translation by J. Rolland, *Introduction à Heidegger* (Paris: Éditions du Cerf, 1985), chapter 1, "*Neokantisme, phénomènologie, existentialisme,*" pp. 11–23. Jacques Derrida first referred to Levinas's work, in light of Husserl's transcendental factuality (*Urtatsache*), as a paradoxical empiricism. See "*Violence et Métaphysique: Essai sur la pensée d'Emmanuel Levinas*" in *L'écriture et la différence* (Paris: Editions du Seuil, 1967), p. 189 ff; *Writing and Difference*, trans. Alan Bass (Chicago: University of Chicago Press, 1978), pp. 151–52. Henceforth cited as *VM*. Note, however, that the ambiguity inherent in phenomenology's approach to the signifying "facticity" of the pre-eidetic earns for it just as well the designation of "concrete, idealist philosophy" (*MA*, 72, 87).

3. Bernard Forthomme, *Une Philosophie de la transcendance: La métaphysique d'Emmanuel Levinas* (Paris: Vrin, 1979). See also Emmanuel Levinas, *Otherwise than Being or Beyond Essence,* trans. A. Lingis (Dordrecht and Boston: Kluwer Academic Publishers, 1991). Henceforth cited as *OB*.

4. See Emmanuel Levinas, *De l'évasion,* ed. Jacques Rolland (Montpellier: Fata Morgana, 1982) and Emmanuel Levinas, *Totalité et infini*

(La Haye: Martinus Nijhoff, 1961); *Totality and Infinity,* trans. A. Lingis (Pittsburgh: Duquesne University Press, 1969).

5. Jacques Rolland remarks in his *"Sortir de l'autre par une nouvelle voie"* (introduction to *DE*) that Levinas's nausea corresponds to the experience of uncanniness, or *Unheimlichkeit,* which Heidegger describes in *Was ist Metaphysik?* (Frankfurt: V. Klostermann, 1969). Thus nausea—as understood by Rolland here, namely as the sentiment of being cut loose from entities and drifting on an open sea—would be the *Stimmung* or uneasy state of mind or soul through which nothingness reveals itself (*DE,* 59). Rolland discusses scrupulously the French translations of *unheimlich* and suggests a relation of virtual succession between the feeling as "not-at-home" and that of being oppressed (*on se sent opprimé*) or being discomfited (*un malaise nous gagne*). Of course, the feeling of "not-at-home" or uncanniness is already characteristic of *Angst* in *Being and Time.* See Martin Heidegger, *Being and Time,* trans. J. Macquarrie and E. Robinson (New York: Harper and Row, 1961), p. 233. Henceforth cited as *BT.* However, Rolland suggests that with nausea (and he reminds us that this insight precedes Sartre's novel of the same name) Levinas has deepened the analysis of anguish characterizing only the suspense in which we ourselves and things fall into indifference (cf. *DE,* 29). This remark is extremely important for its insight into the turning of a state-of-mind or "tonality" *precisely into a passion.* This turning corresponds to a structure found in *Otherwise than Being or Beyond Essence.* There, the turning moves *from* the crispation or contraction of the subject behind itself in obsession and persecution *to* the opening outward of making oneself a sign, of Saying, substitution, and sincerity.

6. See *Being and Time,* p. 435.

7. Indeed, in his notes to *De l'évasion,* Rolland draws a parallel between Levinas's discussion of being tied to being and his remarks about being tied to Judaism, pronounced three years later in an essay entitled "The Spiritual Essence of anti-Semitism according to Jacques Maritain" (*DE,* 105).

8. *De l'existence à l'existant* (Paris: J. Vrin, 1973), first published in 1947; *Existence and Existents,* trans. A. Lingis (Dordrecht: Kluwer Academic Publishers, 1978). Henceforth cited as *DEAE.*

9. As Levinas writes, "The instant is par excellence the fulfillment of existence" (*DEAE,* 130/78). This instant is a relation that does not refer to the future, but rather to the here and now; space as the act of (self-) positing "is not transcended" (pp. 135–38, 82–85, see also *PR,* 289).

10. Emmanuel Levinas, *Totality and Infinity: An Essay on Exteriority*, trans. A. Lingis (Pittsburgh: Duquesne University Press, 1969). Henceforth cited as *TI*.

11. In paying tribute to his friend and sponsor at the *Collège de philosophie*, Jean Wahl, Levinas praises the latter's conception of the paradoxes of transcendence in a language that is as "Levinasian" as it is proper to Wahl: "'Our destiny?' There is a reversal here. In reality 'the metaphysical question . . . puts us ourselves in question as well as it does the world.' The adventure overflows humanity [*l'humain*] and thereby sketches the humanity in which the pulse of this life of transcendence beats. Would not humanity be—of itself—the originary movement of surpassing. . . . Transcendence makes use of humanity, of thought, of consciousness. It is not reduced to the organs or functions to which it calls. It is not reduced to manifestation. Whence the mysterious formulas [of Wahl] such as: 'That of which one is aware [*a conscience*] is that of which one is not conscious. It is that which does not think that thinks. The body as symbol [*Corps symbole*] of this *that which does not think, which thinks* . . .' Consciousness and thought arise therefore in an event which they neither exhaust nor embrace, and which gives rise to them in order to fulfill itself in them. Would this *beyond* be symbolized by the in-side [*en-deça*] of the body for which, according to materialism, consciousness is the epiphenomenon? Or by the flesh in which the spasm is a possibility? The interchangeability of the *beyond* and the *in-side*—or the *very high* [*très haut*] and the *very low* [*très bas*] . . . belongs to the deepest of [Wahl's] thought. Important above all is transcendence. In the metaphysical experience, beyond *knowing*, the human adventure plays out a divine comedy." See Levinas et al., *Jean Wahl et Gabriel Marcel* (Paris: Beauchesne, 1976), p. 21 (my translation). Worth noting is the theme of "divine comedy," or the enigmatic idea of humanity caught up in a relation with what is infinitely beyond it. The theme and the formula is expressed in *Otherwise Than Being or Beyond Essence* at the paradoxical point where transcendence, my desire for the undesirable other, and social justice cross each other (see p. 145 ff.). It is also the title of the fourth section of Levinas's significant 1976 essay "God and philosophy," in *Collected Philosophical Papers,* trans. A. Lingis (Dordrecht and Boston: Kluwer Academic Publishers, 1993), pp. 162–66. Henceforth cited as *CPP*.

12. Also note J. Derrida's discussion of this passage in the light of the logic underlying Levinas's move away from Husserl, toward Heidegger, and subsequently away from Heidegger as well (*VM*, 132 ff.).

13. Levinas, *Time and the Other,* trans. Richard Cohen (Pittsburgh: Duquesne University Press, 1987). See p. 85 for a discussion of the alterity of the "feminine." Henceforth cited as *TA.*

14. Faithful to his thematic of the instant in *De l'Existence à l'existant,* Levinas calls this contraction the "interval" in *Totality and Infinity.*

15. In a passage where the influence of Franz Rosenzweig is palpable, Levinas writes, "The constitution of the interval that liberates the being from the limitation of fate calls for death. The nothingness of the interval—a dead time—is the production of infinity. Resurrection constitutes the principal event of time. There is therefore no continuity in being. Time is discontinuous. . . . In continuation the instant meets its death, and resuscitates; death and resurrection constitute time. But such a formal structure supposes the relationship of the I [*Moi*] to the other [*Autrui*] and, at its basis, fecundity across the discontinuity that constitutes time." (*TI,* 284, trans. modified).

16. In contradistinction to both Heidegger and Sartre, Levinas argues "Life is *love of life,* a relation with contents that are not my being but more dear than my being: thinking, eating, sleeping, reading, working, warming oneself in the sun. Distinct from my substance but constituting it, these contents make up the worth [*prix*] of my life. When reduced to pure and naked existence . . . life dissolves into a shadow. Life is an existence that does not precede its essence. Its essence makes up its worth [*prix*]; and here value [*valeur*] constitutes being. The reality of life is already on the level of happiness" (*TI,* 112).

17. When defined in this way, "need" becomes almost indistinguishable from our quotidian, worldly desire and desires.

18. Note Miguel Abensour's observation in regard to Levinas's first philosophical "formalization" of the space of intersubjectivity as utopian: "The primary concern of Levinas is to find the right place [*la place juste*] of utopia, to determine the element to which it belongs or in which it bathes. . . . The first move of Levinas thus consists in making utopia emigrate from the [anthropological and political] sites in which it loses itself and to return it to its primary element, the inter-human relationship, or better the *human bond.* . . . The [critical] insistence of Levinas upon the anthropology of Buber shows well that for Levinas utopia belongs neither to the order of comprehension, nor to that of sciences [*connaissances*]—of laws of society or laws of history—but, rather, to the register of the Encounter." See Miguel Abensour, *"Penser l'utopie autrement"* in *Cahier de l'Herne: Emmanuel Levinas,* eds. M. Abensour and C. Chalier (Paris: Éditions de l'Herne, 1991), pp. 572–602, here pp. 574–75. English translation by B. Bergo, *Graduate Faculty Philosophy Journal* 20: vols. 2–3 (1997).

19. Yet Levinas kept a deep respect for the contribution of Heidegger's thinking of time. Rather than considering time from the presupposition of time, or space, Heidegger conceived human temporality from human situations. Levinas argues, it seems against Saint Augustine, among others, "The image of a straight line, where the instants are past when they are no longer there, or future when they are not yet there, is a definition of time by time, a tautology. I think then of the importance of notions like those that Heidegger called 'ecstasies of time,' where the past, the present, and the future are considered by Heidegger starting from concrete circumstances of the human being." See G. Petitdemange and J. Rolland, *Autrement que savoir. Emmanuel Levinas* (Paris: Éditions Osiris, 1988), p. 92. Note that Heidegger was not the only object of Levinas's critique. As John Llewelyn has pointed out, *Totality and Infinity* also proceeds as an on-going debate with Hegel's phenomenology. For a discussion of this dimension of *TI,* see J. Llewelyn, *Emmanuel Levinas: Genealogy of Ethics* (London and New York: Routledge, 1995), p. 105 ff.

20. See Adriaan Peperzak, *To the Other* (West Lafayette, IN: Purdue University Press, 1993), p. 202 ff.

21. See Levinas's answer to H. Heering, in "Questions et Réponses," *De Dieu qui vient à l'idée,* 2nd ed. enlarged (Paris: Librairie J. Vrin, 1986), p. 139. "In *Totality and Infinity* the language is ontological because it wants above all not to be psychological. But in reality it is already a search for what I call 'the beyond being,' the tearing of this equality unto self which is always being . . . whatever the attempts to separate it from the present." In precisely this framework, what Levinas calls "ethics" "is like the reduction of certain languages" to what one could call the first shock of their meaning. See *De Dieu,* p. 140 ff.

22. This undertaking resembles Husserl's own struggle against "descriptive psychology" during the period after the publication of the first edition of the *Logical Investigations* and the sketches for the *Ideas.* See Jean-François Lavigne's introduction to *Edmund Husserl: Chose et Espace. Leçons de 1907* (Paris: P.U.F., 1989), pp. 5–19. This is a translation of Ulrich Claesges' edition of *Ding und Raum. Vorlesungen 1907* (The Hague: M. Nijhoff, 1973).

23. This point has been made by a number of commentators, including J. Derrida (in "Violence and Metaphysics") and most recently and succinctly by A. Peperzak in *Toward the Other,* pp. 208, 212.

24. See Marc Richir's provocative remarks on the subject in *Otherwise than Being or Beyond Essence* (See "Phénomène et infini" in *Cahier de l'Herne. Emmanuel Levinas,* eds. M. Abensour and C. Chalier

[Paris: Éditions de l'Herne, 1991], pp. 224–56. Henceforth cited as *PI.*). His use of the term "phenomenological unconscious" would refer to what Levinas calls the structure of sensibility and affect. Richir takes pains to argue that this does *not* refer *just* to the subjectivity invested or called upon by the other, but signifies also the irrecoverable hiatus between the passive openness of sensuous existence (and in-sistence) and the always tautological form of intentionality as noesis-noema.

25. See J. Rolland and S. Petrosino, *La Verité nomade. Introduction à Emmanuel Levinas* (Paris: Éditions La Decouverte, 1984), pp. 131–32.

26. He writes, "But it is here important to underline the possibility of the libido in the more elementary and more rich signification of proximity, a possibility included in the unity of the face and the skin. . . . Beneath the erotic alterity there is the alterity of the-one-for-the-other, responsibility before *eros.*"

27. Marc Richir has done this admirably however. See Richir's "Phénomène et infini" cited above.

28. Thus, as Richir points out, "The amphibology is, as Levinas recalls ceaselessly, that of Being and of the being, of the pure movement of appearing within the stasis from the Same to the Same, to the result or the residue of appearing as such within the appearing of such and such a being, fixated and recognized in the eidetic. . . . The property of this stasis of the Same unto the Same is to temporalize itself in a temporal phase, presence, which is supposed to be homogeneous in so far as it contains in itself *its* memory . . . and *its* anticipation. . . . Phenomenology is thus tautological" (*PI,* 226–27).

29. Gillian Rose, *The Broken Middle: Out of Our Ancient Society* (Oxford, UK and Cambridge, MA: Blackwell Publishers, 1992), p. 262. Henceforth cited as *TBM.* For Levinas's essay, "The Pact," see Sean Hand, *The Levinas Reader* (Oxford, UK and Cambridge, MA: Blackwell Publishers, 1993), pp. 211–26. For his essay entitled "The Ego and Totality" see *CPP,* pp. 25–45 (here p. 30).

30. See, for example, *Totality and Infinity,* p. 213.

31. Rose, *The Broken Middle.* For a concise confrontation of Rilke and Levinas see pp. 252, 254 ff.; for a discussion of Levinas and Kierkegaard, see p. 5 ff.

32. See Levinas, "The Pact,", pp. 98–9. Cited by Rose (*TBM,* 263, emphasis added).

33. This desire, according to Levinas, "finally abolish[es] the distinction between form and content" (*TI,* 51). To be sure, but then the resurfacing of, say, one pole of this duality, however polemical its function here, becomes ambiguous.

CHAPTER 5: SARTRE: DESIRING THE IMPOSSIBLE

1. *L'Imaginaire* (Paris: Gallimard, 1940), p. 246. All translations are mine.
2. A. N. Leak, *The Perverted Consciousness, Sexuality and Sartre* (London: Macmillan, 1989); see chapter 3, esp. p. 65.
3. Jean-Paul Sartre *Oeuvres Romanesques* (Paris: Gallimard, 1981). Henceforth cited as *OR.*
4. See Jean-Paul Sartre *L'Être et le Néant,* 1943; *Being and Nothingness,* trans. Hazel Barnes (New York: Washington Square Press, 1956). Henceforth cited as *EN.* See p. 484 n. 1. Also p. 484 n. 1, and p. 721.
5. See my chapter on Genet in *Sartre's Theory of Literature* (London: M.H.R.A., 1979).
6. *Cahiers pour une morale* (Paris: Gallimard, 1983), p. 485.
7. Jean-Paul Sartre, *Saint Genet* (New York: New American Library, 1963). Henceforth cited as *SG.* I have discussed this more extensively in my chapter on "Notes for an Ethics" in *Sartre: The Necessity of Freedom* (Cambridge: Cambridge University Press, 1989).
8. Sartre's relation to Lacan calls out for an exploration of this point, but that will be another story.

CHAPTER 6: SIMONE DE BEAUVOIR'S DESIRE TO
EXPRESS *LA JOIE D'EXISTER*

1. Simone de Beauvoir, in Hélène V. Wenzel, "Interview With Simone de Beauvoir," *Yale French Studies* 72 (1986), p. 12.
2. For example, in the same *Yale French Studies* volume, Martha Noel Evans, "Murdering *L'invitée*: Gender and Fictional Narrative," pp. 67–86, and Elaine Marks, "Transgressing the (In)cont(in)ent Boundaries: The Body in Decline," pp. 181–200.
3. "Women Have Less Far to Fall," in Alice Schwarzer, *After The Second Sex: Conversations With Simone de Beauvoir,* trans. Marianne Howarth (New York: Pantheon, 1984), pp. 84, 88–89.
4. Simone de Beauvoir, *She Came to Stay,* trans. L. D. Drummond (Cleveland and New York: World, 1954). Henceforth cited in the text as *SCTS.*
5. *L'existentialisme et la sagesse des nations* (Paris: Nagel, 1963), pp. 89–107. Henceforth cited in the text as *LM.* Originally in *Les Temps Modernes* I (April 1946), pp. 1153–63.
6. Simone de Beauvoir, *Force of Circumstance,* trans. Richard Howard (New York: Penguin, 1968), p. 75.
7. Simone de Beauvoir, *The Prime of Life,* trans. Peter Green (London: Penguin, 1965), p. 48.
8. *Sartre by Himself: A Film,* directed by Alexandre Astruc and Michel Contat, trans. Richard Seaver (New York: Urizen Books, 1978), p. 28.

9. Kate Fullbrook and Edward Fullbrook, *Simone de Beauvoir and Jean-Paul Sartre: The Remaking of a Twentieth Century Legend* (New York: Harper Collins/Basic Books, 1994), p. 101.

10. Edmund Husserl, *Méditations cartésiennes*, trans. Gabrielle Pfeiffer and Emmanuel Levinas (Paris: Armand Collin, 1960); *Cartesian Meditations*, trans. Dorion Cairns (The Hague: Martinus Nijhoff, 1960).

11. *Le Malheur de la conscience dans la philosophie de Hegel*, second edition (Paris: Presses Universitaires de France, 1951). See especially "La Place de L'Idée de la Conscience Malheureuse dans la Formation des Théories de Hegel," pp. 10–118.

12. Simone de Beauvoir, *Lettres à Sartre: 1940–1963*, vol. II, ed. Sylvie Le Bon de Beauvoir (Paris: Gallimard, 1990), p. 201.

13. Hegel, *Early Theological Writings*, trans. T. M. Knox (Chicago: University of Chicago Press, 1948), pp. 305–6.

14. Alexandre Kojève, *Introduction to the Reading of Hegel*, assem. Raymond Queneau, ed. Allan Bloom, trans. James H. Nichols Jr. (New York: Basic Books, 1969), p. 12.

15. Toril Moi, *Simone de Beauvoir: The Making of an Intellectual Woman* (London: Blackwell, 1994), p. 129. Henceforth cited as *IW*.

16. Maurice Merleau-Ponty, "Metaphysics and the Novel," in *Sense and Non-Sense*, trans. Hubert L. Dreyfus and Patricia Allen Dreyfus (Evanston: Northwestern University Press, 1964), pp. 32–40.

17. *Witness to My Life: The Letters of Jean-Paul Sartre to Simone de Beauvoir, 1926–1939*, ed. Simone de Beauvoir, trans. Lee Fahnestock and Norman MacAfee (New York: Charles Scribner and Sons, 1992), p. 234.

18. Jacques Deguy, "*L'invitée*, et *Les Mandarins*" in *Roman 20–50*, 13 (June 1992), pp. 53–63.

19. Jean Paul Sartre, *The Age of Reason*, trans. Eric Sutton (New York: Vintage, 1973), pp. 244–45 and 254–56. Henceforth cited as *AR*.

20. Simone de Beauvoir, *The Ethics of Ambiguity*, trans. Bernard Frechtman (New York: Citadel, 1991). Henceforth cited as *EA*.

21. Simone de Beauvoir, *Brigitte Bardot and the Lolita Syndrome*, reprint (New York: Arno Press and the New York Times Press, 1972), pp. 16–17. Henceforth cited as *BB*.

CHAPTER 7: SITUATING IRIGARAY

1. Quotation from Luce Irigaray, *This Sex Which Is Not One*, trans. Catherine Porter with Carolyn Burke (Ithaca: Cornell University Press, 1985), p. 153. Henceforth cited as *TSO*.

2. Luce Irigaray, *Speculum of the Other Woman*, trans. Gillian C. Gill (Ithaca: Cornell University Press, 1985), p. 133. Henceforth cited as *S*.

3. Rodolphe Gasché, *The Tain of the Mirror* (Cambridge: Harvard University Press, 1986), p. 16. Henceforth cited as *TM*.
4. Martin Heidegger, *Introduction to Metaphysics*, trans. Ralph Manheim (New Haven: Yale University Press, 1959), p. 155. Henceforth cited as *IM*.
5. Martin Heidegger, *What Is Metaphysics?* trans. R. F. C. Hull and Alan Crick, in *Existence and Being* (Chicago, IL: Gateway, 1949), p. 355. Henceforth cited as *WM*.
6. G. W. F. Hegel, *The Science of Logic,* trans. A. V. Miller (Oxford: Oxford University Press, 1977), p. 74.
7. Plato, *The Republic,* trans. Desmond Lee (New York: Penguin, 1955), p. 206.
8. Jacques Lacan, *The Signification of the Phallus,* trans. Alan Sheridan, in *Écrits: A Selection* (London: Tavistock, 1977), p. 288.

CHAPTER 8: IRIGARAY'S DISCOURSE ON FEMININE DESIRE:
LITERALIST AND STRATEGIC READINGS

1. Luce Irigaray, *This Sex Which Is Not One,* trans. Catherine Porter with Carolyn Burke (New York: Cornell University Press, 1985), p. 24. Henceforth cited as *TS*. My paper focuses on just a few fragments from Irigaray's texts. I have selected these particular fragments because they provide illuminating examples of the issues I discuss here.
2. I have borrowed this characterization of Irigaray's discourse as "strategic" from Diana J. Fuss's "'Essentially Speaking': Luce Irigaray's Language of Essence," *Hypatia,* winter 1989, pp. 62–80. This is a general characterization. Irigaray uses a number of different concrete strategies—parody, irony, burlesque, etc.
3. Jacques-Main Miller, ed., *Le Séminaire de Jacques Lacan, Livre III, 1955–1966* (Paris: Éditions du Seuil, 1975), p. 286 (emphasis added).
4. Luce Irigaray, "Women's Exile: An Interview," trans. Couze Venn, in *Ideology and Consciousness,* vol. I (1977), p. 65. Henceforth cited as *WE*.
5. One reviewer of this essay suggested that my talk about "getting it right" ("whether it is Irigaray getting it right, or Leland getting it right") obscures a problem that "has to do with theories of truth." As I've constructed her, the literalist thinks that it makes sense to say that some linguistic units (e.g., sentences) can be used to express statements, which are either true or false. But this does not commit the literalist to any particular theory of truth. She may be a Rorty-influenced pragmatist, a Husserlian-style verificationist, an advocate of Tarski's Convention T, and so on. On the other hand, she may

throw up her hands and admit to finding all existing theories of truth unsatisfactory.

6. See, for example, Monique Plaza, " 'Phallomorphic Power' and the Psychology of Women," trans. Miriam David and Jill Hodges, in *Ideology and Consciousness* 4 (Autumn 1978): 57–76. Another example comes from Monique Wittig, "One Is Not Born a Woman," *Feminist Issues,* fall 1981, pp. 47–54. It should be noted that there is more than one version of biological essentialism and that not all critics of Irigaray's biological essentialism agree about which version she is committed to. In addition, not everyone finds Irigaray's commitment to biological essentialism untenable. Diana Fuss's article, cited earlier and incorporated into her book *Essentially Speaking* (London: Routledge, 1990), provides an interesting example of this latter position. See also Naomi Schor, "This Essentialism Which Is Not One: Coming to Grips With Irigaray," in *differences* 1 (1989): 38–58.

7. Judith Butler, *Gender Trouble: Feminism and the Subversion of Identity* (New York: Routledge, 1990), p. 71.

8. Jane Gallop, "Quand nos lèvres s'écrivent: Irigaray's Body Politic," *Romantic Review* 74 (1983): 77–83.

9. Margaret Whitford, "Luce Irigaray and the Female Imaginary: Speaking as a Woman," *Radical Philosophy* 43 (summer 1986): 3–8. Whitford expands on her thesis (and other themes) in her more recent book, *Luce Irigaray: Philosophy in the Feminine* (London: Routledge, 1991).

10. Luce Irigaray, *Le Langage des déments* (The Hague: Mouton, 1973). Irigaray also treats this issue in the essays collected in *Parler n'est jamais neutre* (Paris: Minuit, 1985). More recently still, she has offered a comparative analysis of French, English, and Italian research on the expression of sex differences in language. Some of this research and Irigaray's analysis is collected in *Sexes et genres—à travers les langues: éléments de communication sexuelle,* ed. Luce Irigaray (Paris: Grasset, 1990).

11. See the essays in *Parler n'est jamais neutre* (Paris: Minuit, 1985) for some of Irigaray's best criticisms of the supposed gender neutrality of psychoanalytic theory.

12. Irigaray discusses the psychoanalytic account of mother-daughter relations extensively in her writing, particularly in *Ethique de la différence sexuelle* (Paris: Minuit, 1984) and in *Sexes et parentés* (Paris: Minuit, 1987). This latter work will henceforth be cited as *SP*.

13. Luce Irigaray, "The Three Genres," trans. from *Sexes et parentes* by David Macy in *The Irigaray Reader,* ed. Margaret Whitford (Oxford: Basil Blackwell, 1991), p. 141. References to Whitford's anthology will henceforth be cited as *IR*.

14. Dorothy Leland, "Lacanian Psychoanalysis and French Feminism: Toward an Adequate Political Psychology," *Hypatia* 3 (winter 1989): 81–103.

15. Ann Rosalind Jones, "Writing the Body: Toward an Understanding of *L'Écriture Féminine*," *Feminist Studies* 7 (1981), p. 256.

16. Jacques Lacan, *Intervention on Transference in Dora's Case: Freud-Hysteria-Feminism*, ed. Charles Bernheimer and Claire Kahane (New York: Columbia University Press, 1985), p. 99. Irigaray criticizes Lacan for failing to see that "the problem of a woman's position" is an artifact of male dominance and not a universal law of psycho-sexual development.

CHAPTER 9: A LOVER'S REPLY
(TO ROLAND BARTHES'S *A LOVER'S DISCOURSE*)

1. Unless otherwise noted, all page references refer to Barthes's *A Lover's Discourse*, trans. Richard Howard (New York: Hill and Wang, 1978).

2. Roland Barthes, *Mythologies*, trans. Annette Lavers (New York: Hill and Wang, 1972), p. 246.

3. See Roland Barthes, *Writing Degree Zero*, trans. Annette Lavers and Colin Smith (New York: Hill and Wang, 1968).

4. See Robert C. Solomon, *Love: Emotion, Myth and Metaphor* (Amherst, NY: Prometheus Books, 1990).

5. See Jean Paul Sartre, *The Emotions: Outline of a Theory*, trans. Bernard Roland Frechtman (New York: Philosophical Library, 1998).

6. Jonathan Culler, *Barthes* (Oxford: Oxford University Press, 1983)

CHAPTER 10: IN THIS TEXT WHERE I NEVER AM:
DISCOURSES OF DESIRE IN DERRIDA

1. Jacques Derrida, *Writing and Difference*, trans. Alan Bass (Chicago: University of Chicago Press, 1978). Henceforth cited as *WD*.

2. Jacques Derrida, *The Truth in Painting*, trans. Geoff Bennington and Ian McLeod (Chicago: University of Chicago Press, 1987).

3. See my "Heidegger and Derrida Redux," in *Hermeneutics and Deconstruction*, eds. Hugh J. Silverman and Don Ihde (Albany: SUNY Press, 1985), pp. 219–26.

4. Jacques Derrida, *Cinders*, trans. Ned Lukacher (Lincoln: University of Nebraska Press, 1991). Henceforth cited as *C*.

5. Jacques Derrida, *Memoirs of the Blind*, trans. Pascale-Anne Brault and Michael Naas (Chicago: University of Chicago Press, 1993). Henceforth cited as *MB*.

6. Note that I say here "philosophical" rather than "metaphysical," as Derrida does in a famous footnote to "Violence and Metaphysics": "But perhaps metaphysical desire is essentially virile, even in what is called woman" (*WD,* 321). For more on the maleness of philosophy, especially in the Anglo-American tradition, see my *Is Women's Philosophy Possible?* (Savage, MD: Rowman and Littlefield, 1990).

7. Other forms of permission, and inspiration, in this enterprise came, in addition to the expected sources, from Iris Marion Young, Arlene Dallery, and Vic Lovell.

8. Jacques Derrida, *Glas,* trans. John P. Leavey Jr. and Richard Rand (Lincoln: University of Nebraska Press, 1986).

9. It is eerie, if not *unheimlich,* to read of Artaud's concern with "a bloody tattoo" (*WD,* 187) in light of recent criticisms of the NEA because of a performance in Minneapolis that involved a HIV-positive artist cutting ceremonial figures into another man's flesh and hanging the bloody towels on a line over the audience. If not a direct result of Artaud's work, this piece, like much performance art, truly declares its fidelity to it. "The theater of cruelty . . . is life itself, in the extent to which life is unrepresentable" (*WD,* 234, trans. modified).

10. For another set of consequences of gender-neutrality, see my "What Gilles Deleuze Has to Say to Battered Women," *Philosophy and Literature* 17, no. 1 (April 1993): 19.

11. The links between theater, cruelty, laughter, and women, framed by de Sade and Mallarmé as well as by Hegel and Artaud, are traced in Derrida's "The Double Session," in *Dissemination,* trans. Barbara Johnson (Chicago: University of Chicago Press, 1981), pp. 172–286.

12. The interweavings of this text are getting out of hand here. See *WD,* p. 177, regarding Artaud, and p. 263, for the echo in Bataille. Poetry, criticism, and, of course, Plato, Freud, and Nietzsche (inter)penetrate this fabric at every point.

13. This issue is discussed in the Prologue to *C* (pp. 22–27). Although Virginia Woolf is included in the "dialogue" on page 67 of *C* (but only, of course, as dead prose), there is otherwise no indication that Derrida's voice is not the only one heard here.

14. Jacques Derrida, *The Post Card,* trans. Alan Bass (Chicago: Chicago University Press, 1987).

15. In *Dissemination,* pp. 61–171. For an early commentary on this text, see my "The Treble Clef/t: Jacques Derrida and the Female Voice," in *Philosophy and Culture* (proceedings of the XVIIth World Congress of Philosophy), vol. II (Montreal: Éditions du Beffroi/ Éditions Montmorency, 1986), pp. 654–58.

CHAPTER 11: SPINOZA, NIETZSCHE, DELEUZE:
AN OTHER DISCOURSE OF DESIRE

1. Thomas Hobbes, *Leviathan,* ed. with an introduction by Michael Oakeshott (Oxford: Basil Blackwell, 1946), part 1, chapter 6, p. 32.
2. René Descartes, *The Passions of the Soul,* in *The Philosophical Works of Descartes,* trans. Elizabeth S. Haldane and G. R. T. Ross (Cambridge: Cambridge University Press, 1911), article 57. Henceforth cited as *PS.*
3. John Locke, *An Essay Concerning Human Understanding,* Book II, Chapter 20, Section 6.
4. One could just as easily discuss Freud in this regard, especially concerning his characterization of women's sexual desire in terms of the lack of the phallus. For an extended discussion of this issue, see Luce Irigaray's critiques of Freud in *This Sex Which Is Not One,* trans. Catherine Porter (Ithaca: Cornell University Press, 1985), esp. chapter 3: "Psychoanalytic Theory: Another Look," and *Speculum of the Other Woman,* trans. Gillian C. Gill (Ithaca: Cornell University Press, 1987). In this paper, I have chosen to discuss the productivity of desire in terms of a tradition of discourse that runs from Spinoza to Deleuze. A related account of libidinal productivity, one that can only be acknowledged here, could be undertaken in terms of recent feminist accounts of desire as *jouissance* in the works of Irigaray, Kristeva, Cixous, Spivak, Kofman, and others.
5. Jacques Lacan, *The Four Fundamental Concepts of Psycho-Analysis,* ed. Jacques-Alain Miller, trans. Alan Sheridan (New York: W. W. Norton and Co., 1978), pp. 29, 265. Henceforth cited as *FC.*
6. Jacques Lacan, *Écrits: A Selection,* trans. Alan Sheridan (New York: W. W. Norton and Co., 1977), p. 264. This Hegelian locution appears frequently in the *Écrits* (see also pp. 58, 288–89, 312) as well as *The Four Fundamental Concepts of Psycho-Analysis* (e.g., pp. 38, 115, 158, 235–36). Henceforth cited as *E.*
7. See the following remark by Lacan in reference to the castration complex: "Here is signed the conjunction of desire, in that the phallic signifier is its mark, with the threat or nostalgia of lacking it" (*E,* 289).
8. Jean-Paul Sartre, *Being and Nothingness,* trans. Hazel E. Barnes (New York: Philosophical Library, Inc., 1956), p. 565. Henceforth cited as *BN.*
9. *BN,* p. 615. This sentence, which directly precedes the "Conclusion," reiterates at the ontological level what Sartre earlier discussed at the empirical-psychological level: "Desire is doomed to failure" because its satisfaction (pleasure) precipitates its elimination (see pp. 396–97).

10. In an interview in 1988 in which he was asked to reflect on the trajectory of his published works, Deleuze chose to frame his response in terms of his tending toward "the grand identity Spinoza-Nietzsche." See "Sur la philosophie," in *Pourparlers* (Paris: Éditions de Minuit, 1990), p. 185.

11. Benedictus de Spinoza, *Ethics,* ed. and trans. Edwin Curley in *The Collected Works of Spinoza, Volume I* (Princeton: Princeton University Press, 1985), part III, "Definitions of the Affects 1." Henceforth cited as *SE.*

12. For Deleuze's discussion of Spinoza's identification of desire and *conatus,* see *Expressionism in Philosophy: Spinoza,* trans. Martin Joughin (New York: Zone Books, 1990), pp. 230–31. See also the discussion of *conatus* under the heading "Power" in Deleuze's *Spinoza: Practical Philosophy,* trans. Robert Hurley (San Francisco: City Lights Books, 1988), pp. 97–104.

13. Spinoza, *Ethics,* part III, prop. 9, "Scholium." In *Leviathan,* Hobbes makes a similar point: "But whatsoever is the object of any man's appetite or desire, that is it which he for his part calleth *good"* (part 1, chapter 6, p. 32).

14. The proximity of Spinoza and Nietzsche on this point should not obscure the fact that the relationship between their philosophical projects is an extremely complex one. The affinity Nietzsche felt for Spinoza (see, for example, his postcard of July 30, 1881 to Franz Overbeck, in which he expresses delight at having found a "precursor [Vorgänger]" in Spinoza), and the kinships between their respective naturalistic monisms (for Spinoza, of conatus, and for Nietzsche, of will to power) must not lead us to forget the important differences between them. For a discussion of the similarities and differences between these two "enemy-brothers," see Yirmiyahu Yovel, Spinoza and Other Heretics, vol. 2: The Adventures of Immanence (Princeton: Princeton University Press, 1989), chapter 5: "Spinoza and Nietzsche: Amor dei and Amor fati," pp. 104–35.

15. Friedrich Nietzsche, *Kritische Studienausgabe,* edited by Giorgio Colli and Mazzino Montinari (Berlin: Walter de Gruyter, 1967–1977), volume 12, 2 [77]. Henceforth cited as *KSA.* Wherever possible, corresponding sections from *The Will to Power,* ed. Walter Kaufmann, trans. R. J. Hollingsdale and W. Kaufmann (New York: Vintage, 1968), are given following the initial *KSA* reference. This citation: *WP,* 590.

16. Friedrich Nietzsche, *Twilight of the Idols,* trans. R. J. Hollingdale (Middlesex, England: Penguin Books, 1968), "What I Owe the Ancients," section 2.

17. Friedrich Nietzsche Epilogue, *The Case of Wagner,* trans. Walter Kaufmann (New York: Random House, Inc., 1967).

18. Friedrich Nietzsche, *The Gay Science,* trans. Walter Kaufmann (New York: Random House, Inc., 1974).

19. For an extended discussion of the function of these genealogical criteria in Nietzsche, see my *Nietzsche and the Question of Interpretation: Between Hermeneutics and Deconstruction* (New York: Routledge, 1990).

20. Cf. Nietzsche, *Kritische Studienausgabe,* volume 12, 9 [60]/*WP*, 585, where this idea is suggested as a defining characteristic of the nihilist.

21. Friedrich Nietzsche, *On the Genealogy of Morals,* trans. Walter Kaufmann and R. J. Hollingdale (New York: Random House, Inc., 1967), essay 3, section 12. Henceforth cited as *GM*.

22. Friedrich Nietzsche, *Human, All-Too-Human,* trans. R. J. Hollingdale (Cambridge: Cambridge University Press, 1986), preface 6.

23. Friedrich Nietzsche, *Twilight of the Idols,* "Morality as Anti-Nature," sections 1, 2.

24. Gilles Deleuze, *Nietzsche and Philosophy,* trans. Hugh Tomlinson (New York: Columbia University Press, 1983), p. 62.

25. Gilles Deleuze and Claire Parnet, *Dialogues,* trans. Hugh Tomlinson and Barbara Habberjam (New York: Columbia University Press, 1987), p. 91.

26. "Power in the substantive sense, '*le*' *pouvoir,* doesn't exist. . . . The idea that there is either located at—or emanating from—a given point something which is a 'power' seems to me to be based on a misguided analysis, one which at all events fails to account for a considerable number of phenomena. In reality, power means relations, a more-or-less organized, hierarchical, co-ordinated cluster of relations." See "The Confession of the Flesh," in Michel Foucault, *Power/Knowledge: Selected Interviews and Other Writings 1972–1977,* ed. and trans. Colin Gordon (New York: Pantheon Books, 1977), p. 198. I develop the affinities between Foucault's account of 'power' and Deleuze and Guattari's account of 'desire' in greater detail in chapters 2 and 3 of my *Nietzsche's French Legacy: A Genealogy of Poststructuralism* (New York: Routledge, 1995).

27. Gilles Deleuze and Félix Guattari, *A Thousand Plateaus,* trans. Brian Massumi (Minneapolis: University of Minnesota Press, 1987), p. 399. Henceforth cited as *TP*.

28. Deleuze and Guattari, *A Thousand Plateaus,* p. 399.

29. Gilles Deleuze and Félix Guattari, *Kafka: Toward a Minor Literature,* trans. Dana Polan (Minneapolis: University of Minnesota Press, 1986), p. 56.

30. Gilles Deleuze and Félix Guattari, *Anti-Oedipus,* trans. Robert Hurley, Mark Seem, and Helen R. Lane (Minneapolis: University of Minnesota Press, 1983), p. 26. Henceforth cited as *AO*.

31. Deleuze and Guattari, *Anti-Oedipus,* p. 55. See also Gilles Deleuze, Interview in *L'Arc* 49, second edition (1980): 99.
32. Among other things, this argument is clearly directed against a Marxist philosophy such as Sartre's, which, in *Critique of Dialectical Reason,* "introduces the notion of scarcity as its initial premise." See the footnote on Maurice Clavel in *Anti-Oedipus,* p. 28.
33. See Wilhelm Reich, *The Mass Psychology of Fascism,* trans. Vincent R. Carfagno (London: Souvenir Press, 1970).
34. The research and writing of this paper were made possible through the financial support of the Harris Faculty Fellowship of Grinnell College and the institutional support of the Oregon Humanities Center at the University of Oregon.

CHAPTER 12: DELEUZE AND GUATTARI:
FLOWS OF DESIRE AND THE BODY

1. See Dominique Grisoni, *"Les onomatopées du désir,"* in *Les dieux dans la cuisine* (Paris: Éditions Aubier, 1976), trans. Paul Foss, "Onomatopoeia of Desire," in *Theoretical Strategies,* ed. Peeter Botsman (Sydney: Local Consumption Publications, 1982). Henceforth cited as *OD.* Thanks to Elizabeth Grosz for drawing this important essay to my attention.
2. Judith P. Butler, *Subjects of Desire: Hegelian Reflections in Twentieth-Century France* (New York: Columbia University Press, 1987). Henceforth cited as *SD.*
3. Gilles Deleuze and Félix Guattari, *Mille plateaux, capitalisme et schizophrénie* (Paris: Les Éditions de Minuit, 1980), p. 152; *A Thousand Plateaus, Capitalism and Schizophrenia,* trans. Brian Massumi (Minneapolis: University of Minnesota Press, 1987), p. 121. Henceforth cited as *TP.*
4. Although I am focusing here on the question of desire and social formations, the role of Spinoza and the active body will be the subject of another essay.
5. Gilles Deleuze, *Nietzsche et la philosophie* (Paris: Presses Universitaires de France, 1962); *Nietzsche and Philosophy,* trans. Hugh Tomlinson (New York: Columbia University Press, 1983). Henceforth cited as *NP.*
6. Gilles Deleuze, *Différence et répétition* (Paris: Presses Universitaires de France, 1968); *Difference and Repetition,* trans. Paul Patton (New York: Columbia University Press, 1994). Henceforth cited as *DR.*
7. The term "regime" becomes central in the second volume of *Capitalism and Schizophrenia,* where "regimes of signs" take precedence as

the conceptualization for the organization of desiring and social-machines in various power arrangements. "Regime" also seems to maintain its more conventional French meaning: a set of rules or laws, but also a rate of flow, or a rate of speed—not only do different regimes have different laws or rules—but they occur at different speeds.

8. Friedrich Nietzsche, *The Will to Power,* trans. Walter Kaufmann and R. J. Hollingdale (New York: Vintage Books, 1968), p. 634. Cited in *Nietzsche and Philosophy,* pp. 66 n. 3, 206 n. 17.

9. Gilles Deleuze and Claire Parnet, *Dialogues,* trans. Hugh Tomlinson and Barbara Habberjam (New York: Columbia University Press, 1987), pp. 91, 95. Henceforth cited as *DIA.*

10. See Gilles Deleuze and Félix Guattari, *L'Anti-Oedipe, Capitalisme et schizophrénie,* volume 1 (Paris: Les Éditions de Minuit, 1972); *Anti-Oedipus: Capitalism and Schizophrenia,* trans. Robert Hurley, Mark Seem and Helen R. Lane (Minneapolis: University of Minnesota Press, 1983). Henceforth cited as *AO.*

11. See Alice Jardine, *Gynesis: Configurations of Woman and Modernity* (Ithaca: Cornell University Press, 1984), p. 209. Cited henceforth as *GYN.*

12. This is only partially true since the concept of body is repeatedly articulated and revealed in all its complexity.

13. The body without organs and desiring-production are the focus of the *Anti-Oedipus.*

14. Jacques Donzelot, "Une anti-sociologie," *Esprit,* December 1972, pp. 835–55; "An Antisociology," trans. Mark Seem, *Semiotexte* 2, no. 3 (1977). Henceforth cited as *AS.*

15. Georg Büchner, *Lenz,* trans. Michael Hamburger (Chicago: University of Chicago Press, 1972), p. 44. Henceforth cited as *L.*

16. See, for example, Karl Marx, *Grundrisse,* trans. Martin Nicolaus (New York: Vintage Books, 1973), pp. 85–100, where Marx states that production is preceded by some kind of social organization, and identifies production with both distribution and consumption.

17. Deleuze argues that Hume substituted the external and changing relation "A *and* B" for the internal and essential relation "A *is* B," thereby inaugurating the moving series "and, and, and" which makes way for the concept of *open* systems, unities, or wholes, as opposed to unities that transcend the parts. See *Empirisme et subjectivité: Essai sur la nature humaine selon Hume* (Paris: Presses Universitaires de France, 1953); *Empiricism and Subjectivity: An Essay on Hume's Theory of Human Nature,* trans. Constantin V. Boundas (New York: Columbia University Press, 1991).

18. Such a reading has been suggested by Judith Butler in *Subjects of Desire: Hegelian Reflections in Twentieth Century France* and

Manfred Frank in "The World as Will and Representation: Deleuze and Guattari's Critique of Capitalism as Schizoanalysis and Schizo-Discourse," *Telos,* 57 (fall 1983): 166–76.

19. The notion of "partial objects" is borrowed from Melanie Klein's analysis of the infantile basis of schizophrenia. Klein writes, "In this very early phase . . . the ego's power of identifying itself with its objects is as yet small, partly because it is itself still uncoordinated and partly because the introjected objects are still mainly partial objects. . . . See "A Contribution to the Psychogenesis of Manic-Depressive States" (1935), in *Love, Guilt and Reparation* (Delacorte Press, 1975), p. 363. Presumably this is of use to Deleuze and Guattari because it allows them to talk about bodies or body connections in terms of flows as opposed to complete egos and complete objects which are already totalized and structured in accordance with the Oedipal signifier.

20. This reading differs from Brian Massumi's lucid and creative account in *A User's Guide to Capitalism and Schizophrenia: Deviations from Deleuze and Guattari* (Cambridge: MIT Press, 1992). This reading emphasizes the creative aspects of desiring-production and the breakdowns in desiring-production as opposed to the process of overcoding and capitalist becoming-consumer—even though capital is the point of view of their analysis of history.

21. Eugene Holland, "Schizoanalysis: The Postmodern Contextualization of Psychoanalysis," in Cary Nelson and Lawrence Grossberg, eds., *Marxism and the Interpretation of Culture* (Urbana: University of Illinois Press, 1988), p. 410. Henceforth cited as *SA.*

22. This is one of several critical respects in which Deleuze and Guattari differ from Wilhelm Reich who, in *The Mass Psychology of Fascism* (trans. Vincent R. Carfagno [New York: Noonday Press, 1970]) maintains that fascist governments make use of the Oedipal.

23. Gilles Deleuze, *Proust and Signs,* trans. Richard Howard (New York: George Braziller, 1972), p. 120. Henceforth cited as *PS.*

24. Lucy Lippard, *Overlay, Contemporary Art and the Art of Prehistory* (New York: Pantheon Books, 1983), p. 230.

25. Barbara Kruger, *Remote Control, Powers, Cultures, and the World of Appearances* (Cambridge: MIT Press, 1993), p. 5.

26. Gilles Deleuze, *Logique du sens* (Paris: Les Editions de Minuit, 1969), p. 110; *The Logic of Sense,* ed. Constantin V. Boundas, trans. Mark Lester and Charles Stivale (New York: Columbia University Press, 1990), pp. 89–90. Henceforth cited as *LS.*

27. Alphonso Lingis beautifully articulates the *socius* of "savage" social production in his essay, "The Society of Dismembered Body-Parts," and Jean-Clet Martin articulates that of the despotic social formation

in "Cartography of the Year 1000"; both appear in *Gilles Deleuze and the Theatre of Philosophy,* eds. Constantin V. Boundas and Dorothea E. Olkowski (New York: Routledge, 1994).

28. Alphonso Lingis, *Abuses* (Berkeley: University of California Press, 1994), pp. 11–12. Henceforth cited as *AB.*

29. See Maurice Dobb, *Studies in the Development of Capitalism* (London: Routledge and Kegan Paul, 1959), pp. 177–86. Cited in *Anti-Oedipus,* pp. 267–68, 226.

30. Pierre Klossowski, "Sade or the Philosopher-Villain," trans. Alphonso Lingis, *SubStance* 15, no. 2 (1986): 5–25, here p. 6. For a fuller account of this, see my "Repetition and Revulsion in the Marquis de Sade," in *Sex, Love, and Friendship,* ed. Alan Soble (Atlanta: Editions Rodopi, 1997).

31. Karl Marx, *The Communist Manifesto,* ed. Frederic L. Bender (New York: W. W. Norton, 1988), p. 57.

32. Katherine Q. Seelye, for *The New York Times* in *The Denver Post,* "Dole Throws Down the Gauntlet in Republican Response," Wed., 24 Jan. 1996, p. 12A.

BIBLIOGRAPHY

Adams, Parveen. "Representation and Sexuality." *m/f* 1 (1978): 65–82.
———. "Versions of the Body." *m/f* 11–12 (1986): 27–34.
Agger, Ben. *The Discourse of Domination: From the Frankfurt School to Postmodernism.* Evanston: Northwestern University Press, 1991.
———. *Gender, Culture, and Power: Toward a Feminist Postmodern Critical Theory.* Westport: Praeger, 1993.
Allen, Judith, and Elizabeth Grosz. "Feminism and the Body." *Australian Feminist Studies* 5 (1987).
Astruc, Alexandre, and Michel Contat. *Sartre by Himself: A Film.* Trans. Richard Seaver. New York: Urizen Books, 1978.
Bergo, Bettina, ed. "Levinas's Contribution to Contemporary Philosophy." *Graduate Faculty Philosophy Journal* 20, no. 2/21, no. 1 (1998).
Babich, Babette, ed. *From Phenomenology to Thought, Errancy, and Desire: Essays in Honor of William J. Richardson.* Boston: Kluwer Academic, 1995.
Balbus, Isaac. "Disciplining Women: Michel Foucault and the Power of Feminist Discourse." *Praxis International* 5 (Jan. 1986): 466–83.
Barthes, Roland. *Writing Degree Zero* (1953). Trans. Annette Lavers and Colin Smith. New York: Hill and Wang, 1968.
———. *Mythologies* (1957). New York: Hill and Wang, 1962.
———. *The Pleasure of the Text* (1973). Trans. Richard Howard. New York: Hill and Wang, 1975.
———. *A Lover's Discourse: Fragments* (1977). Trans. Richard Howard. New York: Farrar, Straus & Giroux, 1978.
Bataille, Georges. *Visions of Excess: Selected Writings, 1927–1939.* Trans. Allan Stoekl. Minneapolis: University of Minnesota Press, 1985.
———. *Eroticism: Death and Sensuality.* Trans. Mary Dalwood. San Francisco: City Lights Books, 1986.
———. *Inner Experience.* Trans. Leslie Anne Boldt. Albany: SUNY Press, 1988.
———. *The College of Sociology: 1937–39.* Ed. Denis Hollier. Minneapolis: University of Minnesota Press, 1988.

Baudrillard, Jean. *Forget Foucault.* New York: Semiotext(e), 1987.
———. *Simulations.* New York: Semiotext(e), 1983.
Bell, David, and Valentine Gill, eds. *Mapping Desire: Geographies of Sexualities.* New York: Routledge, 1995.
Bencivenga, Ermanno. "That Obscure Object of Desire." *Philosophy and Phenomenological Research* 48 (March 1988), 533–44.
Benhabib, Seyla, and Drucilla Cornell, eds. *Feminism as Critique: Essays on the Politics of Gender in Late-Capitalist Societies.* Cambridge: Polity Press, 1987.
Bernasconi, Robert, and David Wood, eds. *The Provocation of Levinas: Rethinking the Other.* New York: Routledge, 1989.
Boothby, Richard. *Death and Desire: Psychoanalytic Theory in Lacan's Return to Freud.* New York: Routledge, 1991.
Boundas, Constantin V., and Dorothea Olkowski, eds. *Gilles Deleuze and the Theatre of Philosophy.* New York: Routledge Press, 1994.
Bowie, Malcolm. *Freud, Proust and Lacan: Theory as Fiction.* Cambridge: Cambridge University Press, 1988.
Bracher, Mark. *Lacan, Discourse, and Social Change: A Psychoanalytic Cultural Criticism.* Ithaca: Cornell University Press, 1993.
Brennan, Teresa, ed. *Between Feminism and Psychoanalysis.* London: Routledge, 1989.
Brooks, Peter. *Body Work: Objects of Desire in Modern Narrative.* Cambridge: Harvard University Press, 1993.
Brown, Beverley, and Parveen Adams. "The Feminine Body and Feminist Politics." *m/f* 3 (1979): 33–50.
Büchner, Georg. *Lenz.* Trans. Michael Hamburger. Chicago: University of Chicago Press, 1972.
Buck, Paul, ed. *Violent Silence: Celebrating Georges Bataille.* London: The Georges Bataille Event, 1984.
Burke, Carolyn. "Irigaray Through the Looking Glass." *Feminist Studies* 7, no. 2 (1981): 288–306.
Burke, Patrick, and Jan Van der Veken. *Merleau-Ponty in Contemporary Perspective.* Boston: Kluwer Academic Publishers, 1993.
Butler, Judith. *Subjects of Desire: Hegelian Reflections in Twentieth-Century France.* New York: Columbia University Press, 1987.
———. "Gender Trouble, Feminist Theory, and Psychoanalytic Discourse." In *Feminism/Postmodernism,* ed. Linda Nicholson. New York: Routledge, 1990.
———. "Gendering the Body: Beauvoir's Philosophical Contribution." In *Women, Knowledge and Reality: Explorations in Feminist Philosophy,* eds. Ann Garry and Marilyn Pearsall. London: Unwin Hyman, 1989.
Cameron, Deborah. *The Feminist Critique of Language: A Reader.* New York: Routledge, 1977.

————. "Discourses of Desire: Liberals, Feminists and the Politics of Pornography in the 1980s." *American Literary History* 2, no. 4 (winter 1990): 784–98.

Chanter, Tina. *Ethics of Eros: Irigaray's Re-writing of the Philosophers.* New York: Routledge, 1995.

Chase, Cynthia. "The Witty Butcher's Wife: Freud, Lacan, and the Conversion of Resistance to Theory." *Modern Language Notes* 102, no. 5 (Dec. 1987): 989–1013.

————. "Desire and Identification in Lacan and Kristeva." In *Feminism and Psychoanalysis,* eds. Richard Feldstein and Judith Roof. London: Cornell University Press, 1989

Churchill, Laurie J. "Discourses of Desire: On Ovid's *Amores* and Barthes' *Fragments d'un discours amoureux.*" *Classical and Modern Literature* 8, no. 4 (summer 1988), 301–7.

Ciaramelli, Fabio. "Levinas's Ethical Discourse between Individuation and Universality." In *Re-Reading Levinas,* eds. Robert Bernasconi and Simon Critchley. Indianapolis: Indiana University Press, 1991.

Cixous, Hélène. "The Laugh of Medusa." *Signs* 1, no. 4 (summer 1976): 875–93.

Clayton, Jay. "Narrative and Theories of Desire." *Critical Inquiry* 16 (autumn 1989): 32–53.

Colburn, Kenneth. "Desire and Discourse in Foucault: The Sign of the Fig Leaf in Michelangelo's David." *Human Studies* 10 (1987): 61–79.

Copjec, Joan. *Read My Desire: Lacan Against the Historicists.* Cambridge: MIT Press, 1994.

Cornis-Pope, Marcel. *Hermeneutic Desire and Critical Rewriting: Narrative Interpretation in the Wake of Poststructuralism.* New York: St. Martin's Press, 1992.

Coward, Rosalind. "Female Desire and Sexual Identity." In *Women, Feminist Identity and Society in the 1980s: Selected Papers,* ed. Myriam Diaz-Diocarets. Amsterdam: Benjamins, 1985.

Davis, Erik. "Professor of Desire: Gilles Deleuze at Work and Play." *Village Voice Literary Supplement,* March 1989, 19–20.

Dean, Carolyn J. *The Self and Its Pleasures: Bataille, Lacan, and the History of the Decentered Subject.* Ithaca: Cornell University Press, 1992.

De Beauvoir, Simone. *The Ethics of Ambiguity* (1947). Trans. Bernard Frechtman. New York: Citadel, 1991.

————. *The Second Sex* (1949). New York: Random House, 1952.

————. *Memoirs of a Dutiful Daughter* (1958). Trans. J. Kirkup. Cleveland: World Publishing, 1959.

————. *Brigitte Bardot and the Lolita Syndrome* (1959). New York: Arno Press and the New York Times Press, 1972.

————. *The Prime of Life* (1960). Trans. Peter Green. Middlesex, England: Penguin, 1965.

———. *Force of Circumstance* (1963). Trans. Richard Howard. New York: Penguin, 1968.

———. *Witness to My Life: The Letters of Jean-Paul Sartre to Simone de Beauvoir, 1926–1939,* ed. Simone de Beauvoir. Trans. Lee Fahnestock and Norman MacAfee. New York: Charles Scribner's Sons, 1992.

Deleuze, Gilles. *Empiricism and Subjectivity: An Essay on Hume's Theory of Human Nature* (1953). Trans. Constantin V. Boundas. New York: Columbia University Press, 1991.

———. *Nietzsche and Philosophy* (1962). New York: Columbia University Press, 1983.

———. *Proust and Signs* (1964). Trans. Richard Howard. New York: Braziller, 1972.

———. *Expressionism in Philosophy: Spinoza* (1968). Trans. Martin Joughin. New York: Zone Books, 1990.

———. *Difference and Repetition* (1968). Trans. Paul Patton. New York: Columbia University Press, 1994.

———. *The Logic of Sense* (1969), ed. Constantin V. Boundas. Trans. Mark Lester and Charles Stivale. New York: Columbia University Press, 1990.

———. *Spinoza: Practical Philosophy* (1970). Trans. Robert Hurley. San Francisco: City Lights Books, 1988.

———. *Kafka: Toward a Minor Literature* (1975). Trans. Dana Polan. Minneapolis: University of Minnesota Press, 1986.

Deleuze, Gilles, and Claire Parnet. *Dialogues.* Trans. Hugh Tomlinson and Barbara Habberjam. New York: Columbia University Press, 1987.

Deleuze, Gilles, and Félix Guattari. *Anti-Oedipus, Capitalism and Schizophrenia* (1972). Trans. Robert Hurley, Mark Seem, and Helen R. Lane. Minneapolis: University of Minnesota Press, 1983.

———. *A Thousand Plateaus: Capitalism and Schizophrenia* (1980). Trans. Brian Massumi. Minneapolis: University of Minnesota Press, 1987.

de Rougemont, Denis. *Love in the Western World.* Trans. Montgomery Belgion. New York: Harper and Row, 1974.

Derrida, Jacques. *Writing and Difference* (1967). Trans. Alan Bass. Chicago: University of Chicago Press, 1978.

———. *Dissemination* (1972). Trans. Barbara Johnson. Chicago: University of Chicago Press, 1981.

———. *Margins of Philosophy* (1972). Trans. Alan Bass. Chicago: University of Chicago Press, 1982.

———. *Glas* (1974). Trans. John P. Leavey Jr. and Richard Rand. Lincoln: University of Nebraska Press, 1986.

———. *The Truth in Painting* (1978). Trans. Geoff Bennington and Ian McLeod. Chicago: University of Chicago Press, 1987.

———. *The Post Card* (1980). Trans. Alan Bass. Chicago: University of Chicago Press, 1987.

————. *Cinders* (1987). Trans. Ned Lukacher. Lincoln: University of Nebraska Press, 1991.

————. "At This Very Moment in This Work Here I Am (1987)." In *Re-Reading Levinas,* ed. Robert Bernasconi and Simon Critchley. Trans. Ruben Berezdivin. Bloomington: Indiana University Press, 1991.

————. *Memoirs of the Blind* (1990). Trans. Pascale-Anne Brault and Michael Naas. Chicago: University of Chicago Press, 1993.

————. *The Gift of Death* (1992). Trans. David Wills. Chicago: University of Chicago Press, 1995.

————. *The Politics of Friendship* (1994). Trans. George Collins. London: Verso, 1997.

Descartes, René. "The Passions of the Soul." In *The Philosophical Works of Descartes.* Trans. Elizabeth S. Haldane and G. R. T. Ross. Cambridge: Cambridge University Press, 1911.

Descombes, Vincent. *Modern French Philosophy.* Trans. L. Scott-Fox and J. M. Harding. Cambridge: Cambridge University Press, 1980.

Desmond, William. *Desire, Dialectic and Otherness: An Essay on Origins.* New Haven: Yale University Press, 1987.

Dillon, M. C. *Merleau-Ponty's Ontology,* Evanston: Northwestern University Press, 1998.

————. *Semiological Reductionism: A Critique of the Deconstructionist Movement in Postmodern Thought.* Albany: State University of New York Press, 1995.

————. "Romantic Love, Enduring Love, and Authentic Love." *Soundings* LXVI (1983): 133–51.

————. "Erotic Desire." *Research in Phenomenology* XV (1985): 145–63.

————. "Sex, Time, and Love: Erotic Temporality." *Journal of Phenomenological Psychology* 18 (1987): 33–48.

————. "Desire: Language and Body." In *Postmodernism and Continental Philosophy,* eds. Hugh J. Silverman and Donn Welton. Albany: SUNY Press, 1988.

Doan, Laura, ed. *The Lesbian Postmodern.* New York: Columbia University Press, 1994.

Doane, Mary Ann. "Veiling Our Desire: Close-ups of the Woman." In *Feminism and Psychoanalysis,* eds. Richard Feldstein and Judith Roof. London: Cornell University Press, 1989.

Dobb, Maurice. *Studies in the Development of Capitalism.* London: Routledge and Kegan Paul, 1959.

Dolan, Jill. *Presence and Desire: Essays on Gender, Sexuality, Performance.* Ann Arbor: University of Michigan Press, 1993.

Donnelly, Colleen. "The Non-Homogeneous I: Fragmentation, Desire, and Pleasure in Barthes's *A Lover's Discourse." Southern Review* 21, no. 2 (July 1988): 169–80.

Donzelot, Jacques. "Une anti-sociologie." *Esprit,* December 1972, pp. 835–55. Trans. Mark Seem, *Semiotexte* 2, no. 3 (1977): 27–44.

Duran, Jane. "The Reinterpreting Reader: An Analysis of Discourse and the Feminine." *Philosophy and Social Criticism* 20:3 (1994), 89–101.

Edelman, Lee. "At Risk in the Sublime: The Politics of Gender and Theory." In *Gender and Theory: Dialogues on Feminist Criticism,* ed. Linda Kauffman. Oxford: Blackwell, 1989.

Faurschou, Gail. "Obsolescence and Desire: Fashion and the Commodity Form." In *Postmodernism—Philosophy and the Arts* (Continental Philosophy–III), ed. Hugh J. Silverman (New York and London: Routledge, 1990).

Felman, Shoshana. "Rereading Femininity." *Yale French Studies* 62 (1981): 19–44.

Feral, Josette. "Towards a Theory of Displacement." *Sub-Stance* 32 (1981): 52–64.

Forbes, Ripling. *Hegel on Want and Desire: A Psychology of Motivation.* Wakefield: Longwood Academy, 1991.

Foss, Paul, Paul Taylor, and Allen S. Weiss, eds. "Phantasm and Simulacra—The Drawings of Pierre Klossowski," special edition, *Art & Text* 18 (July 1985).

Foucault, Michel. *Madness and Civilization: A History of Insanity in the Age of Reason* (1961). Trans. Richard Howard. New York: Vintage Books, 1973.

———. *The Order of Things* (1966). New York: Pantheon Books, 1971.

———. *The Archeology of Knowledge* (1969). Trans. A. M. Sheridan-Smith. New York: Pantheon Books, 1972.

———. *Power/Knowledge: Selected Interviews and Other Writings, 1972–1977.* Ed. Colin Gordon. New York: Pantheon Books, 1977.

———. *The History of Sexuality, Volume I: An Introduction* (1976). Trans. Robert Hurley. New York: Random House, 1980.

———. *The History of Sexuality, Volume II: The Use of Pleasure* (1984). Trans. Robert Hurley. New York: Pantheon Books, 1985.

———. *The History of Sexuality, Volume III: The Care of the Self* (1984). Trans. Robert Hurley. New York: Vintage, 1986.

Frank, Manfred. *What Is Neostructuralism?* Trans. Sabine Wilk and Richard Gray. Minneapolis: University of Minnesota Press 1989.

———. "The World as Will and Representation: Deleuze and Guattari's Critique of Capitalism as Schizoanalysis and Schizo-Discourse." *Telos* 57 (fall 1983): 166–76.

Franklin, Sarah. "Luce Irigaray and the Feminist Critique of Language." Women's Studies Occasional Papers, no. 6. Canterbury: University of Kent.

Fuery, Patrick. *Theories of Desire*. Melbourne: Melbourne University Press, 1995.

Fullbrook, Kate, and Edward Fullbrook. *Simone de Beauvoir and Jean-Paul Sartre: The Remaking of a Twentieth-Century Legend*. New York: Harper Collins/Basic Books, 1994.

Fuss, Diana, J. "Essentially Speaking: Luce Irigaray's Language of Essence." *Hypatia* 3 (winter 1989): 62–80.

Gallop, Jane. *Intersections: A Reading of Sade With Bataille, Blanchot, and Klossowski*. Lincoln: University of Nebraska Press, 1981.

———. "Quand nos lèvres s'écrivent: Irigaray's Body Politics." *Romanic Review* 74 (1983): 77–83.

———. "What Gilles Deleuze Has to Say to Battered Women." *Philosophy and Literature* 17, no. 1 (April 1993).

Garry, Leonard M. "The Paradox of Desire: Jacques Lacan and Edith Wharton." *Edith Wharton Review* 7, no. 2 (winter 1990): 1316.

Gasché, Rodolphe. *The Tain of the Mirror*. Cambridge: Harvard University Press, 1986.

Gauthier, Lorraine. "Desire for Origin/Original Desire: Luce Irigaray on Maternity, Sexuality and Language." *Canadian Fiction Magazine* 7 (1986): 41–46.

George, Diana Hume. "'Who Is the Double Ghost Whose Head Is Smoke?' Women Poets on Aging." In *Memory and Desire: Aging, Literature, Psychoanalysis,* eds. Kathleen Woodward and Murray M. Schwartz. Bloomington: Indiana University Press, 1986.

Goethe, Johann W. *Sorrows of Young Werther*. New York: Ungar, 1971.

Griffiths, Morwenna, and Margaret Whitford. *Feminist Perspectives in Philosophy*. New York: Macmillan, 1988.

Grisoni, Dominique. "Onomatopoeia of Desire." In *Theoretical Strategies,* ed. Peter Botsman. Sydney: Local Consumption, 1982.

Grosz, Elizabeth. "Philosophy, Subjectivity and the Body: Kristeva and Irigaray." In *Feminist Challenges: Social and Political Theory,* eds. Carole Pateman and Elizabeth Grosz. London: Allen and Unwin, 1986.

Heidegger, Martin. *Being and Time*. Trans. J. Macquarrie and E. Robinson. New York: Harper and Row, 1962.

———. *Basic Writings,* ed. David Krell. New York: Harper and Row, 1977.

Hans, James S.. *The Fate of Desire*. Albany: SUNY Press, 1990.

Heaton, John. "Language Games, Expression and Desire in the Work of Deleuze." *Journal of the British Society for Phenomenology* 24, no. 1 (Jan. 1993): 77–87.

Hegel, G. W. F. *Phenomenology of Spirit*. Trans. A. V. Miller. Oxford: Oxford University Press, 1977.

———. *Science of Logic*. Trans. A. V. Miller. New York: Humanities Press, 1969.

Hobbes, Thomas. *Leviathan,* ed. Michael Oakeshott. Oxford: Basil Blackwell, 1946.

Holland, Eugene. "Schizoanalysis: The Postmodern Contextualization of Psychoanalysis." In *Marxism and the Interpretation of Culture,* eds. Cary Nelson and Lawrence Grossberg. Urbana: University of Illinois Press, 1988.

Holland, Nancy. *Feminist Interpretations of Jacques Derrida (Rereading the Canon).* University Park: Pennsylvania State University Press, 1997.

———. *Is Women's Philosophy Possible?* Savage, MD: Rowman and Littlefield, 1990.

———. "Heidegger and Derrida Redux." In *Hermeneutics and Deconstruction,* eds. Hugh J. Silverman and Don Ihde. Albany: SUNY Press, 1985.

———. "The Treble Clef/t: Jacques Derrida and the Female Voice." In *Philosophy and Culture* (proceedings of the XVIIth World Congress of Philosophy), volume II. Montreal: Éditions du Beffroi/Éditions Montmorency, 1986.

Howells, C. M. *Sartre: The Necessity of Freedom.* Cambridge: Cambridge University Press, 1988.

Huffer, Lynne (guest ed.). *Another Look, Another Woman: Retranslations of French Feminism (Yale French Studies* 87), 1995.

Irigaray, Luce. *This Sex Which Is Not One.* Trans. Catherine Porter. Ithaca: Cornell University Press, 1985.

———. *Speculum of the Other Woman.* Trans. Gillian C. Gill. Ithaca: Cornell University Press, 1987.

———. "The Fecundity of the Caress." In *Face to Face with Levinas,* ed. Richard A. Cohen. Albany: SUNY Press, 1986.

———. "Sex, Love, and Natural Law Morality." In *The Ethics of Postmodernity: Contemporary Continental Perspectives,* ed. G. B. Madison. Evanston: Northwestern University Press, 1995.

Jardine, Alice. *Gynesis: Configurations of Woman and Modernity.* Ithaca: Cornell University Press, 1984.

Johnson, Galen. "The Colors of Fire: Depth and Desire in Merleau-Ponty's *Eye and Mind,*" *The Journal of the British Society for Phenomenology* 25, no. 1 (Jan. 1994): 53–63.

Johnston, Suzie. "Filling Gaps in the Mythic Landscape of Lack: Feminism, Psychoanalysis, Philosophy and the Challenge of Women's Desire." *De Philosophia* 9 (1992): 39–46.

Jopling, David. "Levinas on Desire, Dialogue and the Other," *American Catholic Philosophical Quarterly* 65, no. 4 (autumn 1991): 407–27.

Kaplan, E. Ann. "Is the Gaze Male?" In *Desire: The Politics of Sexuality,* ed. Ann Snitow et al. London: Virago, 1984.

Kierkegaard, Søren. *Either/Or.* Trans. David F. Swenson and Lillian Marvin Swenson. Garden City, NY: Doubleday, 1959.

———. *Diary of a Seducer.* New York: Ungar, 1966.

Klein, Melanie. *Love, Guilt, and Reparation.* New York: Delacorte Press, 1975.

Klossowski, Pierre. "Sade or the Philosopher-Villain." Trans. Alphonso Lingis. *SubStance* 15, no. 2 (1986): 5–25.

Kojève, Alexandre. *Introduction to the Reading of Hegel.* Trans. A. Bloom and J. Nichols. New York: Basic Books, 1969.

Krieger, Murray. "The Semiotic Desire for the Natural Sign: Poetic Uses and Political Abuses." In *The States of Theory: History, Art, and Critical Discourses,* ed. David Carroll. New York: Columbia University Press, 1990.

Kristeva, Julia. *Desire in Language: A Semiotic Approach to Literature and Art.* Trans. Leon Roudiez. New York: Columbia University Press, 1984.

———. *The Revolution in Poetic Language* (1974). Trans. Margaret Waller. New York: Columbia University Press, 1982.

———. *Time and Sense: Proust and the Experience of Literature.* New York: Columbia University Press, 1998.

Kritzman, Lawrence. "Roland Barthes: The Discourse of Desire and the Question of Gender," *Modern Language Notes* 103, no. 4 (Sept. 1988): 848–64.

Kruger, Barbara. *Remote Control: Powers, Cultures, and the World of Appearances.* New York: Columbia University Press, 1993.

Kuhn, Annette. *The Power of the Image: Essays on Representation and Sexuality.* London: Routledge, 1985.

Lacan, Jacques. *Écrits: A Selection* (1966). Trans. Alan Sheridan. New York: W. W. Norton and Co., 1977.

———. *The Four Fundamental Concepts of Psycho-Analysis,* ed. Jacques-Alain Miller. Trans. Alan Sheridan. New York: W. W. Norton and Co., 1978.

———. "Desire and the Interpretation of Desire in Hamlet." In *Literature and Psychoanalysis,* ed. Shoshana Felman. Baltimore: Johns Hopkins University Press, 1982.

Land, Nick. *The Thirst for Annihilation: Georges Bataille and Virulent Nihilism.* New York: Routledge, 1992.

Lanigan, Richard. *The Human Science of Communicology: A Phenomenology of Discourse in Foucault and Merleau-Ponty.* Pittsburgh: Duquesne University Press, 1992.

La Rochefoucault. *Maximes.* Paris: Larousse, 1941.

Leach, Joan. "Let the Audience De-Side: Possibilities for Postmodern Discourse Ethics." *Social Epistemology* 8, no. 4 (Oct.–Dec. 1994). 383–87.

Leak, A. N. *The Perverted Consciousness: Sexuality and Sartre.* London: Macmillan, 1989.

Lecercle, Jean-Jacques. *Philosophy Through the Looking Glass: Language, Nonsense, Desire.* London: Hutchinson, 1985.

Levinas, Emmanuel. *Totality and Infinity: An Essay on Exteriority.* Trans. Alphonso Lingis. Pittsburgh: Duquesne University Press, 1969.

———. *Existence and Existents.* Trans. Alphonso Lingis. Dordrecht and Boston: Kluwer Academic Publishers, 1978

———. *Collected Philosophical Papers.* Trans. Alphonso Lingis. Dordrecht and Boston: Kluwer Academic Publishers, 1987.

———. *Time and the Other.* Trans. Richard Cohen. Pittsburgh: Duquesne University Press, 1987.

———. *Otherwise Than Being or Beyond Essence.* Trans. Alphonso Lingis. Dordrecht and Boston: Kluwer Academic Publishers, 1991.

Lingis, Alphonso. *Libido: The French Existential Theories.* Bloomington: Indiana University Press, 1985.

———. *Abuses.* Berkeley: University of California Press, 1994.

Locke, John. *An Essay Concerning Human Understanding.* New York: Dover Publications, Inc., 1959.

MacKinnon, Catharine. "Desire and Power: A Feminist Perspective." In *Marxism and the Interpretation of Culture,* eds. Cary Nelson and Laurence Grossberg. Urbana: University of Illinois Press, 1988.

Maffesoli, Michel. *The Shadow of Dionysus: A Contribution to the Sociology of the Orgy.* Albany: SUNY Press, 1993.

Massumi, Brian. *A User's Guide to Capitalism and Schizophrenia: Deviations From Deleuze and Guattari.* Cambridge: MIT Press, 1992.

Merleau-Ponty, Maurice. *Phenomenology of Perception* (1945). Trans. Colin Smith. New York: Routledge, 1962.

———. *Sense and Non-Sense* (1947). Trans. Hubert L. Dreyfus and Patricia Allen Dreyfus. Evanston: Northwestern University Press, 1964.

———. *The Prose of the World* (1952). Trans. John O'Neill. Evanston: Northwestern University Press, 1973.

———. *Signs* (1960). Trans. Richard McCleary. Evanston: Northwestern University Press, 1964.

Meyers, Diana. *Subjection and Subjectivity: Psychoanalytic Feminism and Moral Philosophy.* New York: Routledge, 1994.

Mills, Patricia J. "Woman's Experience: Renaming the Dialectic of Desire and Recognition." In *Writing the Politics of Difference,* ed. Hugh J. Silverman. Albany: SUNY Press, 1991.

Moi, Toril. *Simone de Beauvoir: The Making of an Intellectual Woman.* London: Blackwell, 1994.

Nietzsche, Friedrich. *Human, All-Too-Human* (1880). Trans. R. J. Hollingdale. Cambridge: Cambridge University Press, 1986.

————. *The Gay Science* (1882). Trans. Walter Kaufmann. New York: Random House, 1974.

————. *On the Genealogy of Morals* (1887). Trans. Walter Kaufmann and R. J. Hollingdale. New York: Random House, 1967.

————. *The Case of Wagner* (1888). Trans. Walter Kaufmann. New York: Random House, 1967.

————. *Twilight of the Idols* (1889). Trans. R. J. Hollingdale. Middlesex, England: Penguin Books, 1968.

————. *The Will to Power* (1895). Trans. Walter Kaufmann and R. J. Hollingdale. New York: Vintage Books, 1968.

O'Neill, John, ed. *Hegel's Dialectic of Desire and Recognition: Texts and Commentary.* Albany: SUNY Press, 1996.

Plato. *Symposium.* Trans. W. R. M. Lamb. London: Heinemann, 1961.

Peperzak, Adriaan T. *To the Other: An Introduction to the Philosophy of Emmanuel Levinas.* West Lafayette Purdue University Press, 1993.

————. *Ethics as First Philosophy: The Significance of Emmanuel Levinas for Philosophy, Literature and Religion.* New York: Routledge, 1995.

————. *Beyond: The Philosophy of Emmanuel Levinas.* Evanston: Northwestern University Press, 1997.

Ragland-Sullivan, Ellie. "Seeking the Third Term: Desire, the Phallus and the Materiality of Language." In *Feminism and Psychoanalysis,* eds. Richard Feldstein and Judith Roof. London: Cornell University Press, 1989.

Rapaport, Herman. "Atopos: The Theater of Desire." *New Orleans Review* 11, nos. 3–4 (fall–winter 1984).

Reich, Wilhelm. *The Mass Psychology of Fascism.* Trans. Vincent R. Carfagno. London: Souvenir Press, 1970.

Reineke, Martha. "Lacan, Merleau-Ponty, and Irigaray: Reflections on a Specular Drama." *Auslegung* 14 (1987): 67–85.

Ronell, Avital. *Finitude's Score: Essays for the End of the Millennium.* Lincoln: University of Nebraska Press, 1994.

Rose, Gillian. *The Broken Middle: Out of Our Ancient Society.* Oxford and Cambridge: Blackwell Publishers, 1992.

Rousseau, Jean-Jacques. *Emile.* New York: Basic Books, 1979.

————. *New Heloise.* College Park: Pennsylvania State University Press, 1968.

Saporiti, Elisabeth. "Peircean Triads in the Work of J. Lacan: Desire and the Ethics of the Sign." In *Peirce and Value Theory,* ed. Herman Parret. Amsterdam: J. Benjamins, 1994.

Sartre, Jean-Paul. *The Emotions: Outline of a Theory* (1939). Trans. Bernard Frechtman. New York: Philosophical Library, 1948.

————. *The Psychology of the Imagination* (1940). Trans. Bernard Frechtman. New York: Philosophical Library, 1948. Reprinted, Washington Square Press, 1966.

————. *Being and Nothingness: An Essay on Phenomenological Ontology* (1943). Trans. Hazel E Barnes. New York: Philosophical Library, 1956. Reprinted, Washington Square Press, 1972.

————. *The Age of Reason* (1945). Trans. Eric Sutton New York: Vintage, 1973.

————. *Saint Genet, Actor and Martyr* (1952). Trans. Bernard Frechtman. New York, Braziller, 1963.

————. *The War Diaries of Jean-Paul Sartre.* Trans. Quentin Hoare. New York: Pantheon Books, 1984.

————. *Notebooks for an Ethics.* Trans. David Pellauer. Chicago: University of Chicago Press, 1992.

Schleifer, Ronald. "The Space and Dialogue of Desire: Lacan, Greimas, and Narrative Temporality." *Modern Language Notes* 98, no.5 (Dec. 1983): 871–90.

Schneck, Stephen. "Michel Foucault on Power/Discourse, Theory and Practice." *Human Studies* 10 (1987): 15–33.

Schor, Naomi. "Dreaming Dissymetry: Barthes, Foucault and Sexual Difference." In *Men in Feminism,* eds. Alice Jardine and Paul Smith. London: Methuen, 1987.

————. "This Essentialism Which Is Not One: Coming to Grips With Irigaray." *differences* 1, no. 2 (1989): 38–58.

Schrift, Alan. "Between Church and State: Nietzsche, Deleuze and the Genealogy of Psychoanalysis." *International Studies in Philosophy* 24, no. 2 (1992); 41–52.

————. *Nietzsche and the Question of Interpretation: Between Hermeneutics and Deconstruction.* New York: Routledge, 1990.

————. *Nietzsche's French Legacy: A Genealogy of Poststructuralism.* New York: Routledge, 1995.

Schroeder, Brian. *Altared Ground: Levinas, History, and Violence.* New York: Routledge, 1996.

Schwarzer, Alice. *After "The Second Sex": Conversations With Simone de Beauvoir.* Trans. Marianne Howarth. New York: Pantheon Books, 1984.

Shaviro, Steven. *Passion and Excess: Blanchot, Bataille and Literary Theory.* Tallahassee: Florida State University Press, 1990.

Siebers, Tobin, ed. *Heterotopia: Postmodern Utopia and the Body Politic.* Ann Arbor: University of Michigan Press, 1994.

Silverman, Hugh J. *Inscriptions: After Phenomenology and Structuralism,* 2d ed. Evanston: Northwestern University Press, 1997.

————. *Textualities: Between Hermeneutics and Deconstruction.* New York: Routledge, 1994.

Snitow, Ann, Christine Stansell, and Sharon Thompson. *Desire: The Politics of Sexuality.* London: Virago, 1984.

Soble, Alan, ed. *Sex, Love, and Friendship.* Atlanta: Editions Rodopi, 1997.

Soll, Ivan. "On Desire and its Discontents." *Ratio* 2, no.2 (Dec. 1989): 159–84.

Solomon, Robert C. *About Love.* Roman and Littlefield, 1994.

Solomon, Robert C. *Love: Emotion, Myth and Metaphor.* Amherst, NY: Prometheus Books, 1990.

Sonnenfeld, Albert. "Desire and Fantasm in Joyce/Lacan." In *James Joyce: The Augmented Ninth,* ed. Bernard Benstock. Syracuse: Syracuse University Press, 1988.

Spinoza, Benedictus. *Ethics.* In *The Collected Works of Spinoza,* vol. I. Ed. and trans. Edwin Curley. Princeton: Princeton University Press, 1985.

Spivak, Gayatri Chakravorty. "Displacement and the Discourse of Women." In *Displacement: Derrida and After,* ed. Mark Krupnick. Bloomington: Indiana University Press, 1983.

Stanton, Donna C. "Difference on Trial: A Critique of the Maternal Metaphor in Cixous, Irigaray and Kristeva." In *The Poetics of Gender,* ed. Nancy K. Miller. New York: Columbia University Press, 1986.

Stendhal. *Love.* Trans. Gilbert Sale and Suzanne Sale. Harmondsworth, England: Penguin Books, 1975.

Stockton, Kathryn. *God Between Their Lips: Desire Between Women in Irigaray.* Stanford: Stanford University Press, 1994.

Stoekl, Allan. *Politics, Writing, Mutilation: The Cases of Bataille, Blanchot, Roussel, Leiris, and Ponge.* Minneapolis: University of Minnesota Press, 1985.

Stroud, Joanne. *The Bonding of Will and Desire.* New York: Continuum, 1994.

Suleiman, Susan Robin. "(Re)Writing the Body: the Politics and Poetics of Female Eroticism." In *The Female Body in Western Culture: Contemporary Perspectives,* ed. Susan Robin Suleiman. Cambridge: Harvard University Press, 1986.

Threadgold, Terry. "Language and Gender," *Australian Feminist Studies* 6 (autumn 1988): 41–70.

Ungar, Steven. *Roland Barthes: The Professor of Desire.* Lincoln: University of Nebraska Press, 1983.

Vandevelde, Pol. "The Notions of *Discourse* and *Text* in Postmodernism: Some Historical Roots." *Philosophy and Theology* 6, no. 3 (spring 1992): 181–200.

Virilio, Paul. *Pure War.* New York: Semiotext(e), 1983.

Visker, Rudi. "Habermas on Heidegger and Foucault: Meaning and Validity in the Philosophical Discourse of Modernity." *Radical Philosophy* 61 (summer 1992): 15–22.

Vitz, Evelyn. *Medieval Narrative and Modern Narratology: Subjects and Objects of Desire.* New York: New York University Press, 1989.

Weedon, Chris. *Feminist Practice and Poststructuralist Theory.* Oxford: Blackwell, 1987.

Weiss, Allen. *The Aesthetics of Excess.* Albany: SUNY Press, 1989.

Wentz, Jan. "Desire in Hegel's Realm of Self-consciousness." *Dialogue* 15 (May 1973): 93–98.

Wenzel, Helene V. "Introduction to Luce Irigaray's *And the One Doesn't Stir Without the Other.*" *Signs* 7 (autumn 1981): 56–59.

——— "Interview with Simone de Beauvoir." *Yale French Studies* 72 (1986).

Whitford, Margaret. *Luce Irigaray: Philosophy in the Feminine.* New York: Routledge, 1991.

Willett, Cynthia. "Tropics of Desire: Freud and Derrida." *Research in Phenomenology* 22 (1992): 138–51.

Williams, Linda. *Critical Desire: Psychoanalysis and the Literary Subject.* New York: St. Martin's Press, 1995.

Winant, Terry. "How Ordinary (Sexist) Discourse Resists Radical (Feminist) Critique." *Hypatia* 1 (1983): 609–19.

Wojtyla, Karol. *Love and Responsibility.* New York: Farrar, Straus & Giroux, 1981.

Wyatt, Jean. *Reconstructing Desire: The Role of the Unconscious in Women's Reading and Writing.* Chapel Hill: University of North Carolina Press, 1990.

Yaeger, Patricia. "Toward a Female Sublime." In *Gender and Theory: Dialogues on Feminist Criticism,* ed. Linda Kaufmann. Oxford: Blackwell, 1989.

Yovel, Yirmiyahu. *Spinoza and Other Heretics,* vol. II. Princeton: Princeton University Press, 1989.

Ziarek, Ewa P. "At the Limits of Discourse: Tracing the Maternal Body with Kristeva." *Hypatia* 2 (spring 1992): 91–108.

CONTRIBUTORS

BETTINA BERGO

Bettina Bergo is assistant professor of Philosophy at Loyola College, Maryland. She has translated Levinas's *De Dieu qui vient a l'idée* (Stanford, 1998) and is presently translating his *Dieu, la mort, et le temps* (Stanford, 1999). She is the coeditor of a special issue of the New School for Social Research's *Graduate Faculty Philosophy Journal* (New York) on Emmanuel Levinas in contemporary philosophy (1998). Her publications include *Levinas: Between Ethics and Justice* (Kluwer-Nijhoff 1998) and "The God of Abraham and the God of the Philosophers" in the *Graduate Faculty Philosophy Journal.* Her current research is on the relationship between phenomenology, psychoanalysis, and semiotics.

M. C. DILLON

M. C. Dillon is distinguished teaching professor of philosophy at SUNY, Binghamton. He is author of *Merleau-Ponty's Ontology* (Indiana, 1988; Northwestern, 1998), *Semiological Reductionism: A Critique of the Deconstructionist Movement in Postmodern Thought* (SUNY, 1995), and essays on phenomenology, psychology, literature, and the philosophy of love and sexuality. He is editor of *Merleau-Ponty Vivant* (SUNY, 1991), *Écart and Différance: Merleau-Ponty and Derrida on Seeing and Writing* (Humanities, 1997), and is currently writing a book on the philosophy of love. He is General Secretary of the Merleau-Ponty Circle.

NANCY HOLLAND

Nancy J. Holland received her B.A. from Stanford University and her Ph.D. from the University of California at Berkeley, and is now professor of philosophy at Hamline University. She is the author of *Is Women's Philosophy Possible?* (Rowman and Little-field, 1990), *The Madwoman's Reason: The Concept of the Appropriate in Ethical Thought* (Pennsylvania State, 1998), and editor of *Feminist Interpretations of Jacques Derrida (Re-reading the Canon)* (Pennsylvania State, 1997). She has published papers on the work of Martin Heidegger, Michel Foucault, and Maurice Merleau-Ponty, as well as an essay on images of female desire in the music of Prince.

ELEANORE HOLVECK

Eleanore Holveck has been chair of the department of Philosophy at Duquesne University. Her most recent article is "Can a Woman Be a Philosopher: Reflections of a Beauvoirian House-maid," in *Feminist Interpretations of Simone de Beauvoir,* edited by Margaret Simons (Pennsylvania State, 1995). She is finishing a book on de Beauvoir's philosophical literature, as well as participating in a translation project of de Beauvoir's works not yet in English.

CHRISTINA HOWELLS

Christina Howells is Reader in French at the University of Oxford, and a Fellow at Wadham College, Oxford. She is author of *Sartre's Theory of Literature* (MHRA, 1979) and *Sartre: The Necessity of Freedom* (Cambridge, 1989), and *Derrida: Decon-struction from Phenomenology to Ethics* (Cambridge: Polity Press, 1999). She is editor of *The Cambridge Companion to Sartre* (Cambridge, 1992) and a collection of literary essays: *Sartre* (Longman, 1995). Her research interests center on continental philosophy, literary theory, and modern French literature.

MARC J. LaFOUNTAIN

Marc J. LaFountain is professor of sociology at the State University of West Georgia, where he teaches courses on critical theory, phenomenology, and the sociology of art. His current interests include the body, the erotic, ethics, and art. He is author of *Dali and Postmodernism: This Is Not an Essence* (SUNY, 1997).

DOROTHY LELAND

Dorothy Leland is the director of women's studies at Florida Atlantic University. She is preparing a volume entitled *Husserl, Heidegger, Merleau-Ponty, Sartre: Phenomenology and the Problem of Intentionality.*

DOROTHEA E. OLKOWSKI

Dorothea E. Olkowski is associate professor of philosophy at the University of Colorado, Colorado Springs, and the former Director of Women's Studies. Her publications include *Gilles Deleuze and the Theater of Philosophy,* coedited with Constantin V. Boundas (Routledge, 1994), as well as *Re-Reading Merleau-Ponty: Essays Beyond the Continental Divide* (co-edited with Lawrence Hass) for Humanity Books, and *Merleau-Ponty: Interiority and Exteriority, Psychic Life and the World* (co-edited with James Morley) for SUNY Press. She is completing a book on the philosophy of Gilles Deleuze (combining her work in aesthetics, feminism, and continental philosophy).

ALAN D. SCHRIFT

Alan D. Schrift is professor of philosophy at Grinnell College. In addition to over two dozen articles on Nietzsche and recent French philosophy, he is the author of *Nietzsche's French Legacy: A Genealogy of Poststructuralism* (Routledge, 1995), *Nietzsche and the Question of Interpretation: Between Hermeneutics and Deconstruction* (Routledge, 1990), and co-editor, with Gayle L. Ormiston, of *The Hermeneutic Tradition: From Ast to Ricoeur* and *Transforming the Hermeneutic Context: From Nietzsche to Nancy* (both SUNY, 1990). He has also edited an anthology entitled *The Logic of the Gift: Toward an Ethic of Generosity* (Routledge, 1997).

BRIAN SCHROEDER

Brian Schroeder is Visiting Associate Professor of Philosophy and Religion at Skidmore College. He is author of *Altared Ground: Levinas, History and Violence* (Routledge, 1996) and (with Silvia Benso) Pensare Ambientalista. He is also coeditor (with Lissa

McCullough) of *Thinking Through the Death of God: Essays on the Thought of Thomas J. J. Altizer* (forthcoming). Presently, he is writing two books, *Alterity and Nothingness, or There is Nothing-Other*, a study on Nietzsche, Levinas, and the Kyoto School, and *Altered Geosophy: Grounding Postmodern Environmental Philisophy*.

ROBERT C. SOLOMON

Robert Solomon is Quincy Lee Centennial professor of philosophy at the University of Texas at Austin. He is the author of many books, including *From Rationalism to Existentialism* (Harper and Row, 1972), *The Passions* (Doubleday, 1976), *In the Spirit of Hegel* (Oxford, 1983), *From Hegel to Existentialism* (Oxford, 1988), *Continental Philosophy Since 1750* (Oxford, 1988), *About Love* and *A Passion for Justice* (both Rowman and Littlefield, 1995), and *A Short History of Philosophy* (with Kathleen Higgins, Publisher 1996).

SIMON WALTER

Simon Patrick Walter teaches philosophy at Middlesex University, London, England.

ABOUT THE EDITOR

Hugh J. Silverman is professor of philosophy and comparative literature at the State University of New York at Stony Brook and is currently serving as president of its Arts and Sciences Senate. He has been visiting professor at the Universities of Warwick and Leeds (England), the Université de Nice (France), the Università di Torino (Italy), twice at the Universität-Wien (Austria), the University of Helsinki (Finland), and the University of Sydney (Australia). He is executive director of the International Association for Philosophy and Literature and previously served for six years as executive co-director of the Society for Phenomenology and Existential Philosophy (1980–1986). Author of *Inscriptions: After Phenomenology and Structuralism* (Routledge, 1987; second edition, Northwestern University Press, 1997), *Textualities: Between Hermeneutics and Deconstruction* (Routledge, 1994), and numerous chapters and articles in continental philosophy, aesthetics, philosophical psychology, and literary/cultural/art theory, professor Silverman has lectured widely in North America, the United Kingdom, Ireland, continental Europe, and Australia. He is editor of *Writing the Politics of Difference* (SUNY, 1991) and *Piaget, Philosophy and the Human Sciences* (Northwestern University Press, 1997), and coeditor of *Jean-Paul Sartre: Contemporary Approaches to His Philosophy* (Duquesne/Harvester, 1980), *Conti-nental Philosophy in America* (Duquesne, 1983), *Descriptions* (SUNY, 1985), *Hermeneutics and Deconstruction* (SUNY, 1985), *Critical and Dialectical Phenomenology* (SUNY, 1987), *The Horizons of Continental Philosophy: Essays on Husserl, Heidegger, and Merleau-Ponty* (Nijhoff/Kluwer, 1988), *Postmodernism and Continental Philosophy* (SUNY, 1988), *The Textual Sublime: Deconstruction and Its Differences* (SUNY, 1990), Merleau-Ponty's *Texts and Dialogues: On Philosophy, Politics, and Cultural Understanding* (Humanities Press, 1992, 1996), and *Textualität der Philosophie—Philosophie und Literatur* (Oldenbourg, 1994), as well as the first six volumes in the Continental

Philosophy series: *Philosophy and Non-Philosophy Since Merleau-Ponty* (Routledge, 1988/Northwestern University Press, 1997), *Derrida and Deconstruction* (Routledge, 1989), *Postmodernism—Philosophy and the Arts* (Routledge, 1990), *Gadamer and Hermeneutics* (Routledge, 1991), *Questioning Foundations: Truth/Subjectivity/Culture* (Routledge, 1993), and *Cultural Semiosis: Tracing the Signifier* (Routledge, 1998).